The Constitution o.

Also by George Anastaplo

The Constitutionalist: Notes on the First Amendment

Human Being and Citizen:
Essays on Virtue, Freedom, and the Common Good

The Artist as Thinker: From Shakespeare to Joyce

The Constitution of 1787

A Commentary

George Anastaplo

The Johns Hopkins University Press

Bᴀʟᴛɪᴍᴏʀᴇ ᴀɴᴅ Lᴏɴᴅᴏɴ

This book has been brought to publication with the generous assistance
of Loyola University of Chicago.

The Johns Hopkins University Press, 701 West 40th Street, Baltimore, Maryland 21211
The Johns Hopkins Press Ltd., London

LIBRARY OF CONGRESS CATALOGING-IN-PUBLICATION DATA

Anastaplo, George, 1925–
The Constitution of 1787.

Bibliography: p.
Includes index.
1. United States—Constitutional law. 2. United States—Constitution. I. Title.
KF4528.A53   1988   342.73'02   88–45395
                           347.3022
                 ISBN 0-8018-3605-0 (alk. paper)
                 ISBN 0-8018-3606-9 (pbk. : alk. paper)

The paper used in this publication meets the minimum requirements
of American National Standard for Information Sciences—Permanence of Paper
for Printed Library Materials, ANSI Z39.48-1984.

To
MY BROTHERS
who,
not without considerable personal sacrifice,
have for decades honored
that ancient republican faith
which is grounded in the integrity of the family

Know well, my dear comrade Crito, that these things are what I
seem to hear, just as the Corybantes seem to hear the flutes . . .
—Socrates

Oft have I marked, with silent pleasure and admiration, the force
and prevalence, through[out] the United States, of the principle
that the supreme power resides in the people, and that they never
part with it. . . . There is a remedy, therefore, for every distemper
in government, if the people are not wanting to themselves; if they
are wanting to themselves, there is no remedy.
—James Wilson

That form of government is the best which provides the most effectually for a pure selection of [the] natural *aristoi* into offices of the
government.
—Thomas Jefferson

The Constitution of the United States . . . is internally consistent
in a remarkable degree, an extraordinarily fine example of eighteenth-century legal craftsmanship, and a great credit to Gouverneur Morris and James Wilson whose work it chiefly is. . . .The
scheme of the Constitution is simple and flexible: general national
power, subject only to a few simple limitations, with the state
powers, in the main, continuing for any desired local legislation.
So, if the Constitution were allowed to operate as the instrument
was drawn, the American people could, through Congress, deal
with any subject they wished, on a simple, straightforward, na-
tion-wide basis; and all other subjects, they could, in general, leave
to the states to handle as the states might desire.
—William Winslow Crosskey

We ask, not what this man meant, but what those words would
mean in the mouth of a normal speaker of English, using them in
the circumstances in which they were used.
—Oliver Wendell Holmes, Jr.

The new Constitution is such a plain, calm, sensible Appeal to the Interest, Feelings and Common Sense of our Countrymen that it must by its own intrinsic Weight bear down all Opposition.

—Gouverneur Morris

It is safer to try to understand the low in the light of the high than the high in the light of the low. In doing the latter one necessarily distorts the high; whereas in doing the former one does not deprive the low of the freedom to reveal itself fully as what it is.

—Leo Strauss

Contents

Preface

[J]udicial tribunals, as such, cannot decide upon political considerations. Political reasons have not the requisite certainty to afford
rules of juridical interpretation. They are different in different men.
They are different in the same men at different times. And when a
strict interpretation of the Constitution, according to the fixed rules
which govern the interpretation of laws, is abandoned, and the the-
oretical opinions of individuals are allowed to control its meaning,
we have no longer a Constitution; we are under the government of
individual men, who for the time being have power to declare what
the Constitution is, according to their own views of what it ought to
mean. When such a method of interpretation of the Constitution
obtains, in place of a republican Government, with limited and defined powers, we have a government which is merely an exponent
of the will of Congress; or what, in my opinion, would not be preferable, an exponent of the individual political opinions of the members of this court.

—Benjamin R. Curtis (dissenting),
Dred Scott v. Sandford (1857)

I was surprised to discover, upon preparing these lectures for
publication, that there evidently has not been, since the Ratification Campaign of 1787–1788, any other book-length, section-by-
section commentary upon the United States Constitution proceeding primarily from the original text itself. Even during the
Ratification Period, the longer expositions, as in the *Federalist Papers* and in the State Ratification Conventions, were not systematic but rather were tailored, properly enough, to local interests
and concerns. There have been, of course, many instructive systematic accounts of constitutional law in our own time, but these

have relied far more than I want to do here upon judicial and other official interpretations and applications of the Constitution.

The reader who believes himself to be interested only in the text of the Constitution may want to skip, in his first reading of this Commentary, Lectures No. 1, No. 7, No. 12, and No. 17. The reader who is particularly troubled by the accommodations to slavery in the Constitution of 1787 should perhaps begin with Section VI of Lecture No. 13. There are things said in my opening lectures that are likely to seem much more plausible once the reader begins to get a sense of the Commentary as a whole. The nationalist interpretation of the Constitution I develop here, with a due respect for States' Rights, was anticipated by John Marshall and Abraham Lincoln. I long ago recognized that most of the things I have worked out in reading the Constitution have been found by others long before me. I have also recognized that this is the way it should be.

The Caroline Werner Gannett Bicentennial Lectures upon which my Commentary is based were prepared for audiences made up of undergraduates of the Rochester Institute of Technology, of faculty of its College of Liberal Arts, and of members of the local bench and bar. I delivered fortnightly lectures between September 1985 and May 1986. (Thus, for example, the date drawn upon in the closing paragraph of Lecture No. 6 was November 7, 1985.) Lectures No. 1, No. 7, and No. 12 each served to introduce a set of five lectures in successive quarters of the academic year. (Lectures No. 1 and No. 2 were originally a single lecture, as were Lectures No. 16 and No. 17.)

The lecture series was enhanced by three public forums I conducted at R.I.T. during the 1985–1986 academic year, featuring talks on issues of the day by Anthony Lewis of the *New York Times*, Ramsey Clark of the New York Bar, and Abner J. Mikva of the United States Court of Appeals. Commentators on those talks were Leo Paul S. de Alvarez of the University of Dallas and Laurence Berns of St. John's College. In journeying to New York State to deliver the Gannett Lectures, I felt a certain kinship with the James Madison of the *Federalist*, who also made use of the opportunity provided him in that State to explain the Constitution.

I learned much from the responses of my Rochester audiences as well as from the many comments by readers of the Commentary manuscript before its publication in the Fall of 1986 issue of the *Loyola University of Chicago Law Journal*. The Gannett Lectures were most efficiently arranged by Dean Mary C. Sullivan and Professors Glenn J. Kist, David Murdoch, and John A. Murley, all of the R.I.T. College of Liberal Arts. Critical to the dispatch with which the lectures were developed for law journal and subsequent publication were the efforts of sympathetic student editors, Mary Bird-Murphy, Maria Woltjen, and Andrew J. Majeske, and of three most reliable secretaries, Dana B. Lane of the Rochester Institute of Technology and Christine M. Stack and Louise McDonald of the Loyola University of Chicago School of Law. My wife should also be recognized here, not least for having been able to accommodate herself in Chicago to a year of my predawn departures every other weekend. I also appreciated the unfailing hospitality in Rochester of Dawn H. Murley. Theodora McShan Anastaplo has helped to prepare this Commentary for publication in book form.

The readers of the Commentary manuscript who made many helpful suggestions and corrections before law journal publication include Larry Arnhart of Northern Illinois University, Sotirios A. Barber of the University of Notre Dame, Laurence Berns of St. John's College, William T. Bluhm of the University of Rochester, Leo Paul S. de Alvarez of the University of Dallas, Thomas S. Engeman of Loyola University of Chicago, Stephen M. Heaton, a Loyola University law student, Jamie Kalven of Chicago, J. Harvey Lomax of Memphis State University, Stanley D. McKenzie of the Rochester Institute of Technology, John A. Murley of the Rochester Institute of Technology, Robert L. Stone of the Illinois Bar, and John Van Doren of the Institute for Philosophical Research in Chicago. David Bevington of the University of Chicago and John Alvis of the University of Dallas have been helpful with Lecture No. 7; Mary Cornelia Porter of Barat College and John Kincaid of North Texas State University have been helpful with Lecture No. 12. I have had the benefit as well of comments and suggestions by readers of the law journal version of the Commentary as I have prepared it for publication in book form. These more recent readers include Mervin Block of Chicago and New York, J. Kent Calder of the Indiana Historical Society, who served as copy editor, and Thomas S. Schrock of the University of California at

Santa Barbara. They, along with Laurence Berns and J. Harvey Lomax, have subjected the law journal version to meticulous scrutiny. Also helpful have been comments by Thomas L. Pangle of the University of Toronto, as reader for the Johns Hopkins University Press, and those by Mortimer J. Adler, with whom I conducted a two-week seminar on the Constitution in July 1987 at the Aspen Institute for Humanistic Studies. The text and organization of the book have remained substantially as they were in the law journal version, but with many stylistic and other refinements. All the notes have been prepared since the lectures were given, although some of the material in the notes was originally in the lectures. Appendixes have been added for this book, including the principal constitutional documents drawn upon in my Commentary. I hope to make use, in any future edition of this book, of suggestions and corrections by still more readers.

I have retained the original lecture format for several reasons. This Commentary is directed to the general reader, even as it keeps in mind the training of judges, legislators, and scholars. (I have published elsewhere considerably more technical discussions of a variety of constitutional and legal issues.)[1] There is in Anglo-American law a great lecture-series tradition to which I am contributing. Particularly noteworthy have been the lectures, now books, by William Blackstone, James Wilson, A. V. Dicey, F. W. Maitland, Oliver Wendell Holmes, Jr., and Alexander Meiklejohn. My lecture format should put the reader on notice that comprehensiveness is not to be expected in this Commentary.

Even so, I believe the United States Constitution is examined here with an appropriate rigor, providing a reliable guide for those interested in a coherent account of the 1787 document, including suggestions about the true original intent of its Framers. My hope has been to offer my fellow citizens an account which would exhibit in our Constitution the admirable features that Blackstone was able to find in his:

> Of a constitution so wisely contrived, so strongly raised, and so highly finished, it is hard to speak with that praise which is justly and severely its due: the thorough and attentive contemplation of it will furnish its best panegyric. It hath been the endeavour of these Commentaries, however the execution may have succeeded, to examine its solid foundations, to mark out its extensive plan, to ex-

plain the use and distribution of its parts, and from the harmonious concurrence of those several parts to demonstrate the elegant proportion of the whole. (Commentaries on the Laws of England, IV, 435–36)

I have drawn in this Commentary upon what I have learned in my jurisprudence and political philosophy courses over the years about the nature of law and about natural right, if not even about the nature of nature. Thus, one reader of this Commentary, Laurence Berns, has written to me for publication here:

You are spelling out the virtues, the discipline, the qualities of character and behavior not usually thought about or expressed—though vaguely felt—that went into the making of the Constitution and that are required to make it work as it was intended to work.

Another reader, Harry V. Jaffa, has observed that this is the first time anyone has tried to read the Constitution like a book. He has also prepared for publication the observation that this Commentary "is less a commentary—in the ordinary sense—than it is a communion with the text. In that respect, it reminds one of nothing so much as Leo Strauss's parallel study of Plato's *Laws*."

My constitutional law courses have featured a considerable concern with the Constitution itself. We do not begin to look at cases until several weeks have been spent studying fundamental constitutional documents. One illustration which has always appealed to my constitutional law students might be usefully recalled here. It is about Dizzy Dean, a baseball legend in the St. Louis and Southern Illinois area in which I grew up. He won one hundred twenty games in his first five seasons as a regular pitcher with the St. Louis Cardinals and was only twenty-six when he broke a toe in the All-Star game in 1937. He tried to come back too soon and, favoring his injured toe, ruined his arm. The career of Dizzy Dean reminds us of the distortion that can take place, and the considerable damage that can be done, when one part of a well-constructed system is used to do the work of another part. Consider what has been done with "due process" because the Privileges and Immunities Clause of the Fourteenth Amendment became practically unavailable soon after that amendment was ratified. Consider, also, what led to and resulted from misreadings of the Commerce Clause for more than a century.

I have made few adjustments to the text of this Commentary in the light of highly publicized constitutional and political developments since my R.I.T. lectures were delivered. These recent developments, which are touched upon in note 85 and elsewhere, have tended to support the arguments I had made in my Rochester lectures about the proper relation of the Legislature and the Executive under the Constitution. I have long argued for the rule of law and hence legislative supremacy, despite the natural presumptuousness of the Executive and the intermittent persuasiveness of the Judiciary. Thus, my arguments in Lectures No. 8 and No. 9 are designed, in part, to discipline the inevitable monarchic elements in every great nation.

I try to be of service to my fellow citizens by providing an intelligible account both of the complete constitutional body and of how its parts fit together. This anatomy lesson looks back to sources and ahead to amendments even as it dwells on the original text of 1787. I take for granted throughout this Commentary a general awareness of what courts, legislators, and executives as well as scholars have said about the Constitution. I work, that is, from what "everybody knows." But only if the student of the Constitution secures a reliable grasp of the whole is it possible for him to begin to make sense of what the recognized experts say from time to time. Far more important than the somewhat dubious positions I may seem to take on various issues in this Commentary should be the general plan of the Constitution that I develop here.

It should be evident throughout this Commentary that the Framers knew what they were doing—and that what they did was extraordinarily good. The Constitution that was produced by their Committee on Style in September 1787, after two decades of experimentation and three months of deliberation, must have appealed to the Federal Convention delegates for the same reasons that it can appeal to us. They, too, must have recognized it as a marvelous piece of legal craftmanship. Practice in the proper reading of the Constitution of 1787 can help prepare us to study with due care and imagination not only other well-crafted legal instruments but also the finest works of the mind.

The Constitution of 1787

1. The Constitutions of the Americans

I

The American people, as a people, have had a dozen or so constitutions—if by *constitution* we mean that recognized body of principles which defines a community and guides its conduct. These constitutions, which are interrelated and overlapping, direct the American people to this day. A constitutional roll-call can remind us of what we are all, in one way or another, aware of.[1]

The first constitution, in the broadest sense of the term, of the Americans is one shared with millions of people in what was once the British Empire, now the Commonwealth of Nations. I refer to the language of the English-speaking peoples. This language has been decisively shaped, for moral and political purposes, by William Shakespeare and the King James version of the Bible.

The English language is, so to speak, the sea in which we swim, a sea taken so much for granted that it is rarely regarded as decisive in the constitutional workings of our people. It provides a special guide not only to political matters but also to the human ends that political life ultimately serves. Is it possible to have a sustained constitutionalism on a large scale in the modern world wherever the political and human sensibilities of a people have not been shaped by the language (that is, the thought) of a Shakespeare?

Or, put another way, it is difficult for tyranny to speak persuasively in English.[2] Thus, neither Lenin nor Hitler translates easily into American thought: it can even be hard for us to see why such leaders can be taken seriously, except by the most desperate peoples. I will return to this point in my next lecture. The work of Shakespeare will be drawn upon in some detail in the seventh lecture of this series.

1

II

Another constitution shared by the American people with millions in the Empire and Commonwealth is the British Constitution, the result of centuries of travail and testing in Great Britain.[3] Although largely unwritten, its principles are well enough known (for example, with respect to the workings of Parliament) that they can be described in considerable detail. We notice that parts of that constitution are written, such as Magna Carta and various Acts of Parliament that are obviously regarded as constitutionally significant. But it is the unwritten part of the constitution that determines such things as which acts of Parliament, like the Habeas Corpus Act of 1679, have constitutional significance.

So important was the British Constitution for the American colonists that they invoked it again and again, as British citizens, in their contests in the 1760s and the 1770s with the government of Great Britain. The rights of Englishmen and the British way of doing things were what Americans insisted upon in opposition to the usurpers in London.

The Revolution repudiated the British Constitution, but only in part. Although Americans disavowed that constitution's reliance upon monarchy, they drew upon much of the British Constitution as they organized themselves on various occasions—including that preeminent occasion in 1787 when they drafted a new national constitution. The British Constitution could be several times referred to in the Federal Convention as the best constitution then available in the world, but one that Americans could not reasonably be expected to establish at that time.

Just as the English language must be appreciated if one is to read the United States Constitution of 1787 properly, so the principal features of the British Constitution must be recognized if one is to read and use the Constitution of 1787 as it was intended to be read and used.

III

The first constitution distinctive to Americans is implied and drawn upon in the Declaration of Independence. On that occasion, Americans altered, with a view to natural right, the long-established way. The Declaration both invoked the British Constitution and repudiated ties to Great Britain; it both invoked the rights of Englishmen and transcended them. It implicitly indicated what form of government, or at least what ways of proceeding, Americans would rely upon.

The Declaration of Independence recognized (it did not invent) the standards of government that should guide any people in assessing and in making or unmaking their governments. The Declaration ratified what the Colonists had been doing in several assemblies before 1776 and directed what they would do in many assemblies thereafter until a proper national constitution was explicitly provided for. They retained what they considered sound in their inheritance from Great Britain.

The Americans might have proceeded indefinitely, as they did for almost a decade after 1774, conducting themselves pursuant to the constitutional system implicit in the Declaration of Independence, even though that declaration was primarily a statement of principles brought to bear upon the relations between the Colonies and Great Britain. The way the principles were stated, and the way the grievances were used to invoke and illustrate them, very much depended upon circumstances of the day. Even so, the principles were so stated that they have guided Americans ever since.

IV

Among the still-usable features of the British Constitution was the system of common law—not only the rules of law that had been developed by judges over centuries but also the way that judges went about their work. In practice, the body of the common law includes the statutes that had modified the common-law rulings by judges. Even so, the emphasis was, as it still is, upon the opinions published by judges.[4]

The common law can be seen as the systematic application of human reason, working from generally accepted standards of justice, to the circumstances of the day. It reflects the everyday morality of the community, the application of which is adjusted from case to case as justice and the common good require. It is developed primarily by judges, who find what is good and right to be done here and now, keeping in mind the known practices and expectations of the community. As such, the common law is indeed common—for it is understood to be the law that would be generally accepted by common-law judges, whatever adjustments might be made for peculiar local conditions.

The common law has always displayed great respect both for due process and for property. Some have insisted that the guarantees that bear upon habeas corpus, ex post facto laws, and trial by jury are also common-law rights. In any event, the common law was considered part of the British Constitution. American experience has shown that it can thrive apart from the British Constitution. Throughout the Constitution of 1787, and not only in the vocabulary used, the common law is obviously taken for granted.

V

The common law I have been describing thus far relates both to civil matters, or the law about the relations between persons, and to criminal matters, or the law about offenses against the community. There is as well a kind of common law that deals with public affairs, such as the rules that guide the conduct of parliamentary bodies.

This public common law, or law of public bodies, was repeatedly drawn upon by the British Colonies in North America and thereafter by the American States in the way they organized themselves in deliberative bodies (that is, in conventions and legislatures), as well as in the way they selected the members of various assemblies of government. This law of public bodies is evident also in the way the Federal Convention of 1787, and thereafter the State Ratification Conventions, assembled and conducted themselves.

Much of this law of public bodies was unwritten. What was needed to establish legitimate legislative and other public bodies was widely understood. Perhaps the most important feature of this law of public bodies was the set of rules, or understandings, as to how one might go about drafting and ratifying a constitution. So widely known were these rules that the community at large was fairly united in its recognition of when it truly had a constitution to follow.

Perhaps the most remarkable feature of the considerable constitution-making that went on between 1776 and 1789 was the com-

4

petence with which Americans all over the continent went about the business of establishing and using constitutions, a feat made even more remarkable because of the relaxed confidence with which it was done.

VI

Among the constitutions established were those of the thirteen States in the Union. From 1776 on, State constitutions, unwritten as well as written, were as much a part of the constitutional universe of citizens of the United States as were those constitutions reflected in the language they shared with others, the parts (and hence the spirit) of the British Constitution they had retained, the Declaration of Independence with its recourse to a natural constitutionalism (or the constitutionalism of natural right), the common law that they took for granted, and the law of public bodies that guided the establishment of written constitutions.

For the most part, the constitutions of the thirteen States during the first decade of independence were new. The two exceptions were adaptations of the Colonial charters that had previously governed.[5] In each State, decisions had to be made about how much of the British law would continue in force. Constitutions provided locally, State by State, some of the guidance that the Declaration of Independence provided for the Country at large.

From the outset of Independence, the American people were organized by States. A national system was always taken for granted, however, with the State constitutions themselves recognizing, if only tacitly, a constitution for the Country as a whole, just as the Declaration of Independence took the Union and its governance for granted. Much of the governing of the Country continued State by State while national constitutions were being considered and reconsidered. The States recognized that they had to accommodate themselves to one another for the time being, and they did this well enough, through the Confederation Congress, to prosecute the Revolutionary War to a successful conclusion.

State constitutions exhibited considerable variety. Experiments were tried and adjustments were made to local conditions. It was generally understood that State governments would have whatever proper powers of government that were not national in nature, unless provisions were made in their State constitutions, or in some national constitution, to curtail such powers.

All of the experimentation that went on in the States between 1776 and 1787 served to prepare the people of the United States to develop a proper national constitution.

VII

To say that there was experimentation in the States, as well as in the Continental and Confederation Congresses, is to imply in still another way that there was a set of standards and goals to which the people of the United States looked in determining what constitution they should have and, later on, in determining what amendments should be made from time to time in that constitution. Such a set of standards and goals is explicitly, but not exhaustively, drawn upon in the Declaration of Independence. It was implicitly drawn upon as well in the development and use of the British Constitution and in the development of the common law.

Thus, Americans and, in principle, all Western peoples, have always had an unchanging constitution to guide public action. This guide is, to put it in old-fashioned terms, the naturally right constitution, or the best regime. This enduring constitution is all-pervasive and much drawn upon and yet rarely noticed explicitly. Everyone has some notion of it, but few fully understand it—and a people's grasp of it changes from time to time. Sometimes that grasp can be quite naive, at other times quite sophisticated and yet wrongheaded, as may be seen in various modern ideologies. This points up the importance, in these matters, both of liberal education and of sound moral training for citizens.

One's grasp of the best regime—and hence of what would be better and what would be worse—may be seen in uses of discretion, whether by a people at large or by their public servants. It may be seen, however indistinctly, in the standards by which all judging and choosing are done, including of course the standards used in establishing, assessing, and amending constitutions, as well as in making and unmaking laws and in exercising other powers under any constitution.

The best regime takes for granted a political universe in which reason can study human nature to determine what action is called for at various times. I am talking here about a form of natural right, in the pre-modern sense. A somewhat looser and less instructive way of talking about the best regime is by reference to an "ideal constitution."[6]

To say that a rational political universe is assumed by recourse to the best regime is not to deny that there are irrational factors to be taken into account, including the passions and errors that human beings are prone to. Only because the best regime takes account of persistent irrationalities can it be as sensible, and hence as good, as it is.

For Americans generally, the finest introductions to the best regime are the statement of principles in the Declaration of Independence and the enumeration of goals in the Preamble to the Constitution of 1787, both of which will be discussed in my next lecture and will be referred to many times thereafter.

VIII

The best regime draws upon reason for its understanding of human nature and of the community and political associations appropriate for mankind in varying circumstances. Thus understood, it depends for its rare realization upon quite special circumstances. Yet we are told of another "best regime," but it is in the spiritual realm, not the temporal.

That regime also provides a constitution for Americans, but a constitution which varies from association to association, much as the State constitutions do. That is, religious sects differ, one from another, as to what is considered authoritative.[7] Both sets of ultimate standards, temporal and spiritual, seem to be drawn upon in the Declaration of Independence. Since ultimately there can only be one best regime, there is a tension between its spiritual and temporal conceptions. This tension has been, by and large, healthy and productive in the United States as well as in the West generally.

The best regime in the spiritual sense conventionally looks to revelation for its authority. Traces of this dependence appear in some State constitutions as well as in the Declaration of Independence. An accommodation of sorts between the competing claims of these two versions of the best regime may be seen when the secular statesman appeals to the revelation that happens to be accepted in his community.[8]

IX

A community's allegiance to this or that revelation is of particular interest to the statesman concerned with the character of his people. A set of opinions about what the world is like and about how things should be done is implicit in the character of each people. Such opinions comprise a kind of constitution that guides a country.

Both the character of a people and the form of the revelation that helps shape that character may in turn be shaped by such accidental factors as climate, geography, literature, racial types, and accident or history. Thus, the presence of substantial African slavery in eighteenth-century North America, however much it may have been due to chance, profoundly affected the American character and the alternatives available to American statesmen trying to bring out the best in their Country.[9]

What a political community may properly do to shape, reshape, and perpetuate the character of its people remains a question down to our day. One often hears it said that formation of character should still be left to the family and to the church, that the inculcation of morality is no business of government. Even this judgment as to the best way in our circumstances to provide for character may be a dim and perhaps distorted reflection of the old-fashioned approach that saw such allocations as implicit delegations of authority by the political order. Today, we are apt to overlook the dependence upon political arrangements for the effective operation, if not for the very existence and authority, of such institutions as family and church.

So it was said many times during the Federal Convention of 1787 and during the Ratification Campaign thereafter that the constitution appropriate to and possible for the United States would have to reflect the deep-rooted character of the American people.

X

This introduction to the constitutions of the Americans would not be complete without reference to the Law of Nations, which provided the worldwide political-legal context in which the Constitution of the United States was established.

The Declaration of Independence was concerned with exhibiting "a decent Respect to the Opinions of Mankind." A similar respect, appropriate to the form of the Constitution of 1787, may be seen both in the recognition by the Constitution of the authority of what we call international law and in its acknowledgment of the obligations theretofore entered into by the United States. Such are the duties that accompany the rights and capacity claimed in the Declaration of Independence for the United States upon their "assum[ing] among the Powers of the Earth, the separate and equal Station to which the Laws of Nature and of Nature's God entitle them."

There was then, and there remains to this day, a considerable body of the law of nations—a law (or general understanding in the civilized world) that governs both private and public conduct: for example, with respect to international commercial relations and with respect to the rules of war. Treaties and other undertakings or activities affect those relations, and here, too, there is considerable agreement as to what the world community requires. The United Nations Charter is but one of many efforts to develop the institutions consistent with mankind's understanding of what humanity calls for.

Is not world law, if not some form of world community, implied in all that we now have? Does not humanity make demands upon sovereign nations? With these questions we return to the guidance provided us by the best regime, no doubt an often uncertain guidance. Although there is much that prompts us to defer to the brotherhood of man, there is also much that inclines us to care most for those immediately around us. It may well be that the best regime for human beings on earth is possible only in relatively small communities, where the constitutions and laws appropriate to the character of a people can be developed. This limitation suggests that serious differences between, if not also within, nations are inevitable.

9

XI

Some accommodations to the American character may be seen in the form taken by the first written constitution for the United States, the "Articles of Confederation, and perpetual Union," which more or less prevailed during the decade before the adoption of the Constitution of 1787.

The designation of this document as "Articles" recognized the considerable power claimed by the individual States in the Union. Their association was much more that of a company of sovereigns bound by treaty, or articles, than it was that of a single government for a united people. This kind of arrangement seemed to respect the considerable desire among Americans for local self-government, a desire that persists down to our day and that can be effectively appealed to.

The treaty-like character of this association is reflected in an odd feature of American constitutional history: the Continental and Confederation Congresses began acting pursuant to the Articles of Confederation long before that document was fully ratified in 1781. In a sense, then, formal ratification did not matter so long as the understanding among the States was that the Articles should be in force. One can be reminded of how sovereign nations often conduct themselves; they comply with a treaty that has not yet been fully ratified, especially when it codifies or builds upon existing practices.

However much the Articles of Confederation catered to the American desire for local self-government, they failed to serve adequately the also strong desire for an effective government of the "perpetual Union" many times insisted upon. Some government would have to provide those things that only a general government could provide, such as regulation of the national economy and control of the relations of the United States with other countries. There was, therefore, a campaign to call a federal convention, even as it was generally understood that the States would continue to provide for what was local in, and otherwise special about, various parts of a large and growing Country.

XII

And so, at last in this roll-call of American constitutions, we have reached the Constitution of 1787. It should be evident from what I have said that that Constitution neither can nor was meant to be understood without our taking into account the major elements that contributed to its making.

The Articles of Confederation and the statutes enacted by Congress under the Articles, such as the Northwest Ordinance, must still be reckoned with in interpreting various parts of our present Constitution, as must be the British Constitution, the common law, and the Declaration of Independence. The Declaration, with its affirmation that "all Men are created equal," reminds us of how much of a compromise the 1787 Constitution was in its grudging accommodations to slavery.

Not only must account be taken of the elements that contributed to the making of the Constitution but also of such things that have followed from the original Constitution as the amendments, especially those that conform to the literal meaning of *amendment* (that is to say, *improvement* or *betterment*). It can be salutary to notice that the Bill of Rights amendments did not truly change the powers of the Government of the United States under the Constitution; the liberties and rights (or immunities and privileges) protected by these amendments were implied (or at least were not intended to be threatened) from the beginning. The Tenth Amendment, of which much is made by some, restated what had been done in the Constitution.[10] The Eleventh and Twelfth Amendments clarified what had been attempted in the Constitution.[11]

Various of the amendments make explicit, or confirm, what had been taken for granted or at least had been aimed at from the outset. Even the Civil War amendments—the Thirteenth, Fourteenth, and Fifteenth Amendments—are consistent with, if not called for by, the American constitutional spirit. One must wonder how many of our twenty-six amendments were implicit either in the "created equal" language of the Declaration of Independence or in the related "Republican Form of Government" language of the Constitution of 1787, to say nothing of the language of the Bible, of Shakespeare, and of Magna Carta. In any event, the three Civil

War amendments did ratify the primary intended effects of the Union efforts in that war. However much the relations of the States and the Union were changed by the war, the States remain, in principle, largely independent of the General Government.

XIII

We draw to the end of our roll-call of constitutions that hold sway over the American people by noticing still another constitution, that reflected in my organization here of the comprehensive constitutional system (the dozen interrelated and overlapping constitutions) in which the Constitution of 1787 is found. This system represents a general understanding of things, even "a world view," that includes the recognition of how truly remarkable the 1787 Constitution itself is, something worthy of our respectful attention in the months, decades, and century ahead.

2. Preamble

I begin this discussion of the Preamble to the Constitution of 1787 by returning to a few of the points I made in the opening lecture of this series. It should be useful to spell out these points with a view to my argument on this occasion.

I have suggested that the first constitution of the American people is one shared by them with many others in Great Britain and elsewhere. And I have referred to the language of the English-speaking peoples, a language that has been decisively shaped, for moral and political purposes, by William Shakespeare and the King James version of the Bible. To speak thus is to use *constitution* in the broadest sense of the term, with *language* connoting the traditions, or the accumulated wisdom, of a community.[12]

I have also suggested that an awareness of an enduring body of principles and standards rooted in nature, or "the best regime," has been implicit in the efforts of the American people for more than two centuries now in developing, amending, and using their constitutional arrangements. Without such a body of principles and standards, the doings of politicians, moralists, and teachers cannot make much sense. This is not to say that people can always make explicit what they are in fact aware of and what they rely upon. Such guidance is there nevertheless, and our greatest leaders, among whom Shakespeare should be reckoned, help us understand and refine what we seek.

I have suggested as well that eighteenth-century Americans repeatedly drew upon a law of public bodies to organize themselves in deliberative assemblies such as legislatures and constitutional conventions. How the law of public bodies was applied at the time the Constitution was drafted and ratified depended, in part, upon an assessment by Americans of their circumstances and their needs in light of standards drawn from their awareness of the best possible regime.

The 1776 Declaration of Independence, which was the foundation for both the 1777 Articles of Confederation and the 1787 Constitution, is a particularly vivid manifestation of the language of the English-speaking peoples. The Declaration states, in an authoritative manner, the enduring ends of American government rooted in the inalienable rights of men. The best regime was looked to in the making of prudent judgments about the claims and deeds of the British government. And, of course, a law of public bodies was used by the Declaration in acting upon the judgments reached. Similar observations can be made about the Preamble to the Constitution, the most eloquent part of the 1787 instrument.

The Preamble confirms several key teachings of the Declaration of Independence, especially with respect to both the consent of the governed and the purposes of government. It restates in this context the political principles set forth in the Declaration of Independence.

II

The Preamble provides a transition from the people at large and from the general principles of government into the Constitution itself. And at the end of the Constitution of 1787, Article VII leads out of the document back to the people, as they are organized State by State.

In the First Congress, Elbridge Gerry summarized in this fashion the experience that contributed to the establishment of the Constitution:

> [T]he causes which produced the Constitution were an imperfect union, want of public and private justice, internal commotions, defenceless community, neglect of the public welfare, and danger to [American] liberties.[13]

Gerry's list of the shortcomings endured under the Articles of Confederation obviously follows the order of our Preamble:

14

We the People of the United States, in Order to form a more perfect Union, establish Justice, insure domestic Tranquility, provide for the common defence, promote the general Welfare, and secure the Blessings of Liberty to ourselves and our Posterity, do ordain and establish this Constitution for the United States of America.

The Preamble to the Constitution presents the ends for which "this Constitution" is ordained and established. The last end listed—one might even say the culminating end—is the securing of "the Blessings of Liberty to ourselves and our Posterity." Why should this be so? Is a proper liberty that for the sake of which this people, as a people, ultimately exist?

We notice that it is only with respect to liberty that a concern is explicitly indicated for "our Posterity" as well as for "ourselves." Is not liberty something that is best developed and secured over generations, and that once lost is not easily retrieved? And does not liberty make possible sensible development and repeated appraisals of the measures designed to advance the other great ends of government? In any event, it seems to be something that people can believe they have a duty to preserve not only for themselves but also for those who follow them.

We should further notice that the first of the ends listed in the Preamble indicates which people this Constitution is for—the people of a Union of States. Is not posterity as well as the present generation looked out for by the concern with "a more perfect Union," just as it is by the concern with "the Blessings of Liberty"? Does "Blessings" have a spiritual dimension? Is there not something shining, perhaps even transcendent, about both the "more perfect" and the "Blessings" with which the array of ends in the Preamble opens and closes?

III

Both Union and Liberty, it seems, are to be perfected and thus perpetuated. The central ends in the Preamble's list—the third and fourth ends, to "insure domestic Tranquility" and to "provide for the common defence"—are concerned with perpetuation in a more immediate sense, the simple maintenance of what already is. The concern here is for security both at home and abroad.

Domestic tranquility means, among other things, that it is safe for people to live in the United States. Common defense means, among other things, that it is safe for the United States to live in the world. For many people, assurances of a pervasive safety may be vital to their satisfaction with any particular regime.

Once safety is assured, decent community life and personal development become possible. Some would make safety not only central to, but virtually the comprehensive end of, government. Mere continued existence can easily become an end in itself, with all kinds of sacrifices and impositions willingly endured in order to prolong that existence. Is not this too low a view of things, however important it is to recognize and to provide for the pressing demands of safety?

We all sense that the half-dozen ends of the Preamble are somehow interconnected, at least for this people. Precisely how they may be connected is suggesting itself as we examine the terms of the Preamble on this occasion.

We have noticed both that the first and last (shining) ends are related in several ways to one another and that much turns around the two central (prosaic) ends. This discovery of symmetry can be carried even further by noticing that the other two ends are also related to one another in that they seem to be concerned with the proper ordering of relations among people, either by establishing "Justice" or by promoting "the general Welfare." Does not "Justice" tend to look to reliance upon relations already arranged, while "the general Welfare" tends to look to provision for future relations?

Still another set of correspondences can be noticed. The first three ends of the Preamble—to "form a more perfect Union," to "establish Justice," and to "insure domestic Tranquility"—follow one upon the other. The various States have to be firmly bound together, States that naturally have much in common along with ominous differences. But it is not enough to bind this people together in their respective States. Their relations—the relations of States with one another and of individual citizens with one another—have to be so defined and so conducted that justice will be served. Otherwise, constant turmoil is likely. Justice must be established, and must be generally recognized to have been established, if domestic tranquility is to be secured, that tranquility both among the people of the Country generally and between various

States in the Union. In this way, the formation of a more perfect Union, the establishment of justice, and the assurance of domestic tranquility do follow one upon the other.

The same kind of connections can be suggested between the last three ends of the Preamble: to "provide for the common defence," to "promote the general Welfare," and to "secure the Blessings of Liberty to ourselves and our Posterity." Once domestic tranquility is assured—the tranquility of a people defined by a certain kind of union and reinforced by justice among them—the common defense can be effectively looked to in this Union's relations with the rest of the world. Once peace is provided for at home ("domestic Tranquility") and abroad ("common defence"), the general welfare, particularly with respect to economic and social matters, can be more effectively promoted, especially as a sense of community deepens.

There is as well substantial reciprocity among various of these ends. The common defense is usually better served when the general welfare is promoted, when a people is prosperous and healthy. The same may be said about domestic tranquility. Still, it is instructive to notice as we have the order in which these ends are presented and to suggest how each might have been thought, or naturally sensed, to lead to the next.

Certainly, it is difficult to promote the general welfare in an enduring fashion when a people is repeatedly threatened by troubles at home and abroad. And, in turn, it may be difficult to secure the blessings of liberty when the general welfare is ill-served, when a people is miserable and disaffected.

IV

We return to the opening and closing ends of the Preamble: the forming of a more perfect Union and the securing of the blessings of liberty to ourselves and our posterity. Do not these two ends identify and determine the people of the United States more than do the other four ends? Is not the combination of these ends the distinctive feature of the Preamble?

The other four ends are, after all, the ends of every respectable regime. All governments worthy of the name attempt to minister to justice, to domestic tranquility, to the common defense, and to the general welfare. But this people is identified by a certain kind of Union; and it considers itself a people that is particularly concerned about securing liberty in perpetuity. Critical to true liberty are the practice and prospect of genuine self-government. President Lincoln could speak at Gettysburg of this Nation as having been "conceived in Liberty" and of its form of government as never perishing from the earth.[14]

We notice, however, that liberty may be the only one of the six ends in the Preamble that is not considered an unambiguous good. The blessings of liberty are to be secured, not merely liberty itself, and certainly not the curses of liberty. (One of the curses of liberty, manifested in the desperate determination of some men to continue to hold others in slavery, is touched upon in the next section of this lecture and in Section VIII of Lecture No. 13.)

On the other hand, this end may also be the only one of the six that, insofar as it is good, is desired for its own sake as well as for its consequences. Union, justice, tranquility, defense, welfare—all of those ends seem generally to be desired more, if not sometimes altogether, for their consequences rather than for themselves alone. Is not liberty something we would want for itself alone, even if it did not bring us any other good things, so long as it did not bring us too many bad things? Liberty, as an end, seems to be a manifestation and a celebration of our very existence as rational, choosing beings. Opportunities for sensible choices are provided throughout the Constitution of 1787.

A concern for liberty is evident in the body of the Constitution as well as in the Preamble, not least in its pervasive reliance upon the rule of law. (A proper constitution itself serves as the law of laws.) The rule of law stands for, if it does not assure, a certain kind of liberty. Is liberty likely to endure if the rule of law is not depended upon to help curb the excesses of liberty and otherwise to provide the context within which the meaningful choices might be made that are vital to prudent politics and to moral goodness?

V

Various features of the Preamble, and indeed of the entire Constitution of 1787, can be pointed out by noticing a half-dozen overlapping assumptions about the nature of liberty that are implicit in the Preamble. The more mature opinions of the Framers' day are drawn upon and developed for the compilation I now offer.

The Framers of the Constitution evidently believed that there are such things as "Blessings." That is, they seemed to believe that there was something substantial (we would say objective) about good things. They would not have dismissed opinions about the good and the bad as subjective value judgments. Rather, they hoped for reliable decisions about the moral and the immoral both from judges in their applications of the common law and from statesmen in the exercise of their powers.

The Framers believed that human beings can reliably identify the blessings, the good things, of this world. That is, it is indicated by them that the goodness of things is knowable and known, that it is (or can be) a matter of public knowledge.

The Framers believed that they were entitled to receive and obliged to provide for those blessings. That is, they did not suffer from a lack of confidence as to either their right or their ability to seek out and secure the good things of this world.

The Framers of the Constitution, in their recognition that there are abuses of liberty to be guarded against, can be understood to have learned that the worst is somehow related to the corruption of the best. Liberty could even mean that some men considered themselves free, if not even obliged, to enslave others, thus calling into question the revolutionary insistence in the Declaration of Independence that all men are created equal. (Important elements of equality may be reflected in the provision in the Preamble for establishment of justice and promotion of the general welfare. In addition, the centrality of self-preservation can itself reflect an elementary sense of equality.) I return several times in this Commentary to the limitations upon both liberty and equality represented by the accommodations in the Constitution of 1787 to slavery.[15] The intermittent manifestations of tension between equality and liberty may have contributed to the vitality of our way of life, just as has that tension between the spiritual and the temporal touched upon in Section VIII of Lecture No. 1. We are always being challenged to determine whether the current balance between liberty and equality is indeed the one we should have in the circumstances of the day.

The Framers believed that they could and should look out for themselves, that they should not allow chance passions and desires to determine what happened in their community. That is, they believed in self-government.

The Framers believed that they had a duty to provide for their posterity, which might have been a particularly telling way of looking out for themselves. That is, they believed people should not consider themselves free to do as they please (perhaps another way of saying "as chance determines"). Various problems confronting a community are not merely personal or immediate but also of public or permanent concern.

Thus, the Framers of the Constitution evidently believed that their primary concern should be with their own. That is, they seemed to believe that it is these people and their posterity who must be particularly provided for.

VI

The Preamble puts everyone on notice that the Constitutional arrangements that follow in the body of the document are prepared by and for a people that takes government seriously. Only if one does take government seriously, and especially a government of one's own, may one's own become something that can be of genuine and continuing benefit to others, at least as a guide to how they in turn should conduct themselves and provide for their own.

At the very least, the Preamble indicates that the government being established must and can do the things that the government of a continental empire should be expected to do. Compare the guarded language with which the Articles of Confederation had opened a decade before:

> Whereas the Delegates of the United States of America, in Congress assembled, did . . . agree to certain articles of Confederation and perpetual Union between the States of Newhampshire, Massachusetts-bay, Rhodeisland and Providence Plantations, Connecticut, New York, New Jersey, Pennsylvania, Delaware, Maryland, Virginia, North-Carolina, South-Carolina, and Georgia in the words following . . .

The guarded language continues, as in the first major provision thereafter:

Each state retains its sovereignty, freedom, and independence, and every Power, Jurisdiction and right, which is not by this confederation expressly delegated to the United States, in Congress assembled.

May we not see here a somewhat crippling response to the political trauma suffered in the 1760s and 1770s by the Americans because of impositions by the distant British government that they had been obliged to resist?

The Constitution of 1787 is, somewhat more than the Articles of Confederation, in the spirit of the Declaration of Independence. The language of the Preamble alerts us, just as does the language of the opening lines of the Declaration, to the elevated caliber of the draftsmanship we are about to encounter.

VII

The affinity between the Declaration of Independence and the Constitution of 1787 is further suggested by certain implications of the separation-of-powers approach in the Constitution, a principle that had been severely compromised in the Articles of Confederation.

Various of the grievances in the Declaration of Independence, and the way government itself is spoken of there, presuppose a separation-of-powers approach much like that made explicit in the Constitution. We can even see in the references to divinity in the Declaration of Independence an oblique anticipation of the qualified separation of powers found in the Constitution itself. There are four references to divinity in the Declaration. The first reference, and perhaps the second as well, regarded God as legislator; it is He that orders things, ordaining what is to be. That is, He first comes to view as lawgiver. Next, God is seen as judge. Finally, He is revealed as executive, as One Who extends protection, enforcing the laws that have been laid down, with a suggestion as well of the dispensing power of the executive. Thus, the authors of the Declaration portrayed even the government of the world in the light of their political principles.

In this way, at least, a republican regime is implied by the Declaration of Independence, such a regime as may be seen in various of the State constitutions of that period, in the Constitution of 1787, and even (however distorted in some respects) in the British Constitution. Among the features of the republicanism endorsed by the Declaration are the consent of the governed, a qualified separation of powers, and a proper respect for the inalienable rights of mankind.[16]

I referred in Section VI of Lecture No. 1 to the natural constitutionalism of the Declaration of Independence. Is it not appropriate that the deference in the Declaration to "the Laws of Nature and of Nature's God" should be reflected in the understanding that the best ordering of human things should take as its model the divine ordering of the world?

The Constitution of 1787 can plausibly be taken, then, as an incarnation of the principles revealed in the Declaration of Independence. It is a form of government appropriate for the people of the Declaration—that is, for a people who could produce such a declaration. It is also a form of government that had to defer to circumstances, particularly the long-established institution of slavery. This accommodation left the Constitution deeply flawed, but not without hope of eventual redemption.

VIII

However flawed the Constitution of 1787 was in this respect, it was no more so (although more obviously so) than the Articles of Confederation. Rather, as we shall see in the course of these lectures, the Constitution may even have implied, more than the Articles of Confederation did, the eventual abolition of slavery.

For one thing, the fact that the government under the Constitution was truly a government meant that it could, in appropriate circumstances, do what should be done to serve the great ends set forth in the Preamble. (It was observed in the September 17, 1787, letter of transmittal from the Federal Convention to the Confederation Congress that the considerable powers to be vested in the new government could not properly have been vested in the general government under the Articles, a government that had virtually all its powers assigned to the legislature, and a unicameral legislature at that.[17]) Both supporters and critics of the Constitution knew in 1787-1788 that a much more powerful government was called for by the Preamble and was provided for in the body of the instrument.

We need not be concerned here with how much the Preamble itself empowers the General Government under the Constitution.[18] At the very least, the Preamble assures Americans that the powers elaborated in the body of the Constitution are, and were intended to be, as broad as they seem. Furthermore, it has always been a respectable argument, recognized even in the earliest discussions of the Constitution by both its friends and its enemies, that ambiguities in the body of a document should be resolved so as best to promote the objects, or purposes, that its preamble states. Critics during the Ratification Campaign protested "that the legislature, under this [proposed] Constitution, may pass any law which they may think proper."[19] Although the Preamble has been much neglected the past century or so, it has been substituted for in effect by the expansive use made of the Necessary and Proper Clause, a use that was anticipated during the Ratification Campaign. This exploitation of the Necessary and Proper Clause, natural enough as pressing national problems have been confronted, has sometimes served to conceal from view the superb craftsmanship of the drafters of the Constitution.

IX

However extensive the powers of the General Government under the Constitution may be, the exercise of those powers has always been considered subject to review and restraint by the people organized by States. The continued existence of the States is emphasized in those articles of the Constitution where ratification and amendments are provided for.

The extent of the power of the people is dramatically anticipated, as we shall see in my next lecture, by the opening words of the Constitution, "We the People of the United States." There was, we are reminded, a people available in 1787, and indeed in 1776 and before, a people that could say and do what was said and done in North America from at least 1774 on. The Constitution itself assumes that there are already citizens of the United States in 1787, just as the Declaration of Independence and the Articles of Confederation had assumed the existence of American citizens when those great state papers were drafted a decade earlier.

We shall see in this Commentary various ways in which the ultimate power of the people is taken for granted throughout the Constitution. Consider even what may be seen in the Tenth Amendment,[20] which is made much of by some as a States' Rights guarantee:

> The powers not delegated to the United States by the Constitution, nor prohibited by it to the States, are reserved to the States respectively, or to the people.

It is not inappropriate to regard the first ten amendments (or the Bill of Rights) as a vital part of the great constitutional sowing of the 1787-1791 period. The combination of the Constitution and the Bill of Rights is often considered the original Constitutional arrangement in its entirety. This means, among other things, that ultimate mastery by the people is affirmed not only in the opening words of "the original Constitutional arrangement" ("We the People," with which the Preamble begins) but also in its closing words ("or to the people," with which the Tenth Amendment, and hence the Bill of Rights, ends). Thus, the friends of the Constitution in the First Congress in 1789, upon drafting the amendments to be proposed for ratification, confidently looked beyond the States to the people, just as they had done in the Federal Convention of 1787.

The recognition of the people here is reassuring in that the people can control what the General Government may do with its considerable power. (At times, of course, the people can and should decide that much of this power should lie dormant.) For the people to be able to exercise their control effectively, they must be free to discuss fully what their governments have done, are doing, and propose to do. This means that public deliberation must be brought to bear upon community affairs. The Preamble implies one principle drawn upon in the Declaration of Independence and made explicit in the First Amendment: the people have the right freely to discuss the public business of the Country. (We will return to this freedom-of-speech principle again and again in these lectures.[21]) No people can truly ordain and establish any Constitution, and supervise Constitutional applications and amendments, if they are not free to examine the doings of government.

Nor can the people truly control these matters if they are not competent enough to know what should be done and disciplined enough to do it. Both competence and discipline in a people are served by an informed appreciation of their Constitution, to which we can now turn in some detail, article by article. In the course of this Commentary we will again and again be reminded of, and guided by, the Preamble—by those words, "echoing in part the language of the Declaration of Independence, which breathe spirit into the rest of the Constitution."[22]

3. Article I, Sections 1, 2, 3, 4, 5, & 6

I

The Senate of the United States is said to be a continuing body. Senatorial terms of office are staggered so that one-third of them expire every two years. Thus, a substantial body of Senators in every new Congress is carried over from the preceding Congress. The same may be said of the people of the United States from decade to decade, from generation to generation, beginning well before 1787 and continuing down to our day.

I try in this Commentary to occupy the middle ground between that which preceded the drafting of the Constitution and that which followed upon its ratification—that is, the Constitution itself.

II

Sections 1 through 6 of Article I (the Legislative Article) contain prosaic-looking material, and yet they can be quite revealing.

These six sections begin, "All legislative Powers herein granted shall be vested in a Congress of the United States, which shall consist of a Senate and a House of Representatives." I shall say more about this opening section in Lecture No. 5, when I consider Section 8 of Article I, where various powers of Congress are enumerated, and in Section V of Lecture No. 9, when I compare how Articles II and III open.

Here, then, is a summary of what is to be found in the sections commented upon in this lecture. Section 2 provides for the membership of the House of Representatives. Section 3 provides for the

membership of the Senate. Section 4 provides for the superintending Congressional authority with respect to matters entrusted to
the States in Sections 2 and 3. Section 5 provides rules and procedures for the two Houses of Congress. And Section 6 provides for
the privileges and disabilities of the members of Congress. Let us
see what can be said about, and learned from, these provisions for
legislative routines.

III

Perhaps the most remarkable feature about the 1789 organization of the First Congress under the Constitution, as well as about
the 1787 organization of the Federal Convention pursuant to directions from the Confederation Congress, is that such organizing has
not been generally noticed. There was no serious question about
legitimacy; there was no major controversy about points of order
and the like. Inconclusive selections are rare in the United States to
this day, however vigorously contested elections and appointments may be. It is generally obvious who has been selected according to the prevailing rules. This arrangement respects the
opinion reflected in the Constitution that it is more important to
know who the officer is to be than that it be a particular person or
even the best possible choice.

There have been serious differences from time to time as to what
the best mode of selection is, as to who should be represented
where, and as to whether the States should be equally represented
in the Senate or, earlier, in the Continental and Confederation
Congresses. Also, the Anti-Federalists could report themselves disturbed during the 1787–1788 Ratification Campaign that there
could be only sixty-five members in the House of Representatives
from all thirteen States in the First Congress (1789–1791). But such
differences have not kept Americans from accepting and making
the best of whatever arrangement had been agreed upon, however
deep their reservations might have been about what had been arranged.

Sensible people appreciate the importance of an agreed-upon arrangement. They tend to recognize that whatever arrangement is
made is bound to be arbitrary in some respects and that what is
critical, at least for the time being, is not that the way of proceed-

ing be the best possible way, but that it be a knowable and known way. Americans can put up with extremes in national policy, from accommodation to slavery to wholesale emancipation, so long as the prevailing policy defers to the forms of law.

Another way of describing these matters is to say that Americans generally understand that it is natural to political life that there be conventions, and that a wide range of conventions can be lived with, so long as they are sufficiently identified as arrangements agreed upon for the time being by the community. Rules do matter, even rules that are obviously defective.

Designated persons could show up for the various Continental and Confederation Congresses, for the Federal Convention, and for the First Congress. They could recognize one another as legitimate and could, when enough did show up, get right to work on the business at hand. How many would be considered "enough" depended upon conventions with respect to quorums. It generally makes sense to permit "a Majority of [a Body to] constitute a Quorum"—that is, that number which could prevail even if the entire body were present.

IV

Such confidence and competence depend upon considerable experience in self-government. Much of that experience is manifested in the States, the existence of which is assumed throughout the Constitution. The States relied upon by the Constitution were fairly well defined before the Constitution itself was drafted. They could be counted upon to do the work necessary for the repeated selection of various officers of the General Government, including Representatives, Senators, and Presidents. The States are very much in evidence throughout the Constitution but especially at the beginning, as the Congress comes into being, and at the end, as Ratification of the Constitution itself is provided for.

Of course, State legislatures (and usually bicameral legislatures) were taken for granted. Those legislatures could be counted upon to devise and operate the selection apparatus that would set the General Government in motion. The Constitution does provide a reserve power in the Congress to supervise most of what the States do about the modes of selection upon which the General Government depends, just as it provides in Article IV that the United States should guarantee to each State in the Union "a Republican Form of Government." These Congressional reserve powers with respect to the States have rarely had to be exercised, except in the forms now found in the Fourteenth Amendment.

The State legislatures, then, are recognized to be going concerns, to which qualifications of electors for selection of members of the House of Representatives can be keyed. Behind the State legislatures of 1787–1789 were two centuries of varying degrees of self-government in the British Colonies in North America, colonies that were close enough to Great Britain to be protected from other European powers by British arms and influence but far enough away to be left to their own devices for most everyday matters.

The States, in our Constitutional system, have been largely independent of the General Government and yet have been quite reliable in providing that government what it has needed to be kept in motion. The States, it should be remembered, have never been political subdivisions of, or fully subordinated to, the General Government.[23] This is one reason why the Constitution of the United States may not be suitable for export without considerable modification.

V

Sufficient direction was provided the States for them to produce the members of Congress and the Presidential electors that the emerging General Government needed in 1789. Because it was generally understood that George Washington would be the first President under the Constitution, it was much easier than it might otherwise have been to get things started.

However much the Anti-Federalists complained during the Ratification Campaign that the number of members of the House of Representatives was too small, there was little public criticism then of the proportions allocated to the various States, aside from the controversy over whether and how slaves should be counted. Perhaps this lack of serious criticism was in part because the political power thus allocated was considered balanced by the vulnerability to the direct taxation to which States would thereby be exposed in the same proportions. Such balancing also made it difficult to be sure, at least at the outset, who benefited most from the counting of a slave as three-fifths of a regular citizen. (This mode of counting slaves came out of debates in the Confederation Congress.) For representation purposes, Southerners were willing to have each slave counted as five-fifths of a citizen; for taxation purposes, they preferred that slaves not be counted at all.

Perhaps the initial allocation of seats was accepted not only because Americans had then a fairly good notion of relative State sizes, but also because the constitutionally-required census—to be conducted within three years—would lead soon enough to adjustments in the proportions of seats allocated among the States. The national dedication to equality is reflected in the provision made for a periodic census, after which a reallocation of seats in the House of Representatives would routinely take place.

We do take for granted periodic reallocations of seats, which in turn affect the relative power of the States not only in the House of Representatives but also in Presidential elections. One consequence of such reallocation is that privileged regional or class enclaves cannot easily establish or maintain themselves under the Constitution. It is difficult to overestimate the effects of the equality principle in the American regime, especially since that principle is intimately related to the importance attributed to the liberty of everyone in the Country.

VI

The dedication to equality is reflected in the way the two Houses of Congress are to organize themselves. It is assumed that the members of a House, no matter where they come from, should have equal weight and that, unless otherwise indicated, majority rule should prevail. (I return to this point in Section XII of this lecture.)

It was generally understood in 1789 how members were to organize themselves in the First Congress. The Constitution provided some guidance, but for the most part the experience of the prospective Members of Congress was relied upon. The Framers of the Constitution seem not to have been concerned about what would happen when Congress assembled, perhaps in part because they had been reassured by the ease with which they had themselves organized the Federal Convention of 1787.

The way was smoothed by the justified expectation that a significant number of members in the First Congress would have seen service in Colonial and State legislatures, in Continental and Confederation Congresses, and in the Federal Convention itself. It is remarkable, down to this day, how adept Americans are at organizing deliberative bodies (in government and out). Other gifted peoples of the world treasure adeptness in other human activities, placing far less emphasis than we do upon a moderate political life and genuine self-government.

VII

The principle of equality is consistent with (perhaps even requires) the understanding that the American people are the ultimate authority under the Constitution. The House of Representatives is to be elected by the people directly; the Senate is to be selected by the State Legislatures, which are in turn elected by the people directly (for the most part); and the President is to be selected by electors, who are in turn to be selected in a manner prescribed by State legislatures, which are themselves likely to be directly dependent upon the people. (I return to Presidential electors in Lecture No. 8 and to our system of "coordinated electorates" in Section VII of Lecture No. 16.)

Thus, "the people" take more than one form. We have noticed that the people as countable citizens are provided for in the House of Representatives and that the people as Statewide communities are provided for in the Senate.

We should notice as well that the people are truly in control only when they know what they are doing. There are indications here and there in the Constitution that it is recognized, ultimately by the people themselves, that care must be taken to help the people to bring out the best in themselves and to permit them to seek and to secure what they need and hence truly want.

VIII

Among indications of the advisability of tempering the application of the equality principle are the provisions in the opening sections of the Constitution for the qualifications of members of Congress. The equality principle is not carried so far as to permit the people to select just anyone who happens to please them. The different age, citizenship, and residency requirements for members of Congress (and, varying from State to State, for the voters themselves) are designed to make more likely a reliance upon the appropriate maturity, national loyalty, and local experience.

Although the people's will is to be master, that will, to be sound, must be refined. So refined was this people's will, even before the outset of its activity under the Constitution, that the people themselves could recognize the need for various restraints upon its exercise. These restraints, to be adjusted from time to time as circumstances change, reflect an awareness of what is good and of what is likely to promote or to subvert that good.

IX

The supreme authority of the people in a regime "dedicated to the proposition that all men are created equal" is further recognized in repeated indications by the Constitution that the legislature is ultimately the controlling branch of government. That branch is like the people in action, and it can safely be supreme in the Constitutional system because it is most intimately subject to supervision and control by the people.

I will repeatedly emphasize in this Commentary the legislative supremacy assumed in the Constitution because it is easy today—perhaps it has always been easy—to make much of the President. Certainly, the President is much more visible, much more dramatic, or rather much more easily dramatized. But, as became evident during both the Nixon Administration impeachment crisis and the Reagan Administration Iran arms-Contra aid episodes, Congress does have the final say among the branches of the General Government as to who remains President of the United States.

Impeachment is, however, merely a particularly sensational manifestation of Congressional supremacy, of which there are many other, largely routine, manifestations as well in the Constitution. Although Congress can control significantly the composition, the budget, and most of the activities of both the Executive and the Judicial branches of government, little can be done by the other branches to control Congress in these respects. Although a President or a court may sometimes have something to say about a particular member of Congress (for example, through the criminal indictment and thereafter the trial of that member), the doings of Congress as a body remain largely unchecked except by the electorate. Presidential vetoes and judicial review have a limited place in the original Constitutional dispensation.

In short, the Executive and Judicial branches are dependent upon, and bound by, the laws Congress chooses to make. (The Iran-Contra hearings served to reaffirm the primacy of the laws of the land in the conduct of foreign affairs just as the Watergate hearings had served to reaffirm the primacy of the laws of the land in the conduct of domestic affairs.) For example, although the President is "Commander in Chief of the Army and Navy of the United States," what those forces consist of (or whether they exist at all), as well as what can be done with them abroad as well as in this Country, depends for the most part upon Congress. The courts are similarly dependent. Congress has the power to determine how many courts there will be in addition to the Supreme Court and even how many members of the Supreme Court there will be from time to time.

Let us return briefly to the impeachment provisions in the opening sections of Article I. Each House of Congress has a distinctive part to play. One makes the charges (that is, impeaches); the other passes judgment upon those charges (that is, acquits or convicts). No other branch or officer of government can counteract what Congress does here, no matter how mistaken or wrongheaded Congress may be.

A similar ultimate dependence upon the Legislative branch may be seen in what the Constitution takes for granted about what happens in the States. By and large, except when there is a need for immediate action (as reflected in provisions for when legislatures are not in session), State governments act most significantly through their legislatures. For example, the State legislatures choose the Senators who will serve in Congress, a choice in which the governors of the States do not participate, whatever they may do to fill Senatorial vacancies on an interim basis. (I suggest in Section I of Lecture No. 16 the sense in which the Constitution regards State government as unitary.)

The considerable weight given to the Legislature is apparent as well in the powers assigned to the Senate for approving Presidential nominations, including those of judges, and for ratifying treaties. It is seen in its most pervasive form in the multitude of directives, the interpretation and enforcement of which occupy so much of the time and energy of the Judicial and Executive branches, that are almost all made by, or under the authority of, Congress. No wonder Congress is provided for first in the Constitution. Nothing could be done by the General Government in 1789 until Congress organized itself and got to work.

X

Legislative supremacy can be seen in still another fact so massive and so obvious that it can easily be overlooked: it is reflected in the way the Constitution itself is established and in the place it has in our political life.

After all, the Federal Convention that framed the Constitution resembled in its activities a legislature, not an executive or a court. The State conventions that met to consider the proposed Constitution and to decide whether to ratify it or to reject it were also legislative in character. The activities of these various conventions, whether as framers of the Constitution or as ratifiers of it, were characterized by the kind of deliberation associated with legislatures.

That the Constitution can be understood to be a law of the land points up the doings of the various conventions as lawgivers. The ultimate lawmakers are the people who proclaim themselves in the Preamble as the source for this Constitution. This fact, too, reminds us of the supremacy of the legislative mode.

To emphasize as I have the deliberative character of legislative activity is to remind us of still another facet of legislative supremacy, which is that the Legislature, more than any other branch of government, is empowered on its own initiative to bring human reason to bear upon the issues of the day as it attempts to determine the right thing to do. The Executive and the Courts have to be guided, in decisive respects, by legislative determinations.

Most regimes today find it difficult not to rely upon a legislative assembly as nominally supreme. Even the most tyrannical regime depends upon a certain degree of acquiescence, if not support, from the people at large. When changes in leadership are made in countries like the Soviet Union and China, the ultimate formal authority must rest in a representative body.

The most powerful British monarchs, too, depended ultimately upon the laws of the land for their authority. Except in times of civil war, who became the monarch depended considerably upon how a generally accepted rule defined the succession, a rule that was usually promulgated or endorsed by some more or less representative body. (I return to this matter in Section II(v) of Lecture No. 7.)

XI

The two Houses of Congress are different in critical respects, beginning with the differences in their immediate constituents (the people, for the House of Representatives; the State legislatures, for the Senate).

The Senate is mentioned first in the Constitution. But the House of Representatives is provided for first (in Section 2, with Section 3 reserved for the Senate). The House of Representatives is the distinctive legislative body established by the Constitution, with the Senate resembling much more the Congress under the Articles of Confederation. In addition, the House reflects more immediately the American people's ultimate control of government.

But however different the two Houses of Congress may be, they are both needed for the primary purpose of Congress, the making of laws. The President, too, is involved in the lawmaking process, but his veto can be overridden. He is not needed at all in the amending process. There is, however, no proper way to override the failure of one House either to agree to proposed legislation or to agree to any proposed amendments to the Constitution coming from Congress.

XII

The important differences between the two Houses do not keep the Constitution from laying down rules that apply to both Houses, rules with respect to such matters as when and where the

Houses should meet, how each House is to be governed, what records are to be made of proceedings, and when "the Yeas and Nays of the Members" are to be entered into the Journal.

We can see an occasional apparent exception to the proposition that the majority rules. (I return to this subject in Section I of Lecture No. 14.) Thus, "one fifth of those Present" can require that the *Yeas* and *Nays* be recorded. This defers to the right of the people to learn what has gone on, with a minority of one-fifth being empowered to help the people see who the legislative majority were on any particular occasion. Thus, also, a smaller number than the required quorum (a majority of each House) "may adjourn from day to day, and may be authorized to compel the Attendance of absent Members." This defers to the right of the people to have done on their behalf what may be required for the assembling of the majority needed "to do Business."

The two Houses are the same in these matters, whatever differences they may exhibit in providing for such details as precisely how any absent members are to be compelled to attend. They are the same as well, with no option in either House to be different, in the privileges and disabilities of members of Congress. The members of Congress are to be compensated for their services out of the Treasury of the United States. This provision is a reminder that not even Senators are to be considered merely agents of the States from which they come. Also, all members are exempt from being arrested on certain grounds "during their Attendance at the Session of their respective Houses, and in going to and returning from the same."

Even more important, members of Congress "shall not be questioned in any other Place" "for any Speech or Debate in either House." This recognition of Congressional immunity again reminds us of the freedom-of-speech privilege (available even before the First Amendment was added to the Constitution) of the people of the Country when discussing public business. As I said in my last lecture, it is evident from the ultimate control recognized in the people and from the things the people had to do in order to establish and thereafter to assess and, if need be, to alter, the Constitution that the people have to be left free to discuss both what should be done and what their governments are doing.

At the same time that the privileges of members of Congress are assured, certain disabilities are ordered, such as the limitations upon the capacity of members of Congress to hold certain other offices. These disabilities, as well as the protection of freedom of speech, recognize the weaknesses to which man is susceptible, including both the temptation to advance oneself at the expense of the community and the susceptibility to threats against doing one's duty. Thus, both greed and fear must be anticipated. The freedom-of-speech and the immunity-from-arrest provisions also reflect the opinion that members of Congress should be left free, subject only to being disciplined in Congress itself or at the polls, to conduct the public business as they see fit.

These and other rules about how the Houses of Congress are to work, how members are to be protected, and what they should not do, reflect considerable Anglo-American experience over several centuries with legislative bodies.

XIII

Proper use of experience requires, of course, something more than mere imitation of what has gone before. Circumstances do change, calling for adaptations even in what has worked well. Changes are reflected in, among other things, the names used in the Constitution. The members of the new Congress are to be called *Representatives* and *Senators*, not *Delegates* as under the Articles of Confederation. Delegates are more like ambassadors who represent sovereigns in a league of states. This difference is driven home by the provision for two Senators who vote separately, instead of just one (or a delegation), from each State. We again see that each member of the Senate is somewhat independent of the State legislature that has selected him. Nor is he subject to recall before his term of office expires.

The continued use of *Congress*, however, may have provided a reassuring connection with the past; it is a term that was originally associated with an assembly of ambassadors (such as, later on, the Congress of Vienna) more than it was with a national legislature. Names can conceal changes that have been made—in this case, reassuring those who were afraid that the Constitution prepared the way for a consolidated government that would virtually eliminate the "sovereign States." The same effect followed from the appropriation, by the friends of the Constitution, of the name "Federalists," even though it was the so-called "Anti-Federalists" who were much more inclined to a primarily federal rather than to a national government.

Still, the Constitution obviously came to view as a significant departure from what had been provided for in the Articles of Confederation. Perhaps nothing offered a clearer indication of what lay ahead than the opening words of the Preamble of the Constitution, "We the People." The significance of these words was not lost on so acute an Anti-Federalist as Patrick Henry, who protested in the Virginia Ratification Convention on June 4, 1788:

> I would make this enquiry of those worthy characters [here] who composed a part of the late federal Convention. I am sure they were fully impressed with the necessity of forming a great consolidated government, instead of a confederation. That [the government provided by the Constitution] is a consolidated government is demonstrably clear; and the danger of such a government is, to my mind, very striking. I have the highest veneration for those gentlemen; but, sir, give me leave to demand, what right had they to say, *We, the People*? My political curiosity, exclusive of my anxious solicitude for the public welfare, leads me to ask, Who authorised them to speak the language of, *We, the People*, instead of, *We, the States*? States are the characteristics and the soul of a confederation. If the States be not the agents of this compact, it must be one great, consolidated, national government of the people of all the States.[24]

But however this and like language in the Constitution is to be interpreted, the document displays a remarkable restraint, even what could be called a becoming modesty of speech. Again and again, one encounters the calm and confident elaboration of arrangements, the development and formulation of which had had to come to terms with great and abiding passions that threatened to divide the Country. The discipline found in such language reflects the experience, competence, and civility vital to sustained self-government.

4. Article I, Section 7

I

In recent years both liberals and conservatives have tended to agree that a genuine freedom of speech is necessary in the United States, that citizens should be able to discuss fully all issues of public interest.

Conservatives and liberals are not so likely to agree, however, that among the conditions for an effective freedom of speech are the development and preservation of a citizenry capable of making proper use of this freedom. This topic requires, among other things, an informed consideration of what television has done, and is permitted to continue to do, to the moral character and the political capacities of the American people.

Fruitful deliberation does not just happen. In fact, few peoples in the history of nations have been able to sustain spirited yet disciplined deliberation. And what is true of peoples at large applies also to legislative bodies. Congress, under the Constitution of the United States, provides an instructive illustration of the points I have just made.

We have seen that the freedom of speech of members of Congress is recognized by the Constitution. Congress cannot do its duty properly if members are not left free to discuss, without fear of sanctions elsewhere, whatever they see fit to discuss. Even so, productive discussion is not everyone's talking at random. Some order must be imposed upon the subjects to be discussed. Each House of Congress is empowered, therefore, to establish rules for the governance of its proceedings.

II

But, first, provision had to be made for bringing Congress into being. We have seen how each House of Congress is chosen and what its privileges and prerogatives are as a legislative body. By the end of Section 6 of Article I, sufficient directions have been given to permit the people of the United States, acting in their respective States, to select the members of Congress to which they were entitled—and to permit those members to go about their duties in a workmanlike manner.

In Section 7 *some* directions are given on how a bill becomes a law. Much is left unsaid. The Constitution assumes that everyone knows what a *bill* is and that Congress will determine precisely how something called a *bill* will be transformed into something called a *law*. The Framers evidently did not consider it necessary to say more about these matters than the relatively few things provided for in this section.

At the heart of Section 7 of Article I is the understanding that the making of laws depends ultimately upon Congress. Despite all that is said about the President's part in the legislative process, the account of how a bill becomes a law reflects the ultimate supremacy of Congress among the branches of the General Government.

We will see once again, as we examine this section, the legislative predominance provided for by the Constitution. But we can also usefully bring out here something that we have noticed earlier as well, the extent to which various features of the Constitution are taken from the constitutional history and political experience of the Americans of 1787. The Constitution can be likened to woods which are filled with revealing signs (including tracks of various animals, some of them long gone) that an experienced and alert woodsman can notice. Consider, for example, what is taken for granted by the "Sundays excepted" language in the counting of the days the President has for considering a bill presented to him by Congress. The political-religious presuppositions of Western civilization are casually assumed by this deference to Sundays.

The knowledgeable constitutional woodsman can see where various features of the Constitution came from. For example, passages in the New York and Massachusetts Constitutions of that day anticipated before 1787 much of Section 7 of Article I of the

Constitution of the United States.[25] Other State constitutions of the time, however, had quite different provisions with respect to the matters dealt with in these two State constitutions. This array should remind us that one cannot explain what is in the Constitution of the United States simply by finding antecedents. The Framers of 1787 had a variety of models to draw upon. They had to choose according to some notion of what was best in their circumstances.

III

Sometimes, the Framers seem to have believed, it is good not to provide guidance beyond the barest indications. They assume that, by and large, decisions would be made by majority rule in the legislative bodies. Precisely how each House would go about permitting the majority to have its way was largely left to each of them to determine.

Once Congress is in being, pursuant to Constitutional direction, it controls how legislating is to be done. I refer now only to how laws are to be fashioned, not to what the substantive powers of Congress are nor to what matters Congress may deal with.

Among the things Congress must determine is how the separate doings of its two Houses are to be coordinated with respect to a particular bill. Although each House seems to be left substantially on its own in determining how it will deal with bills, the two Houses must agree upon what constitutes a joint product for presentation to the President. Here, as elsewhere, the Framers obviously relied upon the parliamentary experience of Americans, both before and since 1776.

The Framers also assumed that many of the forms to be relied upon in the fashioning of laws do not really matter, so long as they are both plausible and known and so long as they allow the majority ultimately to have its way after due allowance has been made for the consideration of divergent opinions. I mention this point because one does find in various State constitutions (even more so now than then) detailed provisions for such procedures as how bills are to be framed and how many times they are to be "read." The Framers of 1787, on the other hand, seem to have believed that if Congress could safely be entrusted with vast powers in governing the Country, it could also be entrusted with considerable power in deciding how to conduct its own affairs, especially since it is subject every two years to renewal by the people.

Moreover, Congresses today are properly guided in what they do by the practices and precedents of one hundred past Congresses. Political parties also provide considerable guidance toward the organization of Congress. The First Congress was not unlike Congresses today in that it too had a considerable body of principle and experience to draw upon (but not political parties) when its members sat down to do their work in 1789. They must have believed, as it is easy for people to believe in such circumstances, that the way things had been done, insofar as there was general agreement, must be the natural way of doing things.

IV

Yet is there not something unnatural in what Congress, and indeed any legislature, does—something unnatural, if not even marvelous, to which we are so accustomed that we rarely notice it? I continue to find it astonishing that "all" a legislature ever does officially is to speak—and, even more remarkable, that all the speaking that counts takes the form of *Yea* and *Nay*. The *Yeas* and *Nays* do refer to things that are said about things to be done, but the *Yeas* and *Nays* are what count and what are to be counted. This practice generally assumes, as well as makes it more likely, that all votes will be of equal weight. It also makes majority rule seem quite sensible.

The national laws to be found in our statute books routinely begin, "Be it enacted by the Senate and House of Representatives of the United States of America in Congress assembled . . ." A certain kind of speaking is an action, and so we have "acts of Congress." Words are made flesh, so much so that they may even be said to have teeth. The Executive, on the other hand, is the branch that most often appears to be *acting* rather than "merely" speaking. Our astonishment at all this should be moderated upon recognizing that the significance of the things *said* by Congress does reflect the proper authority of *logos* (or reason) in human affairs.

The Constitution indicates what the authoritative form of legislative saying is to be. There are two major restraints upon the power of Congress to determine when its sayings are authoritative. Most of Section 7 of Article I, on how a bill becomes a law, is devoted to these restraints.

V

The first of these restraints is found in the opening sentence of this section: "All Bills for raising Revenue shall originate in the House of Representatives; but the Senate may propose or concur with Amendments as on other Bills."

Nothing is said here, or elsewhere in the Constitution, as to why revenue bills must originate in the House of Representatives. This is but one of many provisions whose purposes are not expressed. Yet such provisions must be interpreted if they are to be implemented. It may be doubted whether any kind of legal enactment can be properly interpreted without an awareness of its purposes.

This revenue-bill provision is a sign in the woods that the constitutional woodsman can recognize as particularly dramatic, for it reveals much about the constitutional history of the English-speaking peoples for centuries past and about the political circumstances of Americans in 1787.

There is a reminder here of the House of Commons' great quarrel with the Stuarts about who was to determine the sources and amount of the King's revenue. This struggle was exciting, with the loftiest invocations of liberty keyed to the most mundane concerns about property. For Americans this dedication to a property-based liberty took the form of the familiar insistence, "No Taxation Without Representation," which contributed to the Declaration of Independence and the Revolutionary War.

A special form of the concern about the prerogatives of the House of Commons became evident in the Federal Convention of 1787. The decision to designate the House of Representatives as the body in which revenue bills must originate was intimately related to the decision to allow each State, regardless of population, to have an equal number of votes in the Senate. This revenue provision meant, in effect, that a House based on population (and hence on the distribution of property, in the normal order of things) would have the primary influence upon how taxes are to be levied. It was thought improper, at least by the larger States, to allow the small States to have (through the Senate) a decisive voice in determining how much the people in the large States, who would be assessed the bulk of any taxes, would have to pay and in what form.

The revenue-origination provision may also serve to remind us that the House of Representatives is more nearly an exclusively legislative body than is the Senate. The Senate, as we shall see when we discuss the Presidency, shares some of the powers and functions of the Executive branch of the government. This sharing reminds us that "the separation of powers" is qualified.

Sections 2 and 9 of Article I require that direct taxes be apportioned according to population. The revenue-origination provision in Section 7 reinforces what is provided generally in the Constitution about uniformity in taxation. The Framers seem to have agreed that those who happen to have votes should not be able to fleece those who happen to have money.

The concern of the larger States that those who pay more should have the greater say takes many forms. Among nations it may be seen in the recent proposal by the United States that voting power in the United Nations should be somewhat in proportion to financial contributions by nations to that body. At the most local level, such as a faculty meeting, the general principle of equal votes is sometimes tempered by accommodation to the influence of those faculty members who distinguish themselves by their ability to draw students, or by their publications, or by other contributions to the academic community. Against all this, however, is the sense that there should be other prerogatives not based on property, that all are to be treated as if somehow equal. Still, because capital is mobile, those with property (including intellectual property) have to be specially deferred to.

The revenue-origination provision may also serve to remind us of how changes in circumstances may affect, and sometimes nullify, Constitutional provisions. This provision might have been weakened from the outset by the power recognized in the Senate to "propose or concur with Amendments" to revenue bills. Such amendments are, at times, new bills, a practice which the House of Representatives is inclined to resent. Even so, the House that begins the revenue-raising process, especially when the tax bill is complex, can have considerable control over the final version. Amendments cannot usually be as comprehensive as the original bill, and time does run out.

A change in our Constitutional institutions has moderated some of the Framers' concerns here. The Seventeenth Amendment, whereby the Senate is now elected directly by the people in each State rather than by State legislatures, is partly responsible. When this change, which had begun in some States well before the amendment, is combined with the tendency, as through an income tax, to collect monies in ways that do not pit one State against another, the prerogatives here of the House of Representatives seem to diminish.

However, there may still be good reasons for that House to insist upon its prerogatives. There is already much that tends to make the Senate a more prestigious and more attractive place. The Constitutional system depends upon two somewhat different Houses, each of which must enjoy considerable self-respect. (A different aspect of this matter is examined in Section IX of Lecture No. 14.)

VI

I have said that there are two major restraints in Section 7 of Article I to the power of Congress to determine how a bill becomes a law. The first of these restraints is the provision for the origination of revenue-raising bills in the House of Representatives. The second is the assignment to the President of a veto power.

The veto-power arrangement, too, is dependent upon British constitutional experience. The British monarch has, at least in principle, an absolute veto power with respect to bills passed by the House of Commons and the House of Lords. Such a power was exercised by royal governors in various Colonies when the enactments of Colonial legislatures were presented for executive approval.

The Section 7 veto provision may not simply be a diminution of the Congressional power to control the legislating process. It is also intended to insure that the prerogative traditionally claimed by the executive (whatever the status of such a tradition under the

Constitution) should be clearly limited. Still, the Framers knew too much about legislative aberrations not to want to provide a check upon legislative power.

Two-thirds of each House is needed to override the disapproval of the President. Each House considers the bill separately for this purpose; that is, the two Houses are not counted together. The prescribed manner of counting means that instead of a simple majority of 218 in the current House of Representatives, with its 435 members, 290 votes are required to pass a bill over the President's disapproval. Thus, a Presidential veto is worth 72 votes in the House today. Similarly, in the current Senate with its 100 members, 67 votes are needed instead of 51.[26]

Whatever power the President exercises here may be explained by him. The Constitution assumes that Congress is entitled to an explanation since the President must return "with his Objections" any disapproved bill to the House in which it originated.

One may wonder whether a disapproval is constitutionally effective if the Nay-saying President does not provide objections. The Congress, on the other hand, may act to leap over the Presidential barrier without providing any explanation at all. But then Congress routinely does a lot of talking in the course of preparing, debating, and approving bills.

One puzzle is apparent in the otherwise fairly straightforward veto process. Why are bills that are left unsigned by the President not treated uniformly by the Constitution? The fate of such bills depends on whether Congress has adjourned by the time ten days have elapsed. If Congress is there to receive anything the President might send, then his failure to act is treated as if he had signed, and the bill becomes a law. But if "Congress by their Adjournment prevent [a Bill's] Return," any bill he has done nothing about is considered not to be a law. (What constitutes an "Adjournment" has itself come to be an issue in recent years.)

The New York and Massachusetts Constitutions of 1777 and 1780, respectively, indicate that such a provision is designed "to prevent any unnecessary delays" because of executive inaction. We again see, on the other hand, that the Constitution of the United States does not usually bother (except in the Preamble) to explain the purposes of provisions, thus inviting respectful speculation.

The Constitution seems to assume that if the President does not submit a disapproval to a sitting Congress, it may be because he recognizes it is apt to be overturned. In any event, the Constitution anticipates that any disapproval will be accompanied by objections.

But once Congress adjourns, there is no legislature to which the bill may be returned with the President's objections. Still, some might ask, why not require the President at least to record a *Nay* somewhere? Perhaps he is not required to do so because the Constitution, in its parsimony, does not encourage superfluous actions. Besides, is it not preferred that unexplained Executive negatives not be relied upon?

Also, once Congress has adjourned, the only "legislative" power left "in town" is that of the President, but this power pertains only to bills passed by the Congress during the preceding ten legislative days. He is the only one who still has some control over what will become law. Like Congress, in similar circumstances, he need not explain himself; he need only say *Yea*. Thus, when anyone "legislates," a positive action is required.

The Constitution says nothing about the basis upon which the President may approve or disapprove. Presumably, he is entitled to take into account the various considerations (including those of constitutionality, fairness, and usefulness) that Congress might also take into account. Even so, it is much preferred, as we have seen, that he give reasons for any disapproval. It should not be a mere act of will, a monarchical fiat. Once he has acted, Congress is required to record the *Yeas* and *Nays* in any attempt to set aside the Presidential disapproval.

VII

I need only touch here upon another implication of the provision for what happens in the event of a Presidential veto. The considerable detail in this provision dramatizes the complete silence in the Constitution about judicial review—that is, about the supposed duty and power of the National Courts to assess for their constitutionality the laws duly enacted by Congress. Is it likely, one may well wonder, that judicial review was indeed anticipated, when nothing was said about it, considering the care with which executive review was provided for?

Such questions as the following come to mind, especially in the light of the extensive veto provision, about any possible judicial review of acts of Congress: What happens after a court strikes down a law? Is such striking down retroactive to the time the law was enacted? How much of a court does it take to act? Should there be a routine procedure for bringing laws before courts for such review? Which courts are entitled or obliged to exercise this power? What may Congress do in response to such action by a court? Or is a Constitutional amendment the only remedy here— which is to ask, what about the legislative supremacy that is otherwise evident throughout the Constitution?

These questions are stimulated by the arrangements in Section 7 of Article I. We shall consider these matters further when we get to the Judicial Article of the Constitution.[27]

VIII

The concluding part of Section 7 prescribes that every "Order, Resolution or Vote to which the Concurrence of the Senate and House of Representatives may be necessary (except on a question of Adjournment) shall be presented to the President" and shall be responded to by him in the same way, and with the same effect, as bills are presented and responded to. Executive review of bills cannot be avoided by calling a bill something else.

This precaution, to which considerable space is devoted, reflects an awareness by the Framers of how human ingenuity may be used in the service of evasiveness. Efforts will be made to circumvent various limitations. It is also known that it is easier for those who exercise power if they do not seem to be acting against the rules.

In any case, the Framers of the Constitution were very much aware that human nature, in both its lowest and its highest forms, must be reckoned with by statesmen.

IX

I have suggested that the Framers knew, and expected truly political men in government to know, that rules must be both recognized and defensible.

They also knew that many vital rules have to be adjusted to circumstances, and so they left it to each House of Congress to determine precisely how to go about making the laws it was empowered
to help make. Differences in members' ages, in the sizes of assemblies, in powers, in the terms of office, and in constituencies might
well affect what rules would be appropriate in each House from
time to time.

I have also suggested that a considerable experience, both in
Great Britain and in North America, was drawn upon in framing
the Constitutional provisions we have examined on this occasion.
But I have suggested as well that experience, however worthy of
respect, does not alone suffice. Judgment, both moral and political, must be used in determining which lessons of experience are
appropriate in the circumstances one anticipates for oneself and
one's posterity.

5. Article I, Section 8

I

It will be recalled that we saw, in our discussion of Section 7 of Article I, the importance of history for one's understanding of several provisions in that section. We particularly noticed that the Presidential veto provision drew upon antecedents in the State constitutions of New York and Massachusetts, and that the provision for the origination of revenue bills in the House of Representatives drew upon the parliamentary experience of the British people in the centuries preceding.

Section 8 of Article I, too, is derivative of the constitutional history of the Anglo-American people. Many things in this section require acquaintance with constitutional antecedents and with political experience for their accounting. Indeed, it may never be possible to develop a full accounting for this section because chance may affect both what was thought then and what we can learn now about prevailing concerns and precedents in 1787.

The enumeration of some of the Congressional powers had been prompted in large part by a concern about the effect of leaving out powers that had been previously provided for explicitly in the Articles of Confederation or in other constitutional sources. Some of the powers, then, may have been included out of an abundance of caution, especially if they are powers that have been claimed on occasion in Anglo-American constitutional history by either the Executive or the Judiciary.

I will not try to account for the presence of each of the dozen and a half powers enumerated in Section 8. Rather, I will suggest something about the principle of order in accordance with which these

50

powers are organized. Once one sees a plausible pattern, one is likely to approach these powers and the possible significance of their enumeration in a way different from that conventionally relied upon.[28]

Thus, although chance might have been critical here, there may also be an organizing principle which takes chance into account and, to some extent, conquers it.

II

Everyone talks about the Constitution as being an instrument of enumerated powers. Many see the principal depository of such enumerated powers to be Section 8 of Article I. Yet it is evident, upon a careful examination of this section, that considerably more power than is explicitly provided for here is taken for granted. It seems, for example, to be indicated at the outset of Section 8 that the power to lay and collect taxes is to be used, in part, to "provide for the common Defence and general Welfare of the United States." Does not this suggest that a comprehensive mandate for Congress with respect to the general welfare, whatever that may mean, is provided for elsewhere? More is said in this section about powers related to the common defense, with a half-dozen of them collected here. But even these are rather fragmentary, also presupposing thereby that a comprehensive mandate with respect to the common defense has been provided for elsewhere.[29]

All this suggests, among other things, that the Preamble to the Constitution should be taken much more seriously than it usually is, for it is there that the purposes, and hence the powers, of the Government of the United States are authoritatively anticipated. The opening section of Article I can speak of "[a]ll legislative Powers [t]herein granted"—and this *is* to suggest that there are no powers intrinsic to legislatures that Congress inherits, but rather "only" those powers provided for in the Constitution. Still, the powers provided for, either expressly or by implication, may be considerable, far more than the bare enumeration in Section 8 of Article I has led many to believe.

The Anti-Federalists, during the 1787–1788 Ratification Campaign, insisted that the powers of Congress, especially when reinforced by the Necessary and Proper Clause with which Section 8 ends, were vast. Such talk is often dismissed as mere rhetoric, just as are those Federalist counterarguments that consistently played down the extent of the powers provided for by the proposed Constitution. But might not the Anti-Federalists have offered the sounder reading at that stage of the debate?

I anticipate further discussion of the Tenth Amendment by observing that the First Congress, which wrote that amendment in 1789, made sure that the substantive powers granted to Congress by the Constitution of 1787 remained broad, and one assurance of that was the First Congress's refusal to insert the word *expressly* in what is now the Tenth Amendment (so as to make it read, "The powers not expressly delegated to the United States . . ."[30]

Thus, the "party" that prevailed in the Federal Convention, in the Ratification Campaign, and thereafter in the First Congress was determined to recognize a broad grant of powers for the new Congress.

III

We have been more concerned thus far with the emergence of Congress and with its operations than with the powers of that Congress. In this we imitate not only the way the Constitution was written but also the way the Federal Convention conducted its business in 1787. More than a month went by that summer before the Convention considered systematically (if it ever did) the powers the new Congress would have. On June 29, a Georgia delegate expressed the wish "that the powers of the General Legislature had been defined, before the mode of constituting it had been agitated."[31]

. I suspect that this delegate failed to appreciate, or at least did not want to acknowledge, what had been widely understood from the outset of the Convention, that the new legislature would have considerable power. This was reflected in the general agreement quite early in the Convention that the new Congress would be bicameral, thus transforming it into a traditional (and hence full?) legislature instead of the treaty-like conference of "sovereign" States (and hence a body of quite limited powers) that Congress had been under the Articles of Confederation.

The final particular power in Section 8, "To exercise exclusive

Legislation" in certain specified cases, is curiously revealing. This provision implies that the mere grant of power to Congress by the Constitution does not make that power exclusive to Congress, however much Congress's actions may control or preempt what the States might otherwise do. The States can legislate with respect to many of the things that Congress might. Or, put another way, the fact that the States in the early days of the Republic did legislate with respect to many of these things does not mean that Congress was without a superior power here whenever it chose to use it. Or, put still another way for the most important case, Congress has a comprehensive commerce power that the States may share up to the point that Congress chooses to exercise it.

The States did do a considerable amount of the governing in the early days of the Republic. Besides, a sensible Congress would not often want to do things that the States could do about as well, especially since the same people control both the Congress and the State legislatures. There should be no insuperable problems in adjusting the respective claims of Congress and of the State legislatures, especially if the political process is allowed to work.

Any insistence upon "exclusive" powers in Congress is still another illustration of the observation that "more may be less." That is, to insist upon "exclusive" powers in Congress is in effect to deny to Congress various of the extensive powers that the States had been permitted to continue to exercise from 1789 on.

IV

Let us now look in some detail at our text. The first impression made by Section 8 of Article I is that it is a complex collection of powers, made even more so by the apparent lack of order. Still, most of the provisions can be seen as reinforcing and protecting, or filling out, the powers of the General Government over the economy of the Country and over foreign affairs, including the development and uses of the military.

This section ends with an emphatic reminder of Congressional power, its concluding statement saying, in effect, that Congress would indeed have, or could help others to have, fully and effectively the powers indicated here and elsewhere in the Constitution. It may even be said that the Necessary and Proper Clause points to an ultimately comprehensive power in the Congress.

There is something stark about the way Section 8 begins and proceeds. It is matter-of-fact, with no flourishes and with the barest indications of ends or purposes, though, as said, the principal concerns seem to be with commerce, on the one hand, and with war and peace, on the other. Several provisions in this section are ancillary to the concern with commerce; even more are ancillary to the concern with war and peace. Much seems to be taken for granted about the status of property and its uses. The broad tax power provided for does not seem to be given for its own sake, but to permit the General Government to manage as it should both the economy (broadly conceived) and the foreign relations (including the defense) of the Country.

If the powers enumerated in Section 8 are treated as fragments isolated from the rest of the Constitutional scheme, the array does seem arbitrary. But however inexplicable Section 8 may seem on first impression, it stands forth as intelligible once the powers there enumerated are recognized as reinforcements of the General Government's broad powers relating to war and peace and to commerce. Whatever the structure of Section 8, the practice has been (especially with the use of the Necessary and Proper Clause) to provide the General Government quite extensive powers with respect to the domestic life of the Country and with respect to the relations of this Country with other countries. It is not generally appreciated, though, how much this practical (indeed natural?) accommodation has been provided for in the Constitution itself.

The general scope of the Congressional powers in the Constitution is indirectly attested to by the restraints placed upon Congress in Section 9 of Article I. Various of the restraints in Section 9 and elsewhere are upon activities not explicitly mentioned in such parts of the Constitution as Section 8, thereby testifying to a general legislative power in Congress. I again suggest that most of the Section 8 provisions may not be so much granting powers to Congress as recognizing particular powers in Congress, powers that may be already subsumed in grants of general powers to Congress but that, for one reason or another, might be claimed by another branch of government or might even be regarded as nonexistent for the General Government.

When one does try to work out the organization of the powers in Section 8, as suggested in the chart prepared for this lecture,[32] one more easily becomes aware of the general scheme of things assumed in Section 8. This scheme reflects the plenary authority of Congress, especially with respect to both the economy and the foreign relations of the Country. The order to be discerned here requires us to reconsider what is usually said not only about Section 8 but about the Constitution as a whole.

The seventeen sets of powers in Section 8 can usefully be collected in seven categories (as is done in Appendix F). If we accept the conventional interpretations of these powers, the seven categories can be conveniently identified as financial, commercial, monetary, intellectual, judicial, defensive, and managerial (that is, with respect to certain property of the United States). The first three categories are linked in obvious ways. The last three categories indicate Congressional authority with respect to the judiciary, the executive (in its military aspect), and the States (as sources of the property to be managed by the United States). The central category, dealing with post offices and with copyrights and patents, might have been primarily concerned originally with facilitating economic development, but it does look to what may loosely be called the intellectual life of the Country. It is here that steady improvement in the community is explicitly anticipated ("To promote the Progress of Science and useful Arts").

Much of what one says about the arrangement of these seventeen sets of powers in Section 8 is bound to be speculative. (A half-dozen of these sets could be further divided into two or more distinct sets.) I have observed that we simply do not know enough to permit us to be certain about the significance of each set of powers in this context. There must be something that accounts for the arrangement discerned here, for it is obvious that these powers are not collected in the order in which they were agreed upon by the Federal Convention over the summer of 1787. One is challenged to try to figure out what guided the constitutional craftsmen (and particularly Gouverneur Morris and James Wilson, evidently the principal draftsmen of the final version) in putting the Section 8 powers together as we now find them. It suffices for our immediate purposes to suggest a plausible scheme, which thereby makes us more likely to appreciate the integrity of the Constitution as a whole.

Particularly speculative, and hence most tentative, is what I now turn to, supplementing what I have said about the seven categories in which one may collect the seventeen sets of powers found in Section 8. I further suggest that the seventeen sets of powers may be grouped according to the character of those powers before the Constitution was drafted, that is, according to the way those powers were regarded in earlier constitutional documents or in the constitutional thought of the period.[33] It was prudent to explicitly provide Congress those powers once thought, if only by some, to be judicial or executive in character, as well as those powers that had been exercised or claimed either by the Confederation Congress or by the States.

Five such groups, with considerable overlapping, are suggested in Appendix F.[34] The first group of powers might have been considered by some always to have been legislative. If so, they would have been enumerated here either to retain for Congress what the Confederation Congress had had theretofore or to counteract exclusive State claims with respect to those matters. The second group of powers might have been considered by some to have been at one time or another executive (on the civilian or domestic side), especially since there are reflected here various of the prerogatives claimed on occasion by the British monarch. The third group of powers might have been considered judicial by some, and remind us of the authority of the Congress with respect to the courts. The fourth group of powers might have been considered by some to have been at one time or another executive (on the military or foreign-relations side). Was it not sensible to make clear that there is to be no residual executive prerogative with respect to those matters, especially since the President is recognized in Article II as Commander in Chief of the armed forces of the United States? Finally, there is the fifth group of powers, also considered by some always to have been legislative. If so, these powers would have been enumerated for the same reasons the legislative powers in the first group were. The seventeenth set of powers, for example, has the claims that the States might have once had to places acquired by the United States from the States now completely superseded by the claims of Congress. In many cases, therefore, there might have been more than one reason for enumerating a power, the most frequent combination of reasons probably being the desire both to confirm a legislative power for Congress and to suppress executive pretensions.

There may thus be seen in Section 8 an instructive symmetry. The draftsmen of this section moved, in this affirmation of the powers of Congress, from powers previously believed by some to be legislative, to those previously believed by some to be executive, to those previously believed by some to be judicial, to others previously believed by some to be executive, and finally to others previously believed by some to be legislative. A number of subsequent possible claims, arguments, and uncertainties are thus foreclosed, not least with respect to the legislative powers that had been exercised exclusively by the States under the Articles of Confederation.

Has this caution had, however, a perverse effect? The powers listed here primarily to fill out and confirm the authority of Congress and to avoid controversy might have had the unanticipated result of making the powers enumerated here virtually the only recognized powers of Congress. Still, the use of the Necessary and Proper Clause has allowed the expansion of the specific powers listed in Section 8 to secure for Congress almost the full range of any intended powers. But has not this come about in such a way as to obscure the order and symmetry I have been pointing out?[35]

It is when one becomes aware of the organization of Section 8 that one can begin to see that the powers enumerated there may be less independent grants of power and more assurances of the extent of the considerable powers of the Congress, powers that are otherwise provided for or recognized in the Constitution. Much of what I have said here about the character of various Section 8 powers no doubt needs to be corrected or at least refined by scholars versed in the constitutional history of the seventeenth and eighteenth centuries.

V

However Section 8 of Article I is read, it does confirm that Congress, as a working legislature, would have two major powers that Congress under the Articles of Confederation had not had: a direct power over taxes and a comprehensive power over commerce. (A third major power, with respect to foreign relations and the military, had already been exercised by the Confederation Congress and is here reinforced. Because several of the powers listed in Section 8 had been assigned by the Articles of Confederation to Congress, they may be mentioned here lest silence respecting them be taken to mean that the new Congress is *not* to have them.) The power over commerce—over all gainful activity affecting the United States—has proved decisive in determining the scope of the General Government. The United States Supreme Court, in the past half-century, has finally come to acknowledge that the Congress may regulate as much of the economy of the United States as it deems necessary for the common good.[36] In this, it is suggested by my analysis of Section 8, the Court has merely recognized what had been intended from the outset by the Framers of the Constitution, something Chief Justice Marshall had recognized more than a century before.[37]

The Congressional power, especially the power over commerce, is now acknowledged perhaps almost to the extent originally intended.[38] But this has developed in such a roundabout way that it can seem to all too many citizens that the Constitution has had to be circumvented to serve contemporary necessities. This mode of recourse has not provided a salutary lesson for the Country, especially when used to justify the expansion of Executive power as well. The way all this has been done with respect to Congress has not only obscured the craftsmanship evident in the Constitution, leaving gaps in the Constitutional scheme that remain to be filled, but has also been partly responsible for the misconceived "original intent" debate in recent years. The alternative is not "a growing Constitution" but rather a resurrected Constitution.

VI

Much has gotten in the way of a proper reading of the Constitution with respect to the commerce power, including early Southern concerns about uninformed and hence dangerous Congressional interference with slavery. I have indicated that the failure of Congress to exercise many of its powers in the early days of the Republic distorted subsequent interpretations of the Constitution.

Still it became increasingly evident as the twentieth century unfolded that only the General Government could govern the economy of the Country—or, at least, that it was politically necessary for the national government to seem to be attempting to govern that economy. (Did not the misreading of the Commerce Clause mean, in effect, that the American economy was, for a century, left free to develop in an unprecedented manner without comprehensive governmental control?)

We have noticed that virtually nothing is said in Section 8 about the ends of government. But then, little is said about those ends in the body of the Constitution as a whole, and this reminds us of the importance of the Preamble for suggesting the scope of the concerns of the General Government.We should take to heart an observation about the Constitution by Patrick Henry in the Virginia Ratification Convention of 1788 that some must have considered a warning and others must have considered a reassurance: "To all the common purposes of legislation," he said, "[the Constitution] is a great consolidation of government."[39]

If the Constitution does permit a significant consolidation of government, if that government is of the scope that my analysis of Section 8 of Article I suggests, then its ends must be those that governments typically have. Those ends are recognized in the Preamble. They include, in addition to the ends usually served by other constitutions, the special place for liberty in the American Union.

VII

However profound the American respect for liberty, it did not seem prudent to the Framers that the General Government should be so shackled that it could not do the things it needed to do, including the maintenance of the conditions that permit liberty to flourish. A reluctance to shackle government is expressed again and again in the Federal Convention. It is evident that the Government of the United States *is* empowered to do whatever it is intended to do, however important it may be that the people of the United States always be free to examine and discuss whatever that government does.

To say that Congress has great powers does not deny there are limitations upon how those powers are to be exercised. In Section 8 of Article I alone, there are a half-dozen restrictions upon Congress. (Several of the powers listed in Section 8 may be there partly to provide points of departure for limitations collected in this section upon the powers of Congress. Related to this consideration is my discussion, in Section III of Lecture No. 6, of Section 9 of Article I of the Constitution.) These restrictions may be seen in the uniformity that is required as to taxes, and also as to naturalization laws and bankruptcy laws; they may be seen in the limited time for which patents and copyrights may be given, and also the strictly limited time for which army (but not naval) appropriations may be made; and they may be seen in the various powers retained by the States with respect to the militia occasionally in the service of the United States.

In addition, the wording of the powerful Necessary and Proper Clause reflects profound limitations. What is *necessary* depends, of course, largely upon judgment. But must there not be a plausible relation between what is being done and the evident ends of the powers thus being supplemented? What is *proper* depends upon limitations found elsewhere in the Constitution, as well as upon a sense of decency, if not upon natural right itself.

The limitations found in the Constitution may help us appreciate what the ends were intended to be of the government established by the Constitution. I have observed that it is likely that the Congress that wrote the Bill of Rights in 1789 did not believe it was cutting in any way into the substantive powers of the General Government of the United States. In fact, such limitations serve, for a people such as ours, to make it more likely that the Government of the United States is able to advance, with deep-rooted and enduring popular support, the ends it was intended to serve.

With these remarks I have anticipated my next lecture, which will examine the final two sections of Article I of the Constitution and which will look ahead as well to the Bill of Rights.[40]

6. Article I, Sections 9 & 10

I

The discipline reflected in and permitted, if not required, by the Constitution should be evident from a careful reading of the document. Discipline is reflected in the care and competence with which the Constitution is put together. Discipline is called for if the public servants authorized by the Constitution are to exercise in a salutary manner the powers entrusted to them.

We have glimpsed in this Commentary the kinds of sources upon which the Framers of the Constitution drew. These sources are evident to students of the constitutional documents that precede the United States Constitution. They are evident as well to those familiar with the early history of the United States and the proceedings of the Federal Convention of 1787.

We have also seen that there is a sense to the whole of the Constitution, that the document can be thought about, part by part as well as in terms of the relations among the parts. This *thinking* about the Constitution—the very insistence that it can be thought about—is critical to these lectures. This Commentary, then, is an exercise in how to read not only the Constitution but anything serious.

We can see how the two parts of the Constitution with which we are primarily concerned here, Sections 9 and 10 of Article I, illuminate each other. Various of the provisions in Section 9 seem, standing alone, to be directed at all governments in the United States. Even if the first and last of the eight provisions in Section 9 did not conclusively indicate that only the Government of the United States is being addressed throughout Section 9, then Section 10, which is obviously addressed to the States, would make it clear that this is so. Several provisions from Section 9 are repeated in Section 10 (with respect to bills of attainder, ex post facto laws, and titles of nobility). It would not have been necessary to repeat these provisions in Section 10 if Section 9 were intended to apply to the State Governments as well as to the Government of the United States. My immediate purpose in pointing out these relations is to illustrate what it means to say that the Constitution invites and requires careful reading, a reading that takes each part seriously even as it keeps the whole in mind.

I can now turn to a more or less systematic consideration of Sections 9 and 10 of Article I. A full consideration of these two sections would have to say much more than I can here about the sources of various of its provisions in the materials upon which the Constitution of the United States draws. It is one consequence of the success of the constitutional statesmanship of 1787 that the Constitution itself has come to be regarded as if it stood virtually alone, and this can have the unfortunate effect of helping make the Constitution seem less meticulously organized than it is. We have seen in our discussion of Section 8 of Article I that one must make an effort today to discern the care with which the seemingly divergent parts of the Constitution are put together. A Constitution that proved to be remarkably successful in large part because it was so well crafted has, because of its eclipse of its predecessors, come to be regarded as in some degree haphazard and therefore as far less well crafted than it was originally recognized to be.

II

Section 9 follows immediately upon the development in Article I of the Legislature and of much of the legislative power of the United States. Restraints are placed in Section 9 upon how that legislative power is to be exercised, upon how revenues may be raised, and upon how expenditures of such revenues are to be made.

This section begins with a guarantee for twenty years of the right of *the original States* to engage in the international slave trade. It is fitting and proper that this was thus exposed to view, rather than hidden among the tax and commercial provisions later in this section, because it was one unhappy but obvious condition for perpetuation of the Union. Two of the States, South Carolina and Georgia, evidently persuaded the Federal Convention that they and North Carolina would not accept the proposed Constitution without this guarantee, a guarantee reinforced by a restraint upon any use of the tax power to accomplish the same thing that was feared from a commercial regulation by Congress of the slave trade. If those three States had stayed out, there was no telling what effect that would have had either upon other Southern States or upon European powers interested in meddling in American affairs.

The second and third provisions of Section 9, dealing with habeas corpus and with bills of attainder and ex post facto laws, are, in effect, an insistence upon the rule of law that it is well to have after such great powers had been recognized for the Government of the United States as are evident in Section 8. Perhaps this insistence upon the rule of law is particularly to be treasured by a people who could see, in the slavery institutions with which they had come to be saddled, the despotism that a perversion of the rule of law can lead to.

The fourth, fifth, and sixth provisions of Section 9, dealing with direct taxes, with export taxes, and with preferential treatment of some ports at the expense of others, exhibit a concern lest the revenue, and to a lesser extent, the commerce, powers of the United States be used to favor some States at the expense of others. This lively concern, that all States be treated the same, continues down to our day, as may be seen in contemporary legislative struggles about policies that favor, say, "the Sun Belt" as against "the Frost Belt."

The seventh provision of Section 9 proceeds, naturally enough, to precautions about how the money collected, in a fair fashion, by the United States is to be distributed and to be accounted for. It seems appropriate that immediately following these severe restrictions upon the distribution of money there should be even more severe restrictions, in the final provision of Section 9, upon the distribution of titles of nobility by the United States. Some like money, we are thus taught, and others like honor. Therefore, checks have to be placed against abuses that may conceal from the self-governing American people how things really stand with respect to where the funds in the Treasury go and where the merit among them is to be found. (Appendix L displays an 1810 attempt to limit further the distribution of titles of nobility among Americans.)

III

The restrictions found in Section 9 reinforce what we have seen in the preceding sections of Article I about the extent of the legislative powers and about the relation of the Legislative branch of government to the Executive and Judicial branches. It has been suggested that it is the Appropriations Clause of Section 9 "that, more than any other , gives Congress control over the acts of other branches of government . . . since all depend on Congress for money to carry out their functions."[41] The implications of various of the Section 9 provisions can thus be appreciated.

The constitutional scholar whom I have just quoted can dismiss the slave-trade provision as "of historical interest only" at this time.[42] To take this approach, however, is to neglect a most revealing, and hence instructive, feature of the Constitution. For it can be quite useful to ask what the twenty-year guarantee of an exclusive international slave-trade power in the States implies about the original power of Congress to regulate the slave trade. Does not this guarantee implicitly recognize that without it the Congress would have been able, at once, to forbid Americans to engage in the international slave trade? A further question: If so, what would have permitted Congress to do this? The answer: The Commerce Clause, with its grant of power to Congress to "regulate Commerce with foreign Nations." This leads to still another question: What does the grant of power to Congress to "regulate Commerce . . . among the several States" permit Congress to do about the slave trade moving between the States of the Union, to say nothing of slavery's influence and effects upon the commercial life of the Country as a whole? Does not the twenty-year international slave-trade guarantee tacitly recognize a quite broad commerce power in the Congress of the United States, and perhaps also a broad general-welfare power? The insistence by Georgia and South Carolina upon this temporary curtailment of Congressional power can be read as eloquent testimony to the great dormant powers of the

64

General Government under the Constitution.

These, and like, analyses suggest that the powers provided for by the Constitution were intended to be, from the beginning, far more extensive than they are yet recognized to be in principle, however broad they may now be in practice. It can still be said by scholars that "there is no general power granted to Congress to legislate for the general welfare." Rather, we are told, the principal, if not the only, general-welfare power to be exercised by Congress comes from the power given it in Section 8 of Article I to "lay and collect Taxes, Duties, Imposts and Excises . . . [in order to] provide for the common Defence and general Welfare of the United States."[43] It should be evident to those who have found merit in the way I have interpreted the Constitution thus far that it is unlikely that the only power given Congress to provide for the general welfare should come in the form of a power given it to lay and collect taxes in order to provide for the general welfare. It is remarkable that this language in Section 8 should not have led judges and scholars to the rather obvious conclusion that an extensive Congressional power to provide for the general welfare must be otherwise accounted for in the Constitution. For this we can look to the Preamble of the Constitution, if not to the very nature of a legislative body for the Country as a whole. We can look as well, as we have only begun to do here, to the general-welfare power, and the other great powers, taken for granted in the very restrictions placed upon Congress in Section 9 of the Constitution.

I again observe that when we read the Constitution in this fashion and apply it to contemporary problems, there is no need for the Constitution to "grow." It was, in principle, fully grown from its outset, subject to the profound challenge with respect to slavery, evident in the original Constitution, which was eventually faced up to by the Thirteenth, Fourteenth, and Fifteenth Amendments.

We now return to Section 9 by observing that there is much in that section to confirm what is generally evident in the Constitution—to confirm what James Wilson, who was later to serve on the United States Supreme Court, said in the Federal Convention on August 13, well after the Constitution had begun to take its final form: "War, Commerce & Revenue [are] the great objects of the General Government."[44]

IV

If the Government of the United States was intended from the outset to be a government of extensive powers, what safeguards were there to protect against the abuses of such powers? The principal safeguards evident in the Constitution itself are, first, the qualified separation of powers (which means, among other things, that no one officer or body of men can have its way without gaining the cooperation of others, with Congress itself divided into two largely independent bodies); second, the significant place left for the States in the complete Constitutional system; and third, the ultimate control by the people, who retain the power to review what their public servants are doing.

Much was made during the 1787–1788 Ratification Campaign of the absence from the Constitution of a bill of rights, the preparation of which had been briefly considered in the Federal Convention. I suspect that if it had been anticipated by the Convention delegates how much of a fuss would be made during the Ratification Campaign about the lack of a bill of rights, a separate compendium of the rights and privileges of citizens would have been prepared by them, drawing upon what was available in various State constitutions of the day.

Even so, it has been noted, "Section 9 and Section 10 [of Article I] were originally looked on as a kind of bill of rights."[45] Several of the provisions found in these sections are to be found in State bills of rights of the day, particularly the guarantees with respect to habeas corpus, bills of attainder, and ex post facto laws. Those particular rights, coming as they do in the Constitution after the Legislative branch is established, serve as reminders that this government should indeed proceed through laws. This insistence upon the rule of law, which may be seen throughout the Constitution, is sometimes regarded as significantly different from what may be seen in the Bill of Rights we now have. The rule-of-law emphasis may be somewhat more political, and less personal, in orientation than our contemporary concern with rights. But one should not make too much of this, since not only is the habeas corpus concern in Article I rather "personal" in interest but so are the jury-trial and perhaps the treason-trial guarantees found in Article III of the original Constitution.

Besides, many of our Bill of Rights guarantees very much depend upon, or aim at, the rule of law. This means it is recognized that our rights and privileges presuppose established government and a civilized way of life. An insistence upon the rule of law may be seen, for example, in the freedom of the press recognized in the First Amendment. A substantial part of that guarantee looks to keeping government from instituting a system of censorship. The "no previous restraint" rule included in "freedom of the press" means that publishing will be subjected only to the kind of rule of law that other human activities are routinely subjected to.

Still, as we have noticed, freedom of speech and of the press were taken for granted by the Constitution even before the First Amendment was adopted. After all, there is considerable reliance in the Constitution upon discussion. It is obviously taken for granted in the exercise of the power recognized in the people to ratify and to amend the Constitution (in Articles VII and V), in the Republican Form of Government Guarantee for the States (in Article IV), in the protection of the freedom of speech of legislators (in Article I), in the opportunity provided the President to state his objections when he vetoes a bill passed by Congress (in Article I), and of course in the periodic recourse to elections (in Articles I and II). Even before the Constitution was prepared, there had been, for some two decades, a vigorous public reliance upon the most uninhibited freedom of speech. And so the First Amendment was in a sense superfluous. This is not to deny that it is important to retain the amendment, once we have had it and have relied upon it, lest its removal be taken to mean a national repudiation of our vital freedom of speech.

Whatever one may think about the necessity for the Bill of Rights, one thing about it should again be emphasized as we prepare to draw to a close our principal consideration of the legislative powers of the Government of the United States. The Bill of Rights did not cut in any significant way into any of the substantive powers of that government. I pointed out in my last lecture that it is hardly likely that the very men who wrote the Constitution would, upon taking control of the Congress two years later, have set out to dismantle what they had so painstakingly built up during the summer of 1787. They did intend that the General Government should be able to govern, especially with respect to commerce and to war and peace; they also intended that Congress should have the tax power to properly finance such governing. The freedom of citizens to examine and discuss what their government is doing does not mean that that government cannot do the things it is empowered to do. In fact, we can again say, the government is better able to do what it is empowered to do precisely because people can freely examine whatever may be done.

We need not go further into what freedom of speech is and how it and other rights contribute to a proper government in these United States. It suffices to assure ourselves that the Framers of the Constitution did not go to the trouble they did in order to empower the new government to abridge freedom of speech, to quarter soldiers improperly, or to deny any person his life, liberty, or property without due process of law.

Due process, which is primarily a courts-based guarantee, may be temporarily set aside in grave circumstances, as can be seen in the habeas corpus provision. It seems to be suggested, by its being placed thus in the Legislative Article, that only Congress can order, or authorize (if only retroactively?) the President to order, a suspension of the privilege of the writ of habeas corpus. But, one must wonder, why was not a similar provision put in Section 10 to control State governments, especially since the bill of attainder and ex post facto provisions in Section 9 were repeated with respect to the States in Section 10? May this suggest something that few recognize even today, that it was intended from the beginning that improper arrests in the States could be reached by means of a habeas corpus action in a national, or "federal", court, or at least that Congress could authorize access to the National Courts for this purpose (and this well before the Fourteenth Amendment)?[46] Or does it merely suggest that sufficient habeas corpus protection in the States is implied by the Republican Form of Government Guarantee for the States? Some clarification of all this can be hoped for when we consider the judicial power of the United States in Lectures No. 10 and No. 11.

It should be instructive to notice here how the habeas corpus privilege is provided for. It seems to be indicated that this long-established privilege is not to be infringed except in special circumstances. The Framers obviously built here upon the common-law privilege, a privilege similarly available in most, if not all, of the

States at that time. This should remind us that common-law privileges and immunities were always considered by early Americans to be constitutionally available to them, independent of what any document might say from time to time. One risk of a bill of rights was repeatedly pointed out during the 1787–1788 Ratification Campaign, and that was that the formal enumeration of certain rights might be taken to repudiate other long-established rights. (This risk is related to what we have noticed in Section IV of Lecture No. 5 about the perhaps unintended consequences of the enumeration of powers in Section 8 of Article I.) So well recognized were common-law, and hence constitutional, privileges and immunities among the English-speaking peoples that Americans could confidently invoke them when they drew up their grievances against Great Britain in the Declaration of Independence. They obviously did not need a bill of rights to do that, and to make it stick.

I have already referred to the suggestion that a formal bill-of-rights approach might have encouraged a greater emphasis upon the personal than upon the political in the way citizens approach their governments. Does this follow from, or does it make more likely, a greater emphasis upon judicial review, and hence judicial governance, than was exhibited in the early days of the Republic? Even so, it should be noticed, much of what the United States Supreme Court has been doing, with the Fourteenth Amendment and perhaps with other Constitutional provisions, may be somewhat similar to what English common-law courts did in the seventeenth and eighteenth centuries in building up the great body of common-law privileges and immunities recognized under the British Constitution. I shall say more about this subject, too, when I examine Article III.

One more point should be made before we turn from these Bill of Rights considerations to a systematic inquiry into Section 10 of Article I. It should be evident, from a study of all of the provisions we have discussed, that the Framers of the Constitution were hardly relativists. We see again and again, including in Sections 9 and 10, qualifications and exemptions that do not make sense unless the language thus modified would otherwise be unqualified and hence absolute in effect. We also see provisions that are presented without qualifications or exceptions, reflecting in this way the Framers' beliefs in absolutes.

V

Let us turn now to a consideration of the arrangement of the provisions in Section 10, a consideration that can be briefer than it might otherwise be because of what we have already said about Section 9. There are some fourteen provisions collected in three paragraphs. The first paragraph sets forth complete, or absolute, prohibitions upon the States; the second and third paragraphs set forth qualified prohibitions upon the States, that is, prohibitions that Congress may suspend from time to time.

The first five provisions, comprising roughly the first half of the first paragraph, help make sure that the Government of the United States will not be interfered with by the States in its exercise of its Constitutional powers with respect to foreign relations (the first two provisions) and with respect to monetary matters (the next three provisions). Thus, the United States is to be able to act as a sovereign abroad and is to have virtually unlimited powers over the domestic economy.

The latter half of the first paragraph contains the bill-of-rights-type provisions I have already discussed. The States are limited with respect to these matters as is the Government of the United States. The "sleeping giant" here is the "Obligation of Contracts" provision, something not found in Section 9. Almost all scholars see the Contracts Clause as a special form of an ex post facto prohibition, extending to contracts already made a special immunity from retroactive State interference.[47]

The remainder of Section 10, in its second and third paragraphs, places restraints upon the exercise by the States of their tax powers (in the tenth and eleventh provisions of this section) and upon various things the States might do that affect foreign relations (in the twelfth, thirteenth, and fourteenth provisions of this section). These restraints may be waived, and the exercise of these State powers may be supervised, by Congress. It has ultimate control over the relations among the States and over the relations with foreign nations that these restraints are designed to keep particular States from disturbing.

We can again see how extensive the great objects of the Government of the United States were intended to be, especially with respect to the national economy and to foreign relations. One might wonder whether even the bill of attainder and ex post facto restraints upon both the States and the General Government exhibit a considerable concern that property rights, and hence commercial activity, not be improperly interfered with by government. Or does it suffice to see these restraints as contributing, along with the titles-of-nobility restraint, to the necessity of maintaining republican governments if a continental republic is to survive? If so, these bill-of-rights-type provisions are not primarily for the sake of citizens but for the sake of the Union itself.

The "without the Consent of the Congress" qualifications in Sections 9 and 10 once again remind us not only of the broad powers of the Government of the United States but also of the primacy of Congress among the various branches of the General Government. When the Government of the United States speaks to the States, it is primarily through Congress. We can thus see here, still another time, the extent and character of legislative supremacy under the Constitution. I keep making this point not only because it is so much neglected today, but also because various sections we have come upon suggest problems that cannot be satisfactorily explained without a recognition of legislative supremacy. All this testifies as well to how carefully crafted the Constitution is, how meticulously the parts fit together and reinforce one another.

VI

It will not do, however, to leave things as they now are. For it is well to be reminded that, for Americans, "the government" includes, along with the General Government, both various local governments and the people themselves in their capacity as the ultimate governors.

Although the "Consent of the Congress" qualifications reflect the supervisory power of Congress in our system, especially with respect to the economy, military matters and foreign relations, a good deal is left for the States to do. It is well to emphasize again that the States are not subdivisions of, or simply subordinated to, the Union. The slave-trade provision with which Section 9 opens includes a rare instance of a special privilege for some States ("any of the States now existing") as distinguished from other States. The rarity of such advantage for any State points up the essential equality not just among the original States but among all States, whether original or subsequent.

The restrictions upon the States also suggest that they are the loci of special interests (some have ports, others do not) as well as the loci of special vulnerabilities (some may be invaded when others are not). It is repeatedly recognized in the Constitution that the passions of men can have distorting effects that should be guarded against. Here, the passion for gain has to be disciplined (not simply eliminated, but disciplined), which means that States cannot be permitted to take improper advantage of other States in order to make themselves prosperous; and the passion of fear has to be deferred to by permitting people to defend themselves without having to wait upon a distant government to act.

VII

Greed and fear help account for many of the problems to be faced. Consider, for example, the opening and closing provisions in Section 9. The section opens with a recognition (if not even the protection) of slavery; it closes with a repudiation of titles of nobility. It thereby moves from a blatant denial of equality to an insistence upon a degree of equality that perhaps no other modern people had ever had. Why were the slavery interests compromised with? In part because of legitimate concerns both with respect to commerce, or property, and with respect to war and peace, or self-preservation. These concerns affected what could be done about slavery, once again reminding us of the tension that can arise between personal rights and community needs. Even so, it is evident from Section 9 that slavery would become even more vulnerable after 1808 than it already was in 1787, and this the Southern slaveholder came to appreciate as the Country moved for some four score years toward the crisis that would considerably advance the great task begun by the Declaration of Independence.

We notice also that the Legislative Article to which we have been primarily devoting our attention thus far ends with a recognition that war, or the prospect of imminent invasion, takes precedence over the limitations placed in the latter part of Section 10 upon the powers of the States. Such a recognition of the inexorable requirements of war may be seen elsewhere as well, as in the habeas corpus provision in Section 9. Thus, the natural demand upon mankind of self-preservation is recognized. It is this demand, sometimes compelling, which can make the Executive seem so attractive—and this I will discuss in my next three lectures. We need not wait until then, however, to notice that the recognition of the compelling character of the desire for self-preservation should remind us, if reminder we need, that the Constitution, and the government set up pursuant to it, are not ends in themselves. They must ultimately be seen in terms of their service to life, liberty, and property or, put another way, in terms of their service to genuine and enduring human happiness, something in need of serious and repeated examination.

We the people of the United States have been conducting such an examination, off and on, for some two centuries. We should not be discouraged if the work done in one generation has to be reconsidered in the next, for that seems to be the way of a self-governing people (if not of every civilized people), a way that is reflected in the Constitutional provision for amendments. Nor should we be discouraged by the fashionable belief that we live in too different a time to be able, or perhaps to need, to understand what the Framers of the Constitution meant and said. They were very long ago, of course, but they can be quite near as well. It depends, in part, on how one looks at it:

A man born in 1787, the year the Constitution was drafted, and who lived seventy years, which we no longer consider a remarkably long life, would have died in 1857. A man born in 1857 and who also lived seventy years would have died in 1927. By that time, someone my age today was already two years old. Thus, three lifespans separate us from the men who sat in the Federal Convention in Philadelphia. So we can say, and be heartened by our ability to say, that the Constitution is both old—the oldest written political constitution in effect today—and, depending upon how one figures, young. This means that the Constitution of the United States can be venerable and yet vital, something we can all wish not only for our institutions but also for ourselves personally.

7. Anglo-American Constitutionalism

I

My principal undertaking here is to read the Constitution of the United States, working as much as possible from the text of 1787.

I have devoted most of my efforts in the first third of this Commentary to a somewhat detailed consideration of Article I of the Constitution, the Legislative Article. Most of the last third of the Commentary shall be devoted to a somewhat detailed consideration of the fourth, fifth, sixth, and seventh articles of the Constitution, which are very much concerned with the relations of the States to the Union.

The middle third of this Commentary will be devoted to Article II, the Executive Article, and Article III, the Judicial Article. The Presidency will be discussed in my next two lectures; the Judiciary will be discussed in the two lectures thereafter.

Although the principal activity in the Commentary consists of interpretation of the Constitutional text itself, I indicate here and there the background and foundations that the Constitution takes for granted. The Constitution of 1787 presupposes such things as the British Constitution, the Common Law, the Law of Nations, and that which I have called the Law of Public Bodies (which provides, among other things, guidance to what is to be taken to be both a constitution and its adoption). In addition, the Constitution presupposes such American instruments as the Declaration of Independence, the State Constitutions, and the Articles of Confederation. The character of the American people very much affects what it is possible to do here, a character that has been shaped by and that bears upon what is generally believed about the best regime, either temporal or spiritual. That character, which helps determine the constitutional and political principles and aspirations of our regime, is also shaped by the language of the English-speaking peoples, a language that incorporates and reflects Anglo-American opinions about the most important moral and political matters.

When we wonder what it was that the Framers brought to their Constitution-making, we must remember the influence upon them of the greatest English authors as well as the Bible. Thus, a half-century after the Federal Convention of 1787 at Philadelphia, Alexis de Tocqueville reported in his *Democracy in America*, "The literary inspiration of Great Britain darts its beams into the depths of the forests of the New World. There is hardly a pioneer's hut which does not contain a few odd volumes of Shakespeare. I remember reading the feudal drama of Henry V for the first time in a log cabin."[48]

The hold of Shakespeare upon nineteenth-century Americans, often in quite primitive circumstances, is testified to again and again. Consider this account, by a nineteenth-century rancher, of what could happen among cowboys in the West:

> The Englishmen brought a lot of culture into the West. There were practically no books out there, but an Englishman always brought Shakespeare with him: it was the decent thing to do. And they read their books, read them aloud to the cowboys, many of whom never got any further in their schooling than the rudiments of reading and writing. I've seen a bunch of cowboys sitting on their spurs listening with absolute silence and concentration while somebody read aloud. . . . I remember once after we'd been listening to *Julius Caesar*, one of them said to me, "That Shakespeare is the only poet I've heard who was fed on raw meat." When I sold my ranch in Montana, I divided my books among the riders, and eighteen out of twenty-one wanted Shakespeare.[49]

I do not mean to suggest that Shakespeare was the only author to whom early Americans would look, for there were also Milton, Locke, Bunyan, and Blackstone, but Shakespeare was the one who probably provided early Americans with a comprehensive moral and political account of things. They encountered in his plays an entertaining instructor in constitutional principles, an obviously wise man who could teach them about the most important temporal things (just as the Bible was generally believed to guide them with respect to spiritual things). The way Shakespeare spoke about the things he described—the moral presuppositions underlying what he said—helped shape generations of Americans. Because the things he described included a rather extensive account of the constitutional history of England, he offered early Americans an apparently authoritative guide to an understanding of their own constitutional antecedents. James Wilson, in the Federal Convention, could take it for granted that his fellow delegates would understand his reference to "the project of Henry the 4th & his Statesmen."[50] Where else but from Shakespeare's English History Plays (except perhaps from David Hume) would the typical American, or his teachers, have gotten fairly reliable opinions about Henry IV and his ministers, as well as about his predecessors and successors? I myself have been struck by how much Shakespeare and Blackstone agree in their accounts of English constitutional history.

Let us consider then, with a view to our own examination of the Constitution of the United States, what early Americans could have learned (or, at least, could have believed they learned) about constitutionalism from these plays about English history. It should become evident how all this bears upon what we have already seen, and upon what we have yet to see, about what may be found in the Constitution of 1787. It should also be encouraging, and not only for those citizens who may be drawn more to literature than to political treatises, to see how much one can learn about constitutional matters from a great playwright.

My first lecture of this series surveyed the dozen constitutions of the Americans. In this lecture we shall see again, but from the perspective of noble fiction, various elements of those interrelated and overlapping constitutions. I turn now to brief observations, suggested by a reading of Shakespeare's English History Plays, observations which bear upon the presuppositions and purposes of American Constitutionalism.

II

i

We see in the History Plays one great account of English constitutional history, a history during which constitutional government of sorts is taken for granted by the kings, nobles, and commoners portrayed there. These plays draw upon episodes that extend from 1199 to 1533. This span of three and one-third centuries begins with *King John* (which may have muted references to Magna Carta) and ends with *Henry VIII* (which concludes with the birth of the great Elizabeth). "When Elizabeth came to the throne," we are told,

> England was already in some ways a "limited" monarchy. Parliament, and especially the members of the House of Commons, claimed prerogatives of their own and were steadily gaining in both experience and power. In the mid-1560s, for example, the Commons made repeated attempts to use parliamentary tax-levying authority as a means of obliging Elizabeth to name a Protestant successor to the throne. . . . She never claimed or exercised the right to establish law; that was Parliament's prerogative. She needed all her considerable diplomatic skills in dealing with her Parliaments and with the English people, self-reliant and proud of their reputation for independence.[51]

We are reminded that England during Shakespeare's lifetime (1564–1616) was "a small nation by modern standards":

> Probably not more than five million people lived in the whole of England, considerably fewer than now live in London. [London's population stood at perhaps one hundred thousand people within the walls and as many more in the suburbs.] England's territories in France were no longer extensive, as they had been during the fourteenth century and earlier; in fact, by the end of Queen Elizabeth's reign (1558–1603), England had virtually retired from her once-great empire on the Continent. Her overseas empire in America had scarcely begun. Scotland was not yet a part of Great Britain.[52]

This account continues with a description of Shakespeare's country that late eighteenth-century Americans could have readily applied to their own as well: "By and large, England was a rural land. Much of the kingdom was still wooded, though timber was being used increasingly in manufacturing and shipbuilding. . . . England's chief means of livelihood was agriculture."[53]

ii

Among the lessons taught by Shakespeare in these and other plays is the importance of the political. When the political life of a country is unhealthy, we are taught, the private as well as the public life of the community can be contaminated.

We wonder, in passing, what it means when political matters are often spoken of in nonpolitical terms, as happens now and then in these plays. This may be seen in our own time by the considerable use of sports imagery in the discussion of politics.

iii

The English History Plays testify to the importance of peace and liberty, with both of these somehow grounded in justice. There are indications in Shakespeare (not only in the History Plays) that there is much to be said for a republican tradition. Even in the History Plays, in which a monarchical regime is taken for granted, there are repeated references to ancient Rome, especially to the Republic, as providing the finest models for citizenship.

It may well be that we have to look beyond the History Plays, indeed to *The Tempest*, for development of the opinion of what would truly be the best regime for Shakespeare. But the regime of *The Tempest* is not faced, in the way the History Plays are, by "historical realities." Shakespeare can celebrate the aspirations and some of the accomplishments of the British regime even as he graphically records (more so than does Blackstone) its shortcomings.

iv

Critical to English constitutional order is a respect for the rights of Englishmen. Protection of property is taken for granted, and one can see, especially in *Richard II*, how much mischief can be generated for decades to come by arbitrary royal confiscations. One can also see in these plays the grave risks run by a king and his ministers when they have recourse to oppressive taxation.

Throughout the History Plays it is evident that good government depends upon citizens' being able to tell the truth to their sovereign. Again and again kings who do not avail themselves of proper counsel from their ministers suffer harm.

The importance of being able to state one's grievances is recognized, as well as the sensibleness of those sovereigns who want to learn what their subjects' grievances are and who then do something to deal justly with them. At times, when a grievance is severe and longstanding and there is no prospect of redress by the acknowledged authorities, a right of revolution seems to be tacitly recognized.

V

The most obvious authority in the History Plays is the king of the day. (He often legislates, something the Framers of the Constitution of 1787 took precautions against in providing for the Legislative power and in placing restraints upon the Executive power.) But even in these plays, there are indications (guarded, but nevertheless to be taken seriously) that who the king is depends, if there is to be a sustained dynasty, upon parliamentary or other such determinations. Force is not enough to secure the throne, although force can be significant. No one dares to say publicly, in any of the plays, "I am king simply because I have had the power to seize and hold this throne." Again and again, an interpretation of the rule of succession is invoked. What the rule is generally understood to be matters, as well as what are generally understood to be the facts to which the rule is to be applied.

When one talks about a rule of succession, one is talking ultimately about the dictates of some legislative body, or of a kind of common law produced over centuries by the community as legislature. True, the parliamentary power of earlier days often rested largely in the hands of the nobles. True, also, the nobles could be very much influenced by their king or by some other claimant to the throne. Nevertheless, it is recognized that one is not truly king until one has been properly crowned (a ceremony for which a parliamentary determination, or a judgment pursuant to a long-established rule, can be decisive); and one is not safely king unless in accordance with an established and known rule, because otherwise someone else will surely come along who can persuasively invoke the appropriate rule to justify his own effort to seize the throne.

This is not to deny, of course, that a king, even when his power is nominal, can be quite dramatic in appearance, whereas parliamentary bodies, and certainly parliamentarians, tend to appear pedestrian. But this disparity in appearances does not settle the question of where the ultimate power lies.

vi

Not much is said in the History Plays about the status of the judiciary in the English constitutional system. Perhaps the most dramatic recognition of the desirability of an independent judiciary is seen at the end of *2 Henry IV*, when the newly elevated Henry V endorses the integrity and rigor that had been exercised by the Chief Justice even against himself as Prince Hal.

Much is suggested about the nature of the judicial process and hence about judicial prerogatives in what is taken for granted throughout the plays about the rule of law.

vii

But it is the monarch who holds center stage in the History Plays. So great is his allure, or magic, that these plays are, in large part, Shakespeare's version of Machiavelli's *Prince* (of which Shakespeare is aware, not without respect, but about which he has serious reservations).

Various of the kings' attributes and prerogatives in the plays anticipate those of a chief executive anywhere, except perhaps where a constitution is so clear about allocations of powers that the implied powers of the executive are quite limited. In the History Plays, the king serves as symbol of his country. The integrity or unity of the country may depend upon him, especially since the nobles tend to head off in the diverse directions dictated by their respective local loyalties. It is the king who speaks for the country as a whole when it deals with other countries.

One can see in these plays how much divinity does hedge about a king. There is a tendency (a natural tendency?) to make much of the lone executive, once he is singled out. The man thus raised up can seem godlike, someone whom others can be guided by in ways great and small. Henry V can assure the French princess whom he is courting, when she informs him that "It is not a fashion for the maids in France to kiss before they are married," that "We are the makers of manners, Kate; and the liberty that follows our places stops the mouth of all findfaults . . ."

So dramatic is the monarch that concerns about treason can turn around him, with any denials of his title to office constituting a capital offense. Perhaps this is in part due to the necessity for vesting in one man supreme control over decisions about war and peace. (Even in our republican Constitution, we see that the President is designated "Commander in Chief of the Army and Navy.") Such supreme control means that the proper commander must have the capacity, and the power, to be shrewd, tough, perhaps even cruel and deceitful, if need be. The Archbishop of Canterbury can speak over the infant Elizabeth's cradle of a sovereign's servants being "peace, plenty, love, truth, *terror*."[54] Some two hundred years later Gouverneur Morris, in the Federal Convention, could regard the President of the United States as "the general Guardian of the National interests."[55]

I shall say more about these matters when we come, in Section II of Lecture No. 9, to the problem of the implied powers of the President under the Constitution. Perhaps such an inquiry can be taken as also examining, in effect, how much the supposed powers of the monarch in the History Plays were more show than substance.

viii

It should be no wonder, then, that the mode of selection of so exalted a personage as the Chief Executive should be made much of, as we see both in the History Plays of Shakespeare and in the Constitution of the United States.

There are rules for determining who he is. These rules are likely to be followed. Furthermore, we have noticed, it is the function of some legislature—which can be, in the case of constitution-framing itself, the entire people of a country—to declare or at least to define such rules. This led to different rules in France from those in England.

We shall see that it is usually vital to the interests of the community that there be an immediate, clear designation of who the Chief Executive is.

ix

A perennial problem in assessing any claimant to the post of Chief Executive is whether legitimacy depends upon some form of merit, especially in those circumstances where the one who is next in line is clearly inferior by nature to another with less of a legal claim.

In the English History Plays, the rule of succession is often treated as if natural. It is sometimes suggested that a royal nature asserts itself even in adverse circumstances. The comic version of this may be seen in Falstaff's justification of his cowardice on one occasion, when he was badly frightened by Prince Hal in disguise: instinct, he explained, had kept him from striking the true prince.

Still, installation of the legal successor means that someone naturally better may have to be set aside. Troublesome as that may be, personal merit is generally not enough to justify disregarding legitimacy. There is a considerable momentum to the lawful claim.

Even so, the ultimate dependence of law upon merit, or justice, may be seen in the bloody fate of the tyrannical Richard III. For he was, by the end of his career, the man with the best claim to the throne according to the rule of succession. Of course, to get where he was he had to kill a brother and two nephews with better claims.

By the time the History Plays begin to draw to an end, the audience should be prepared to concede that mere legality does not suffice. The right of revolution begins to be recognized, the right that was to put the kings of England in their proper and permanent place a century later in Great Britain and two centuries later in North America.

X

Americans can see, upon working their way through the History Plays, what those titles of nobility can mean that have been forbidden by the ninth and tenth sections of Article I of their Constitution.

Hereditary claims can be quite complex matters in the plays. The nobility, which then held much of the effective legislative power of England, were most respectful of royal claims of succession, not least because their own titles to considerable lands and privileges also depended upon such claims.

Among the consequences of a dependence upon heredity is the importance of honor. (This means hereditary enmities as well as hereditary alliances.) A Falstaff can provide a healthy corrective: he suggests that honor is made too much of by his countrymen, that honor is the man who died last Wednesday. But however much of a corrective is provided both for the pretensions of honor and for the claims of heredity, the rules of succession have to be complied with. No matter how much Henry IV laments the undisciplined conduct of his elder son and heir apparent, it is taken for granted by all loyal subjects (as well as by the king himself) that Prince Hal will succeed his father, if he survives him.

xi

The nobility are thought to have a certain character by nature; the same can be said of the people at large. One of the strengths of England is that it has no permanently depressed classes, no institution of slavery. Henry V can say at Agincourt that those who fight with him that day will be ennobled by their achievement, however base their birth.

He, perhaps more than any of the other monarchs we see in these plays, can thus encourage the people to identify their interests with his. His distinctive merit may be, partly because of his extended association with Falstaff and other dubious company, that he has some access to both the high and the low.

We see again and again in the History Plays that the good sense and sound character of the people at large have to be reckoned with, that the people are sensitive to the shortcomings of their betters, including the King and those around him. At times, one suspects, ultimate control by the people is indicated, along with the passions (both questionable and inspired) to which the people are susceptible.

xii

The oaths of office required by the Constitution of the United States are provided for against the background of constitutional developments, depicted in the History Plays, in which it very much mattered who swore allegiance to whom. Although oaths of allegiance are repeatedly violated in the plays, we are given to understand that this cannot be done without grave risks. Sophistic arguments can be made as to how oaths might be set aside, but we are repeatedly shown the dreadful effects of perjury.

A special form of oath-taking, of great importance in the History Plays, is that seen in marriage vows, which are vital to legitimacy and to a proper succession. It is here that the influence of the Church is perhaps most felt, since the Church has much to say about what the rules are by which families, and hence claims to succession, are constituted. Here, too, we can discern how different our own regime is in decisive respects, including the relative insignificance among us of the institution of marriage as political action. The two monarchs in the History Plays who are shown to have married for love (Edward IV and Henry VI) are looked down upon for having allowed their lust to override their better judgment, if not even their monarchical duties.

xiii

Once allegiances are prescribed by law, the risks that follow upon rebellion are serious, even when there has been great provocation. It can take generations to cure the wounds left by usurpation. In the History Plays, the War of the Roses can finally be settled only when claimants from the two lines join in marriage.

One does not strike down a king, whether he is legitimate or a usurper himself, without the risk of dire consequences. We have seen in the United States the remarkable dislocations brought about by Presidential assassinations. Even the peaceful surrender of office by a President threatened with impeachment has had traumatic effects. That is, there simply may be no good way of doing this sort of thing.

On the Continent, during the period covered by the History Plays, the English monarchy became known as remarkably unstable. And so it could be said by Spanish ambassadors, when their monarchs considered allowing Katherine of Aragon to marry the son of Henry VII, "Bearing in mind what happens every day to the kings of England, it is surprising that Ferdinand and Isabella should dare to give their daughter at all."[56]

However that might have been, the History Plays teach that if one gains power through disloyalty, one cannot hope to be secure. More important, one sees, as in *Richard III*, what can eventually happen because of usurpations and civil war: there is a general corrosive effect, with a widespread deterioration of trust and mutual respect, as the monstrous takes over.

xiv

We have already noticed that Edward IV and Henry VI allowed passion to override considerations of policy in their marriages. We are repeatedly reminded in the History Plays of the relation of moral virtue to political virtue, and hence to the happiness of the community. Rulers have a not always dormant moral sense in the community to reckon with.

This is related to what we can see in these plays of the place of religious faith and of conscience in the life of the community. One teaching of these plays, easily picked up by Americans, is that religious institutions should be kept somewhat separate from the political order. This is not to suggest that the plays assume that religion is not properly useful to the statesman. But it is evident that religion—or, at least, ambitious churchmen—can get in the way of good government. Sometimes the Church appears as a foreign state, or as another state within the state.

We further see that the determinedly pious prince can be far less effective, and hence less virtuous politically, than he should be. Early and late warnings are provided, in the careers of Richard II and Henry VI, of princes unfitted by their piety for proper rule. Love and policy are thereby distinguished.

On the other hand, a complete lack of piety will not do either. Impious villains are shown as eventually failing and suffering. Shakespeare *is* bound somewhat by the historical record, but he accounts in his own way for what is generally known to have happened. By and large, the truly good prevail. The playwright suggests, by the way he presents the troubles England was subject to, that for several generations there was no one both strong enough and good enough to lead the country properly. Another way of putting this is to say that Shakespeare brings together history and nature.

xv

A standard of the common good seems to be evident throughout the History Plays, even though it is often only implicit. One continuing problem is what, precisely, constitutes *the country* to which kings, nobles, and commons should be dedicated. How much should England claim as its own? Is France worth repeated campaigns? What about Ireland, which requires constant attention? Is it not enough of a challenge for English leaders to deal properly with Wales and Scotland, to which they at least have ready access?

The History Plays leave open the question of what should be

made of French expeditions by the English kings. Does nature suggest what is properly British? We can, in *1 Henry VI*, see Joan of Arc fairly easily persuade the Duke of Burgundy to abandon his allegiance to the English king and to align himself with other Frenchmen. We can also see that the most glamorous of the English kings, Henry V, resorts to his exciting French adventures upon the advice of his dying father, who, aware of the fragility of his own claim to a usurped throne, counsels his son to unite the country behind him by engaging in a foreign war.

All this reminds us of something that can be disturbing about the political life depicted in these plays: there is surprisingly little evidence of sacrifice by any monarch of his personal interest to the common good, although the rejection of Falstaff by Henry V may appear to be such a sacrifice. Most, if not all, of the kings tend to look out first, if not only, for themselves, even as they call upon their subjects for great sacrifices.

One wonders how the regime established by the Constitution of the United States undertakes to make it more likely that the common good will take precedence over personal interests in the careers of public servants.

xvi

Fortunately, it usually is clearly in the interest of English sovereigns in the History Plays that the rule of law should be respected. For one thing, as we have seen, a fully proper succession presupposes the rule of law. A lawyer in *1 Henry VI* sides with the Yorkist claim to the throne on the basis of what the law provides.

So much is respect for the rule of law emphasized that even tyrannical executions, except in the most dreadful cases, routinely require a written order in due form. The considerable power exercised by the Lord Mayor of London in maintaining law and order among the quarreling nobles attached to the royal court also reflects this respect.

The plays make clear that even during these days of usurpation, of intrafamily killing and of civil war, total breakdown of the rule of law is not to be tolerated. They show throughout that a standard of justice is repeatedly looked to, a standard that respects property, law-abidingness, and even culture. This respect for the established way is dramatized by the barbarity of the rebellious Jack Cade in 2 *Henry VI*. Shakespeare repeatedly reminds his English-speaking audiences what radical self-serving can mean. Here it is seen in a commoner; in *Richard III*, it is seen in the king himself. In both cases, the villain is shown abandoned (naturally abandoned?) by all supporters with any shred of decency left in them as he faces remorseless destruction at the hands of the righteous.

xvii

Jack Cade's determined attack upon law and culture—even to the extent of killing anyone whom he finds to be literate—has, as one effect, a reminder of the civilization required for constitutionalism. Civilization nourishes, and is in turn sustained by, proper government. Thus, we are also reminded, the nonpolitical aspects of life are important as well. We are reminded, that is, of the human things that political life ultimately serves.

Religion, properly used, makes a contribution here. So does philosophy, however rare its appearance. The happiness of the community—for nobles, people, and kings alike—is held up by the English History Plays as a worthy objective. We can see here an anticipation of that "Pursuit of Happiness" celebrated in the Declaration of Independence and to which American Constitutionalism is dedicated.

III

This discussion of the English History Plays has not been primarily concerned with them as works of art but rather as indications of the principles and aspirations that early Americans inherited with the education provided them in the English language.

I have drawn upon these plays for useful guidance to Anglo-American constitutionalism, even though I recognize both that many other plays by Shakespeare are much better as plays and that various works by other authors have also been important for the education of Americans. The History Plays, insofar as they address both the problem of what happens when rulers are not properly selected and the problem of what happens when rulers, however selected, do not conduct themselves properly, very much touch upon issues and concerns that should be evident to us as we examine the provisions in the Constitution for the Executive and for the Judiciary.[57]

Our problem now is not with the authoritative making of laws, to which I have devoted my opening lectures, but with the interpretation and execution of laws, to which I now turn. In my next lecture, I will discuss the opening section of Article II and the Twelfth Amendment to the Constitution. In the lecture following, the remainder of Article II will be discussed, in which the powers of the Presidency are dealt with, those powers which are subordinated both to the laws made by Congress and to the law, or constitution, made by the people.

We will continue, in our examination of these texts, to see how the various parts of the Constitution fit together, thereby further reassuring one another that the Constitution can indeed be thought about.

8. Article II, Section 1

I

Much is made in this Country of the President of the United States. Much is made as well of Presidential elections—of how Presidents are selected, of campaign strategies, and of the lives and times of Presidents. Would we make as much as we do of the Presidency if we recognized the role chance plays in determining both which particular man becomes President and what he personally can do? (Chance may have far less to do with which party or which policy is chosen from time to time than it does with who the candidate of a party is.) The President may be looked up to because he seems to be in control, or because we hope that *someone* is in control. But is it not rare for anyone to control either his becoming President or his principal doings as President? Only two or three Presidents in the twentieth century, if that many, can be said to have been substantially in control of their Presidential careers.

The careers of legislators and judges are much more predictable. One can have reasonable ambitions, with respect to either Congress or the Courts, and thereafter one can have, if one is both talented and somewhat fortunate, a career that is substantially what one had planned. Citizens in various private careers may have even more control over their destinies than do those with ambitions in public life. The natural unpredictability of public life is probably compounded wherever ultimate control rests in the people at large.

This is not to deny that there is something spectacular about the Presidency. It looks big, and Presidents themselves tend to make a lot of the Presidency. These assessments are reinforced by what is

89

said by "Presidents' men" and by chief executives of other countries, who also see themselves as truly special. So remarkable is it when any particular man makes his way to the Presidency that it is tempting to regard his rise as providential.

Quite trivial things, however, can chance to derail a Presidential candidacy and sometimes even a Presidency. Lest one be troubled by the realization of how vulnerable Presidents and would-be Presidents are, it should be remembered that much, perhaps most (if not even all), of the important things a President does are dependent upon other people, particularly upon what Congress makes as laws and upon how the National Courts interpret those laws. To the extent that the regime provided for by the Constitution encourages moderation, it usually does not matter much who the President is or even what political party is in power.[58]

Yet we keep tinkering with the mode of selecting the President in order to be sure, as if it always made all the difference in the world who is chosen. We may well ask, "In order to be sure of what?" Probably the only thing we need to be sure of, most of the time, is that we have indeed designated someone clearly enough for the office, so that there is no lingering uncertainty or festering resentment about the final selection made among candidates who have been adequately screened during the public nominating process for their competence and integrity.

Most of the material I consider in this lecture is devoted to the process for choosing the President. A discussion of this process, and of various changes that have been proposed, permits us to see how one might think sensibly about the Constitution. Some features of the Constitution here may most usefully be seen by delving into other ways of doing the same things.

II

I exaggerate the role of chance in the selection of a President, partly because it has long seemed to me that far too much has been made in recent decades of the Presidency. It is also salutary to be reminded as well of how much chance determined the particular mode of Presidential selection that we use. This is one major provision in the Constitution that could easily have been quite different in critical respects.

The major provisions in the Constitution for the selection of other officers of government, and especially members of Congress and of the National Courts, are largely what they were bound to be, once it was decided (as it was decided, perhaps, even before the Federal Convention first met in May 1787) that the new national government should have broad powers with respect to commerce, foreign affairs (including war and peace), and taxation. Even the distinctive American division of the Congress could have been somewhat expected, at least to the extent that it was likely that the interests and demands of both the large and the small States would have to be respected. That legislative division had been anticipated in various State constitutions before 1787. The powers, as distinguished from the mode of selection, of the President were determined in large part by the decisions made about the powers that the Congress would have.

The complicated mode of selecting the President does not matter as much as it may sometimes seem to us, however much we allow ourselves to get caught up by the superficial aspects of political contests. The character and talents of any particular President are not likely to be important, at least when compared to the circumstances of his time and to the policy that Congress is prepared to lay down on vital issues of the day.

We can be thankful that we rarely require a Washington or a Lincoln. Nor have we done badly with the "accidental" Presidents we have had in the twentieth century, the men who completed the terms of their predecessors. However the President is chosen and whoever he may happen to be, what is likely to be decisive are the character of the people and the caliber of the continuing deliberation in the community at large, which deliberation the Congress and the President may contribute to, of course, and which they are in any event likely themselves to be shaped and guided by.

III

Although most of this discussion will be devoted to the mode of electing the President, I should first touch upon the length of his term of office. This issue was much debated in the Federal Convention, as was the related issue of whether the President should be able to succeed himself. Good arguments were made in support of various positions on these issues. It is difficult to assess any of the delegates' arguments, however, since the proposals made from time to time were keyed to other proposals already tentatively adopted. The important thing to notice is that the delegates understood that there would be a series of complex consequences that depended upon the combination of proposals adopted.

There was not much concern in the Convention either about the lengths of the terms of members of Congress or about whether they should be able to succeed themselves. As for judges, the Convention provided for them the lifetime appointments that British judges had. About this there does not seem to have been much controversy, however much uncertainty there might have been about precisely how judges should be selected.

The issue of whether a President should be able to succeed himself was much agitated in the Federal Convention. George Washington's emphatic refusal to seek a third term proved decisive for a century and a half. Franklin Roosevelt's willingness and ability to get himself elected four times overrode the Washington precedent and moved Congress and the Country to make sure it would not happen again, and so we have the Twenty-second Amendment limiting a President to two elected terms.

One argument against such a limitation is that it may deprive the Country of the services of the very man most needed in perilous times. Whether this argument makes too much of the Presidency, and of particular men, is a question related to the one with which I opened this lecture. Are there not good reasons for limiting a President to two terms? After a decade of acting "Presidential" (that is, during one's first election campaign and then while in office), one is not apt to be well informed about what is happening among the people of the Country no matter how instructive and disciplining political campaigns may be. One is likely to have spent a decade in which one's contacts with people have been unnaturally limited and one's information has become considerably restricted, however bolstered by specialized secret intelligence. One is likely, therefore, to become simply "out of touch," adept only for ceremonial occasions. Perhaps most crippling is the lack of time the typical President has for serious reading, extended conversation, and sustained reflection. He is even more constrained in these respects than members of Congress, who are also far too busy.

One consequence of the Twenty-second Amendment is that it has thus far imposed a restraint only upon the political party that pushed it. The Eightieth Congress proposed the amendment, the only Republican Congress since the days of Herbert Hoover a half-century ago. Subsequent to the amendment's ratification in 1951 the only Presidents with substantial prospects of third terms have been Republicans. Not only should this remind us of one of the beauties of the rule of law—one can be hoisted by one's own petard—but it should also remind us that the consequences of Constitutional changes can be far-reaching and difficult to discern.

IV

James Wilson reported that the problem of determining the mode of selecting the President had been one of the most difficult before the Federal Convention.[59] The delegates struggled with this problem repeatedly. Even so, the system they settled upon—a complex system utilizing electors who would be chosen in each State and who would in turn be free to choose a President and a Vice President—soon required revision, the Twelfth Amendment, ratified in 1804. This amendment is itself as long and as complex as the provision it was intended to correct, separating as it does the electors' votes for the Presidency from their votes for the Vice Presidency.

But to recognize a provision as being long and complicated is not to regard it as truly important in itself. I have indicated that it is far more important that it be clear what the Presidential-selection provision is than that it be this or that provision. However important the President may or may not be, it is vital that it should be generally and, preferably, immediately apparent who he is once the votes have been counted in whatever way has been agreed upon for doing so, provided that that way is not perceived as unsuitable. One reason so much is made of being sure who the President is at any particular moment is that much of the considerable power he does have depends upon public opinion, not upon lawmaking authority, as for Congress, or upon argument, as for judges.

The present arrangement for choosing the President, with its dependence upon the allocation of votes according to States (with the smaller States getting more votes per capita than strict allocation by population would warrant), reflects the federal element in the Constitution. The federal character of the arrangement is reinforced by the general practice, for a century and a half now, of assigning the electoral votes of each State on a winner-take-all basis.

One possible system, the selection of the Chief Executive by lot from among an array provided by an appropriate screening process, would produce a President adequate to the times in most circumstances but is nevertheless obviously unsuitable. The difficulty here would not be that of developing the screening process, for we have always had that in the form of party caucuses, conventions, or primaries. Rather, the difficulty would be that of admitting to an out-and-out recourse to chance, which would undermine the salutary belief that the people are in fact governing themselves. The use of a lottery, therefore, would probably be bad for political morale. Still, as I have suggested, much of what we do in choosing a President is dependent upon chance anyway, but in a much more expensive and burdensome way than an out-and-out lottery would be. But we do not choose to recognize this publicly, and there may be a sound instinct at work here.

We are obliged to recognize, however, that chance plays a considerable part in the choice of Vice-Presidential candidates and in the determination of which Vice President succeeds to the Presidency, as eight Vice Presidents have done in completing their predecessors' terms.[60]

V

The mode of selecting the President culminates in what happens in Congress once the votes in the several States have been recorded and sent to the President of the Senate of the United States, pursuant to Constitutional direction. We are once again reminded of the general supervisory power of Congress in the Constitutional system. Until Congress acts, there is no President chosen. This means that Congress may provide the rules, and hence the standards, by which the votes counted and recorded in the States are to be in turn received, counted, and dealt with by Congress. There is something of the pageantry of an ancient ceremony about all this, a ceremony that dramatizes the penultimate power in Congress, which in turn is immediately subject to the electorate.

It is instructive to see how this ceremony is conducted, as recorded in the *Congressional Record* for January 6, 1977 (following upon the Carter-Ford election contest in November 1976).[61] This is how the *Record* reports the Joint Session of the two Houses of Congress that day, a session held pursuant to the provisions of a concurrent resolution:

> At 12 o'clock and 55 minutes p.m., the Doorkeeper, the Honorable James T. Molloy, announced the Vice President and the Senate of the United States.
>
> The Senate entered the Hall of the House of Representatives, headed by the Vice President and the Secretary of the Senate, the Members and officers of the House rising to receive them.
>
> The Vice President took his seat as the Presiding Officer of the joint convention of the two Houses, the Speaker of the House occupying the chair on his left.
>
> The joint session was called to order by the Vice President.
>
> The VICE PRESIDENT. Mr. Speaker, Members of the Congress, the Senate and the House of Representatives, pursuant to the requirements of the Constitution and the laws of the United States, have met in joint session for the purpose of opening the certificates and ascertaining and counting the votes of the electors of the several States for President and Vice President.
>
> Under well-established precedents, unless a motion shall be made in any case, the reading of the formal portions of the certificates will be dispensed with. After ascertainment has been made that the certificates are authentic and correct in form, the tellers will count and make a list of the votes cast by the electors of the several States.
>
> The tellers on the part of the two Houses will take their respective places at the Clerk's desk.

The tellers, Mr. CANNON and Mr. HATFIELD on the part of the Senate, and Mr. DENT and Mr. DICKINSON on the part of the House, took their places at the desk.

The VICE PRESIDENT. The Chair will now hand to the tellers the certificates of the electors for President and Vice President of the State of Alabama, and they will count and make a list of the votes cast by that State.

Mr. DICKINSON (one of the tellers). Mr. President, the certificate of the electoral vote of the State of Alabama seems to be regular in form and authentic, and it appears therefrom that Jimmy Carter of the State of Georgia received nine votes for President and WALTER F. MONDALE of the State of Minnesota received nine votes for Vice President.

The VICE PRESIDENT. There being no objection, the Chair will omit in further procedure the formal statement just made for the State of Alabama, and we will open the certificates in alphabetical order and pass to the tellers the certificates showing the vote of the electors in each State; and the tellers will then read, count, and announce the result in each State as was done in the case of the State of Alabama.

Is there objection?

The Chair hears no objection.

There was no objection.

The tellers then proceeded to read, count, and announce, as was done in the case of the State of Alabama, the electoral votes of the several States in alphabetical order.

The VICE PRESIDENT. Gentlemen and gentlewomen of the Congress, the certificates of all of the States have now been opened and read, and the tellers will make the final ascertainment of the results and deliver the same to the Vice President.[62]

After the tellers delivered to the Vice President a statement of the results, the ceremony continued with this announcement:

The VICE PRESIDENT. The state of the vote for President of the United States, as delivered to the President of the Senate, is as follows:

The whole number of the electors appointed to vote for President of the United States is 538, of which a majority is 270.

Gov. Jimmy Carter, of the State of Georgia, has received for the Presidency of the United States 297 votes; President Gerald R. Ford, of the State of Michigan, has received 240 votes; and Gov. Ronald Reagan, of the State of California, has received 1 vote.

The state of the vote for the Vice Presidency of the United States, as delivered to the President of the Senate, is as follows:

The whole number of the electors appointed to vote for Vice President of the United States is 538, of which a majority is 270.

Senator WALTER F. MONDALE, of the State of Minnesota, has received for Vice President of the United States 297 votes; and Senator ROBERT DOLE, of the State of Kansas, has received 241 votes.

This announcement of the state of the vote by the President of the Senate shall be deemed a sufficient declaration of the persons elected President and Vice President of the United States, each for the term beginning on the 20th day of January, 1977, and shall be entered, together with a list of the votes, on the Journals of the Senate and the House of Representatives.

Members of the Congress, the purpose for which the joint session of the two Houses of Congress has been called, pursuant to Senate Concurrent Resolution 1, 95th Congress, having been accomplished, the Chair declares the joint session dissolved.

(Thereupon, at 1 o'clock and 34 minutes p.m., the joint session of the two Houses of Congress was dissolved.)

The House was called to order by the Speaker.

The SPEAKER. Pursuant to Senate Concurrent Resolution 1, the Chair directs that the electoral votes be spread at large upon the Journal.[63]

We can see here, in this thirty-nine minute performance, the formal compliance there routinely is with the Constitutional duty of Congress to determine in early January every four years who is to become President of the United States on the 20th of January. We can also see reflected here various other features of the Constitutional provisions we are examining. The 538 electors identified as "the whole Number of Electors appointed" to vote for President of the United States are derived by adding together (in accordance with Section 1 of Article II, as supplemented by various amendments) the 100 members of the Senate, the 435 members of the House of Representatives, and the 3 votes from the District of Columbia.

Particularly impressive in all this—although very much taken for granted by us—is that a Vice President of one party can preside over a ceremony that marks the ouster of an incumbent of his own party from the Presidency and, of course, his own ouster from the Vice Presidency. An odd feature on the 1977 occasion was the single vote for Ronald Reagan, who had not been on the ballot in the State of Washington, where one Ford elector voted for him. This action by that elector bears on the proposals for electoral reform which I will soon be discussing.

But first, it is instructive to notice how much there is, not only in the ceremony we have just witnessed but throughout Article II, that testifies to the concern of the Framers of the Constitution that the President be thoroughly hedged in. It is recognized that the President, however limited he may be by the laws made by Congress, still has considerable prestige, to say nothing of the potential for usurpation (especially since he *is* designated "Commander in Chief of the Army and Navy"). And so the irrepressible Patrick Henry protested in the course of the Ratification Campaign in Virginia that the proposed Constitution "squints toward monarchy."[64] The prestige likely to attend "the God-like prince," the single man at the top (no matter how he gets there), can be reinforced by the patronage he is likely to have at his disposal, the discretion he must exercise in the execution of laws (to say nothing of a virtually unfettered pardoning power), and the contact he has with others abroad (which includes, as was said again and again in the Federal Convention, the temptation to be bribed).

The Framers' concern for the integrity of the Presidency is indicated by their providing in this case only that the incumbent must be "a natural born Citizen." In addition, the President has a higher age requirement than any other officer of government. True, it is only five years higher (35) than that for a Senator (30), which in turn is only five years higher than that for a Representative (25), but the principle is nevertheless indicated. The President is considered more august, even though the age used for him is so low as not likely to have much effect in practice.

It seems to be understood that the principal locus of abuse of power lies in the Presidency and in Presidential selection. This understanding is reflected in various precautions. For example, "The Congress may determine the Time of chusing the Electors, and the Day on which they shall give their Votes; which Day shall be the same throughout the United States." This provision was primarily designed to reduce improprieties, or the appearance of improprieties, in bargaining among States for votes. Improprieties are also guarded against in the limitations upon who can serve as electors: "but no Senator or Representative, or Person holding an Office of Trust or Profit under the United States, shall be appointed an Elector." Some of these people may be too much under the influence of an incumbent President; others, the Senators and Representatives, have to receive and certify what the electors do and, in some contingencies, may have to choose the President themselves. More stringent restrictions are placed upon the changes that may be made in the compensation of the President than in the compensation of other officers, partly to protect him and partly to hold him in check. Moreover, he alone has a specific oath provided for him in the Constitution.

Finally, it should not be considered accidental that the impeachment power introduced in Sections 2 and 3 of Article I, which applies to other officers of the General Government as well, should have been returned to at the end of the Executive Article (in Section 4 of Article II). It is instructive that this article, which began with identification of the power of the Presidency as the "executive Power" (that is, the power to execute the laws made by legislatures), should end with a reminder of the control by Congress of who remains President of the United States.

VI

The question of who becomes—or rather, of how someone becomes—President of the United States continues to vex American citizens down to our day. We have seen that considerable space was devoted to this question in Article II and less than two decades later in the Twelfth Amendment. Related questions were returned to in Amendments XX, XXII, XXIII, and XXV. Almost half of the space devoted to amendments is allocated to provisions for the mode of selection and for the term of office of the President, much more than is allocated to any other subject.

If various politicians, and an even larger number of political scientists, have their way, considerably more language will be added to the Constitution to guide the selection of the President. For we hear much, from time to time, about abolishing the "Electoral College," especially the customary arrangement whereby the votes of each State are allocated as a unit to one Presidential candidate. There has been so much said about all this that it would not be useful to repeat at length. I need only touch upon this problem here and there as part of my overall effort to suggest how the Constitution in its entirety should be thought about.

What is at the bottom of the anxiety about the Electoral College? Primarily, the possibility that the man who obtains the most popular votes in a Presidential election may not be the man who gets the requisite number of votes in the Electoral College. Typical of the concerns expressed is the observation by President Carter in March 1977:

> Under the Electoral College, it is always possible that the winner of the popular vote will not be elected. This has already happened in three elections, 1824, 1876, and 1888. In the last election [in 1976], the result could have been changed by a small shift of votes in Ohio and Hawaii, despite a popular vote difference of 1.7 million.[65]

Allied to this kind of observation, which has been made again and again in recent decades, is the kind of warning issued by an editorial writer after the 1976 election:

> Imagine the mood of the nation right now if one of the presidential candidates had won a majority of the popular vote on Tuesday but had failed to garner the 270 votes needed to seal his victory in the electoral college. Such an indecisive result unquestionably would have intensified disillusionment with the electoral process just at the time when the nation is beginning to get rid of the aftertaste of Watergate.[66]

What "the mood of the nation" would be in such circumstances would depend upon how the Country had been taught to see any disparity between the popular vote and the Electoral College vote.

How should these matters be understood by the people?

It should be noticed, first, that it is rare when there is such disparity. But much more important to notice is that a disparity between the Electoral College vote and the popular vote need not be taken as significant, however much the increasing emphasis upon equality may lead us to magnify the significance of popular votes. If it were known in advance that only the popular vote would count, then the popular vote would indeed mean more than it does now. What is to be made, for example, of a light turnout in a large State when it is known in advance that that State will go by a wide margin to a particular candidate? When voting is conducted under the present dispensation, it does not make sense to be agitated about precisely who happens to have the largest total popular vote Countrywide. Not only does it not make sense, but it is irresponsible for any commentator to magnify the significance of that vote. It would be as if we counted up all who voted for Democratic candidates for the House of Representatives and all who voted for Republican candidates for the House of Representatives, and then insisted upon allocating the House seats between these two parties in accordance with such totals. There is always the possibility of a discrepancy between the total popular vote and unit-by-unit determinations wherever there are local units that do matter in any political arrangement. Yet are there not good reasons for having units that matter? On the other hand, there may be no good reason for having the selection of the President be, or seem to be, more democratic than the selection of Congress.

It is curious that those proposing amendments can be satisfied with eventually settling upon a candidate who may have had a plurality of only 40 percent in the popular vote, under their proposed arrangements, while they are troubled by the prospect of someone's winning with only 49.9 percent, under the present arrangement, if someone else happens to have 50.1 percent. It is also curious that some blithely accept the prospect of fairly frequent runoffs and other uncertainties under their proposed arrangements. Intellectuals have been unduly influential here, the very people who should have thought through what the present system does. They should be much more appreciative than they evidently are of the obvious fact that the system has worked as well as it has for so long.

The arguments for the present arrangement, or something close to it, are many and sound, including arguments that see it as encouraging respect for the States as States, permitting the smaller States more participation than they might otherwise have in the national choice, moderating resort to nationwide demagoguery, limiting the attractiveness of election fraud (or at least localizing its consequences), and making for quicker and surer determinations of who the winner is in accordance with the announced rules. Should not the burden of argument rest with those who would change what has been so successful for almost two centuries? We are told that people are concerned. But are not those concerns due at least in part to the arguments of those who have not explained properly either how things truly stand or what the consequences of change could be?

VII

The concern now expressed is that we should guard against the possibility that the popular winner may lose. It is not generally appreciated how much the leading amendment proposals would expose us to all kinds of unpredictable developments.

I have suggested that it is already largely a matter of chance which particular man becomes President of the United States. But that is the kind of chance we can expect, can adapt ourselves to, and perhaps even make good use of. However much our present mode of selecting a President may itself also be due to chance, there are various important and useful institutions, expectations, and practices that have naturally formed around that mode. It is one thing to recognize both the inevitable play of chance and that accommodations to it must be made; it is quite another thing gratuitously to expose ourselves to the vagaries of chance, to increase the number of important activities that become unpredictable.

The proposed popular-election change need not—and once resorted to, might not—be limited, in principle, to the mode of choosing Presidents. Should the choice of Senators also be keyed to a national vote, that is, in a manner that allocates Senators according to population? Or if that should seem somehow subversive of the traditional balance of the Congress, what about another change so as to rely more upon popular votes: why not require

Constitutional amendments to depend upon three-fourths of the vote in a national referendum rather than, as now, upon three-fourths of the States voting as States? We can see that the mode of choosing Presidents is not the only Constitutional device we use that does not defer to the total popular vote. Yet should we not be reluctant to rely upon Countrywide popular votes in the two situations I have just mentioned? (I return to this question in Section VI of Lecture No. 14.)

The many unpredictable consequences of the Presidential-selection proposals could mean that nothing important would be changed if any of the proposals should be ratified. Or they could mean that many vital things would be changed, including the significance of the States in the Union, the mode of campaigning, and the role of political parties. Such things (to which I will return) are somehow keyed to the present mode of selecting the President, however accidental some features of the present mode are bound to be.

It may seem odd to defend as desirable, that is, on the basis of nature, conventions that have been accidentally developed. But that happens all the time, as may be seen for example with the language of a people or with our much-respected institution of trial by jury. In any event, the present mode of Presidential selection does have the advantage of being venerable, of having worked quite well for a long time, and of having other institutions, some of them perhaps as yet unrecognized by us, adapted to it.

A change now could subvert further the federal elements in our Constitutional arrangement, going even beyond the centralization and consolidation that the economic life of the Country may require and that the communications industry promotes. One thing I have emphasized about the proposed changes is the unpredictability of what could happen, and this should make us cautious, considering both how important Presidential elections seem to be among us and how smoothly our long-established system has worked. Nothing is to be gained by making it uncertain (for days, if not for weeks, at a time) who has actually been anointed according to whatever the prevailing rule may be. It is, as I have indicated, one merit of the present dispensation that things are almost always settled promptly, unlike what can be expected under the proposed amendments, which may encourage much more vote fraud and recounting than we now have and which may, according to their proponents, require frequent runoffs.

Perhaps an even more serious consequence of a popular-vote amendment would follow upon the efforts to be expected to get out the vote at all costs, with the related changes in the way issues are discussed, personalities are presented, and campaigns are run. Also, it would be difficult to have a national popular-vote election for President without eventually taking away from the States the considerable control they retain over elections and vesting that power completely in Congress. Yet, as we know, political parties in this Country continue to be organized for the most part within States. Politics for us remain mostly local politics, and there may be something healthy about this, in that it permits the people to control, to the extent possible, what is happening. A subversion of local politics, in the name of a supposed national popular control, could undermine effective self-governance by the very people in whose name the popular election of Presidents is being advocated. The Framers of the Constitution recognized that there are better ways and worse ways of organizing the institutions through which the ultimate power of the people is exercised.

VIII

I have not tried to show that the present mode of selecting the President is preferable to various possible alternatives. It suffices to show where the burden of argument lies and that the case has not been made for a change. I have also suggested the ways things could change, and for the worse, with an alternative mode of selection. Should it not be said, on the basis of all this, that it simply may not be prudent to change at this time? Yet there are problems that should be addressed. For one reason or another people have come to be somewhat disturbed (in part because of the influence of those who should have known better) by the system we now have. Certain genuine, though minor, defects in the long-established Presidential-selection system might well be addressed, lest agitation about them undermine respect for the entire Constitutional system.

There is, for example, the threat of the "faithless elector," as exhibited most recently (as we have seen) by the Presidential elector from the State of Washington who voted, in 1976, for Ronald Reagan, when he had been elected on a Gerald Ford slate. Rare as this kind of infidelity has been, people can be disturbed by the prospect of much more of it some day. There no longer seems to be any reason for leaving an option with the Presidential electors chosen in each State. The general understanding is that they should vote as they have been pledged to vote. To take care of the danger that people anticipate, however, changes in State laws or an act of Congress should suffice, requiring Presidential electors to vote in accordance with their pledges. No Constitutional amendment is needed to deal with this problem.

Other people are more concerned about the practice of having each State's votes cast as a unit in favor of one Presidential candidate. It is not generally appreciated that this practice, too, is a product of State law; it is certainly not required by the Constitution. The States, one by one, could decide to have their votes allocated according to the popular vote for each candidate.[67] Those who would like to see this done nationwide should perhaps experiment in a few States to determine what its effects may be.

It should be recognized that there would still remain people who would not be satisfied with the two experimental, State-by-State remedies I have suggested for consideration. We live in an age when it is easy for many to believe that there is something wrong when the popular vote of the Country at large does not seem to count for anything. It may not be prudent therefore simply to dismiss such a concern. Perhaps the popular vote of the Country at large can be used in those rare instances when the Electoral College approach does not produce a winner. Under the present arrangement, the election of the President then goes to the House of Representatives. The popular vote could be used either directly or indirectly to identify a winner in such a contingency.

The direct way would be to allow the total national vote itself to be used. This poses many of the difficulties I have already indicated, including the impetus it would give to efforts to establish national election laws, even a national election board. Such a vote could be misleading, again for the reasons I have given, since that popular vote might not reflect what the vote would have been if it had been generally known in advance that the popular vote might mean something "this time." Perhaps, then, the popular vote should be used indirectly, in the rare contingency I have referred to, by having the members of the House of Representatives vote individually on the President, rather than, as now, State by State, with each State having one vote.[68]

Thus, the changes that it might be useful to consider here are these: first, that the Presidential electors be eliminated, with the votes of the States credited directly to the appropriate candidates; second, that the votes of each State continue to be allocated as a unit, but be subject to change by State law with the approval, if not at the direction, of Congress; and third, that in the event the States' electoral votes do not elect a President, the House of Representatives just chosen in the same national election would do so, with each member of the new House, along with appropriate representatives from the District of Columbia, voting individually.

But, I should at once add, the critical problem here is not with the matters I have been discussing, despite the agitation one hears from time to time. Rather, the critical problem here is with how Presidential campaigning is done under the present system, including how primaries are arranged. An informed national debate is needed on this issue, with a view to developing a policy that makes sense, one that reduces both the kind of demoralizing happenstance found in the primary system we now have as well as the increasing reliance, both in primaries and in general elections, upon advertising techniques and huge expenditures.[69] Our concern should not be with scenarios conjured up about unlikely Electoral College contingencies that would not matter much anyway if they did come to pass. Rather, our principal concern should be with the corruption of the political process that is going on around us all the time and that should be addressed by sound deliberation about what we want our election campaigns to be and to do. Certainly, care should be taken not to permit reliance on public opinion polls, nor recourse to a popularly elected Presidency, to convert our sound republican system into an undisciplined plebiscitary government.

IX

The common good ultimately depends in this Country not upon the mode of electing Presidents or upon who the President happens to be at any particular time or indeed upon precisely what the Constitution says about any number of things. The common good ultimately depends, instead, upon the caliber of the discussion that the American people continually engage in. The kind of discussion engaged in and the conduct permitted and promoted depend upon the character of the American people. That character, in turn, is shaped and perpetuated by the kind of discussion engaged in.

It is that continuing national discussion upon which we depend. We should not allow the splendor of the Presidency to seduce us from our republican virtue. For the more we make of the Presidency (whose proper powers I will be discussing in my next lecture), the less apt we are to think for ourselves and the more apt we are to be manipulated. Among the bad effects of this distortion is an undue concern about how the President is chosen, instead of recognizing that all we can reasonably hope for is a well-established plausible mode of selection that is generally agreed upon.

I should not conclude this discussion of the Constitutional text for this lecture without saying something more about the Vice President. It was accepted, upon the death of the first President in office in 1841, that the Vice President becomes President, not merely Acting President, in filling out the term of a departed President. This well-established Constitutional custom has now been ratified by the Twenty-fifth Amendment, which provides at length for an "Acting President" in various other contingencies. (Might it not be even better in our circumstances, considering how Vice Presidential candidates have come to be selected, if we routinely make use hereafter of the Twenty-fifth Amendment in choosing all Vice Presidents? We would be apt to get sounder choices for Vice President if the President knew he had to offer someone whom the Congress would be willing to confirm.) We need say no more on this occasion about the Vice President than what was said in 1793 by John Adams, while serving as our first Vice President: "My Country has in its wisdom contrived for me the most insignificant office that ever the invention of man contrived, or his imagination conceived."[70] It is salutary to be reminded of Vice-President Adams's attitude, which distinguished, in effect, between the present power and the great potential of his office. It is salutary to be reminded of this in part because, if I am correct, even the far more significant Presidency promises much more than it can usually produce. It is also salutary to be reminded of what happens to the power of the man serving as President when he leaves office. He usually becomes little more than a helpless celebrity, pampered and yet bedeviled by his countrymen. This, too, should make us wonder about how much power the typical President truly has when in office.

Much can be made by theorists of the will and efficiency of the President, especially if he is regarded as a single man acting decisively. But is he not usually much more dependent upon, if not even the captive of, a horde of assistants than the typical member of Congress? Is it not much more fitting for us to look to Congress as the branch of the General Government that ordains and establishes what we are to do? For Congress is the branch that relies most upon political deliberation and that requires, and can get, more reliable guidance from the people. It is the branch that the people can know best as they choose among the men and women most familiar to them in their local districts. It is upon Congressional elections that all our self-government, as a Country, is properly grounded, not upon whatever President may happen to be made available to us from time to time by chance.

9. Article II, Sections 2, 3, & 4

I

I stand with this lecture at the midpoint of my Commentary on the Constitution of 1787. It is appropriate that this series should turn upon a lecture concerned with the powers of the President, for it is a chronic problem among us today what the status of the President should be. It is important, that is, to insist that the President is very much confined by the Constitution.

The Constitutional article devoted to the Presidency indicates at the outset that the President's power is to be known as the "executive Power." This designation recognizes, as we have seen, that the President is to execute laws that serve the policies laid down by Congress.

The executive power means very little, at least under this Constitution, without Congressional direction, which includes, of course, the directives deposited in the statute books over the centuries by one Congress after another. The extent of the powers of the Government of the United States is determined for the most part by the extent of the powers of Congress.[71]

Even when the mass media and others make so much of the Presidency, the personal popularity of a President does not mean much unless he can put it to effective use in persuading the people at large to act—to so act as to prevail upon Congress to do this or that. If the people do not respond or if, in turn, the Congress does not respond to the popular opinion of the moment, the President is left with little more than the appearance of power.

This is not to suggest that the President does not have a variety of powers. One can have various powers and yet not truly have much power, if the exercise of one's powers very much depends upon what others do. For example, the President's powers as Commander in Chief of the army and navy may not amount to much if the Congress should decide to establish or finance no more than a token military force.

It is instructive to notice what the powers of the President are and how they are organized. This we now do by considering the second and third sections of Article II, where the President's principal powers, aside from the veto power spelled out in Article I, Section 7, may be found. Thereafter we will reconsider the fourth section of Article II, which I touched upon in Section V of my last lecture. (This lecture and the preceding one are perhaps the most cautionary, if not the most polemical in this Commentary, partly because so much of the Presidency is regal, and otherwise extraconstitutional, in character. One can be reminded here of the salutary jealousy exhibited by the Senate toward the Consuls for whom it was responsible in the Roman Republic at its height.)

II

Section 2 can be conveniently divided into two parts. The first part includes the President's power as Commander in Chief, his power to require certain written opinions of the principal officers in each of the Executive departments, and his power to grant reprieves and pardons.

How far do the powers of the President go? Are there implied powers? Should not the powers granted to the President be read with their broadest meanings? But it need not be assumed that he also has the power to do all things "necessary and proper for carrying into Execution" the powers he is granted. The Congress itself has such a "necessary and proper" power because the Constitution explicitly gives it that power. Why should one assume, therefore, that the President has implied for him a sweeping power that had to be explicitly granted to Congress in order for it to have it? Furthermore, why would the President require such a sweeping power if Congress is adequately empowered to make all laws necessary and proper for carrying into execution the powers vested by the

Constitution in the President? (I return to this in Section V of this lecture.)

We are obliged to consider, as we did in our efforts to understand the principle of order of various Article I provisions, why these three powers (with respect to being Commander in Chief, to requiring certain written opinions, and to granting reprieves and pardons) should have been the first ones set out among the powers of the President in Sections 2 and 3 of Article II.

These three powers are those that the President exercises more or less independently of Congress. But, as suggested, not even these powers can be exercised altogether independently of Congress. Not only does Congress determine what kind of an army and navy we are to have but also what Executive departments there are to be.

We have also noticed that the appropriations that Congress chooses to make provide the material foundations for all activities of the Executive branch. Related to these are both the laws upon which the very existence of the Executive departments rests and the Congressional actions, such as declarations of war, which are supposed to determine much of what the Executive may do. We should remember as well that all of the laws that Congress makes can be made without the approval of the President, a fact of profound Constitutional significance.

III

The second part of Section 2 of Article II provides for the President's power to make treaties and to appoint various "Officers of the United States." The powers enumerated here are not exercised independently of Congress. Treaties require the concurrence of "two thirds of the Senators present"; ambassadors, judges and other officers of the United States whose appointments are provided for by the Constitution require the concurrence of the Senate (probably by a majority, although it may be left to the Senate to designate what constitutes its concurrence); and the appointments of other officers established by law may also be subject to the concurrence of the Senate or may have their appointments vested by Congress, "as they think proper, in the President alone, in the

Courts of Law, or in the Heads of Departments." (I consider in Section VI of Lecture No. 4 and in Section I of Lecture No. 14 the Congressional numbers required on various occasions.)

Recess appointments are then provided for, "which shall expire at the End" of the next session of the Senate. The need for an interim, or emergency, power of appointment is recognized, even as an ultimate dependence upon Senate concurrence is again affirmed. If the Senate does not choose to act upon a recess (or any other?) appointment, after it returns, the appointment expires at the end of the session.

The arrangements in Section 2 with respect to treaties and appointments take it for granted that the Senate can be depended upon to be as well equipped as the President to know, or at least to be told, what is needed by the Country from time to time. The Senate shares the Executive power here, however convenient it may be to vest in a single man the negotiation of treaties and the nomination of particular men for various posts. The President is not assumed to know things the Senate does not know or that the Senate cannot be told in appropriate circumstances.

There is a parallel here to the sharing by the President in the legislative process, with the use of the veto power, but with this critical difference: the Congress is permitted to override a Presidential veto in the course of making laws, whereas the President is not permitted to override a Senatorial refusal to concur in a treaty or in an appointment. Permitting the use of "executive agreements" and other devices to circumvent the Senate prerogative here is like permitting Congress to disregard a Presidential veto.

It is well to emphasize this because all too many people like to believe that the President knows and feels things that the rest of us, and especially those in Congress, cannot. The Constitution does not count upon such Presidential superiority. Some people are no doubt superior to others, but there is little reason to believe, either from the Constitutional arrangement or from the experiences we have had, that those superior beings are apt to be found more in the Presidency than in Congress or in other walks of life. That a noteworthy superiority *can* be found in the Presidency is testified to by the final appendix to this Commentary.

IV

Certain emergency situations may require that one person be able to act promptly or until Congress can be assembled to act. But we should be reluctant to acknowledge other emergency powers than those provided for in the Constitution. One such power, as we have seen in reviewing the powers of Congress, has to do with the suspension of the privilege of the writ of habeas corpus. Another emergency power, of sorts, has to do with the Presidential recess appointments we have noticed. We thus see that the Constitution does provide for extraordinary circumstances.

Yet we hear complaints about the President's being handcuffed in his conduct of foreign affairs by the War Powers Resolution of 1973[72] and by other laws. Such complaints fail to appreciate both the extent to which emergency power is (and is not) provided for by the Constitution and the significance of the requirement that the Senate routinely pass on treaties and various appointments. The foreign-aid, defense, and other appropriations by Congress, along with related legislation, do far more than the things most Presidents do most of the time to determine what the United States will be in the world at large.

Some critics of our current arrangements argue, "Congress shares in the determination of foreign policy, but the President is responsible for its conduct."[73] They can be troubled by developments whereby "the President's essential freedom of maneuver has been restricted by a series of laws, amendments, and continuing resolutions that transfer responsibility for the conduct of foreign policy, especially its military aspects, to a deliberative body."[74] They can be further troubled by the recognition that "the President must now consider, not the efficacy of his actions, but the reaction of Congress to them."[75] (We can again notice that the Roman Senate had to be reckoned with by the Consuls. This did not keep the Consuls from remarkable successes, and may even have put their successes on a firmer footing.)

Related to such concerns are those that find critics disturbed when the President has to take into account the opinion of the people of the United States about what he is doing. Such critics can even observe that the rule of law (of which the Constitution is the highest written form among us) can be such as "to give free play to [Fidel] Castro in Angola, who [is] not similarly restrained by a Cuban legislature."[76] There are many things that dictators can do, however, that our Presidents cannot. Should we not recognize that we are stronger, and better, because of the restraints we place upon government?

Arguments on behalf of unfettered Presidential discretion are not new. Perhaps the classic Supreme Court case on the subject followed President Truman's seizure of the strike-threatened steel mills during the Korean War.[77] The problem, simply stated, was that the President wanted to exercise a power that Congress had debated giving to him but had deliberately denied him. The President might even have believed it would be disastrous for the Country if he did not exercise the extraordinary power he did in the circumstances, circumstances that could easily have been taken care of with emergency legislation if the Congress had wanted to do so.

But then, Congress does, or fails to do, all kinds of things that Presidents do not like. Suppose that a President decides the Country desperately needs a substantial increase in taxes but the Congress refuses to raise taxes. May he then raise taxes on his own? Surely not. Or suppose a President decides the Country should go to war but Congress refuses to declare war or to appropriate funds to conduct a war. May he go to war or secure such funds on his own? Surely not, the Framers of the Constitution assumed, however much well-intentioned usurpation there might have been here in the twentieth century.

President Lincoln's extraordinary measures in the absence of Congress, which did not reassemble until several months after his inauguration, are often pointed to as justification for strong Presidents. It is natural that in the most devastating circumstances, as when the Union is breaking up, unanticipated, even extra-constitutional, measures may have to be taken in behalf of the Country, and not only by the President. But, thank Heaven, this is certainly not the typical situation. Today, there is no doubt but that the President is, or can be, empowered by various acts of Congress to fend off or to respond to sudden threats to the United States. Such empowerments of the President go back to the First Congress.

Moreover, the President can let us all know whenever he believes that even more powers are needed for emergency purposes. The lack of sufficient empowerment by Congress is not the primary complaint of critics, however, but rather the Constitutional understanding that the President simply is not on his own in the conduct of the grand affairs of the United States, whether at home or abroad.

It remains to be seen whether the War Powers Resolution of 1973 effectively restrains Presidents. There may be something wrong with the War Powers Resolution both in that the Congress has had thus to assert its Constitutional authority and in that so many respectable people regard such an expression of Congressional integrity as itself a usurpation. And so it can be said, "We have, through the War Powers Resolution and through the amendments that have followed it, institutionalized Neville Chamberlain as the model for American Presidents."[78] This is a misdirected argument, considering that the lack of a War Powers Resolution did not keep a Neville Chamberlain from acting as he did. Nor did the British parliamentary system, a system that makes much of Executive power and Cabinet accountability, spare Great Britain from ineffective government in the late 1930s and at various times since then. It is prudent to recall that it is not this act or that, or even this institution or that, which ultimately determines how a country acts, but rather the understanding and the soundness of the people, at least in a liberal democracy. This is well to keep in mind, especially when troubled times abroad and economic distress at home tend to enhance the status of the President of the United States.

Much is made these days of modern technology and of the need for the General Government to be able to act with speed. Does not the ever-growing technological power available to and threatening all mankind call for more, not less, deliberation out in the open, deliberation in which everyone can share who may have something to contribute, and deliberation that all of us can listen to and judge? Instead, we are asked to permit more and more manipulation and maneuverings among the often-faceless advisors of Presidents, hidden away in the recesses of the White House and elsewhere.

We learn, for example, that a prospective Secretary of Agriculture had "jarred political sensibilities at the White House" by having been so bold as to insist upon "direct access to the President."[79]

We also learn that a White House Chief of Staff "would never agree to permit [this (or any other?) Cabinet officer] to bypass him and go directly to the President."[80] What is most startling about this quite remarkable state of affairs is that it should be so casually accepted that Cabinet officers, "the Heads of Departments" provided for in the Constitution and subject to Senate confirmation, should be treated as subordinates by Presidential aides who are not confirmed by the Senate. Consider, also, the National Security Advisor, also not confirmed by the Senate, who can cavalierly take over many of the duties of the Secretary of State and of the Secretary of Defense in one administration after another.

Yet Heads of Departments are again and again regarded by the Constitution as officers of considerable stature. We see in Section 2 of Article II that Heads of Departments may be permitted by Congress to make appointments on their own, as may the President and the National Courts.[81] So independent are the Heads of Departments under the Constitution that the President had to be empowered to "require the Opinion, in writing, of the principal Officer in each of the executive Departments," and then only "upon any Subject relating to the Duties of their respective Offices."[82] The continuing Constitutional importance of the principal officers of the Executive departments is dramatically testified to by the Twenty-fifth Amendment provisions with respect to Presidential incapacity.

Much is to be said, therefore, for returning to the spirit as well as to the letter of the Constitution, a constitution that takes it for granted that the people of this Country are the ultimate rulers here, with Congress as their principal agent among the branches of the General Government. It should also be said that the people, as rulers, have both the power and the duty to require Congress to conduct itself, and to appear to conduct itself, much better than it now does.

V

Section 3 of Article II can be conveniently divided into three parts. The first part reads, "He shall from time to time give to the Congress Information of the State of the Union, and recommend to their Consideration such Measures as he shall judge necessary and expedient . . ." (This is as close as the President gets to the "necessary and proper" power of Congress.)

It is evident here that information about the State of the Union need not be limited to an annual speech (or to any speech at all), but rather may be given "from time to time," which probably means whenever the President chooses to communicate with Congress (unless Congress provides otherwise?). It seems to be assumed that the President may sometimes have information that the Congress does not have. What readily comes to mind is what he may learn in the course of conducting military operations and what he may learn from the ambassadors and other public ministers he is empowered to send and to receive. It is apparent that such information is not authoritative, in the sense that Congress has to accept as binding whatever the President reports. He can do no more than "recommend to their Consideration such Measures as he shall judge necessary and expedient." If Congress does not agree that the recommended measures are truly necessary and expedient in serving one or more of the goals set forth in the Preamble, then the President must make do with what Congress has already provided while he marshals whatever additional information and arguments he may be able to muster to persuade Congress, either directly or through the people.

Is it not clear here as well that Congress is to have the decisive, or authoritative, voice as to what the controlling measures of the United States are to be? Such provisions as this indicate how limited any inherent or implied powers of the Presidency are under the Constitution. Again we notice that there is not given to the President anything comparable to the Congressional power found in the Necessary and Proper Clause. The specificity with which Presidential powers are provided suggests that the President has only the powers indicated, and even these are usually circumscribed by or are dependent upon powers of Congress.

This is consistent with the oath laid down for the President in precise terms. He is to "faithfully execute the Office of President." That is, he will perform the duties and exercise the powers provided by the Constitution, not the duties and powers other executives elsewhere may have from time to time. Among his duties is that he will, to the best of his ability, "preserve, protect and defend the Constitution of the United States." Notice that he is not personally pledged to serve the people or the Country or even the good and just, but rather the Constitution, which would seem to discourage the invocation by any President, except perhaps in the most catastrophic circumstances, of supposed prerogatives rooted in the people or in the Country at large or in any extra-constitutional standards. He, like all the other officers of the General Government and of the State Governments (referred to in Article VI), must conduct himself in accordance with the Constitution. But, more than for the others, his office is strictly defined by the Constitution, whereas some of the other officers have powers and prerogatives independent of the Constitution, which is true, for example, of State Government officers and may be true as well of Judges of the United States, especially if they are to serve as traditional common-law judges. Should not all this be inferred from the way Article II opens, speaking simply of "The executive Power," *not* of "The executive Power of the United States" in the fashion of Article III with its opening words, "The judicial Power of the United States"?[83]

The President of the United States may thus be more strictly confined than any other major officer of the General Government because the Framers recognized that anyone who happens to be singled out as President, no matter how limited his formal powers may be, tends to be made much of by his fellow citizens, especially in a large country. To discipline the President as we do is to reaffirm the rule of law among us.

VI

The second part of Section 3 of Article II is devoted to what the President may do, "on extraordinary Occasions," to convene both or either of the two Houses of Congress. It is devoted as well to what he may do, in special circumstances, to "adjourn them to such Time as he shall think proper." The adjournment power has rarely if ever been used by any President. Congress, if it conducts itself sensibly, makes such Presidential intervention unnecessary. Also, with Congress sitting virtually all the time now, few occasions arise for a President to convene either or both Houses of Congress.

In any event, we can again see that emergency contingencies are provided for by the Constitution, thereby pointing up the limitations of the President in situations in which he is not thus empowered to act. It should be evident, upon examining the Constitution, that there can be innumerable situations in which one branch of the General Government refuses to do something that another branch of that government considers vital to the welfare of the Country, and there may be nothing that can be done about such refusal in the immediate circumstances. That is one of the risks of constitutional government and of any separation of powers. But then, the branch of the General Government that refuses to act may be doing precisely what is required for the common good. Besides, the other branches of that government, and the people at large, are still left free to explain to the recalcitrant branch what may seem to them to be so desperately needed.

We can also see in these provisions of Section 3 the sense in which the President may be regarded as a presiding officer, especially with respect to Congress.[84] The powers given here to the President to convene and to adjourn are no more than supplements to the broad legislative powers given to the two Houses of Congress. These powers are designed to be much less than those once exercised by the Executive under the British Constitution to dissolve Parliament, and everything can turn on that difference. The President's powers to convene and adjourn Congress are minor when compared to the veto power given to him, which can routinely affect in a significant way the legislation that Congress enacts.

VII

The power given the President to "receive Ambassadors and other public Ministers" may be placed immediately after the convening-and-adjourning power because the receiving of diplomats is something like the calling together (the "receiving"?) of the Congress. This power could thus fit into the second part of Section 3.

Or should we consider it as leading off the third part of Section 3? That part includes as its principal provision that "he shall take Care that the Laws be faithfully executed, and shall Commission all the Officers of the United States." Is detailed conduct of affairs, both at home and abroad, to be left to duly certified officers who are commissioned by the President? If so, these three powers may reflect facets of Presidential activity. The conduct of foreign affairs may be seen in the receiving of diplomats; the conduct of domestic affairs may be seen in faithfully executing the laws; and the conduct of both domestic and foreign affairs may depend upon "all the Officers of the United States" commissioned by the President.

Or is it merely chance that brings these three powers together at the end of Section 3? That is, these may simply be powers left over and in need of inclusion somewhere, especially if they happen to have been executive powers that the Congress under the Articles of Confederation had exercised, which means that it is prudent to specify them for the President if he is to have them. Still, the last empowerments of the President in Article II reminds him of his duty to see that the laws are faithfully executed. We have seen that this is the foundation upon which all else necessarily and properly rests for his office.[85]

I have observed that we may never be able to work out in as much detail as we might like precisely why each part of the Constitution is where it is. In political matters, particulars and hence chance can play a considerable, sometimes even a mysterious, part. Does not this suggest the limits of the practical life, even one so active as that of the chief executive of a great country?

VIII

The limits of political life are indicated in still another way in the final section of Article II, where the institution of impeachment, introduced in Sections 2 and 3 of Article I, is returned to with the provision, "The President, Vice President and all civil Officers of the United States, shall be removed from Office on Impeachment for, and Conviction of, Treason, Bribery, or other high Crimes and Misdemeanors." To provide for impeachment is to recognize that political judgments can be mistaken. Certainly, the people may not know all that they need to know to choose properly on any particular occasion.

One gets the impression here that the offenses from which impeachment might follow are to be of a serious character, not something light and transient. It is suggested in Article III that impeachments relate (usually, if not always) to "Crimes."

Is it not significant that the last words in the Executive Article are devoted to the possibility of impeachment, thereby not only pointing up the Framers' concern with the conduct of the Presidency, but also once again reminding us of the ultimate superiority of Congress among the three branches of the General Government?

IX

With this reminder of Congressional superiority, we return to the problem of what we have allowed the Presidency to become. Concerns about what has recently been called "the Imperial Presidency" have been expressed from the beginning of the Republic under the Constitution, and even before that beginning.

Always in view, of course, was the British monarchy with its extravagant claims a century or two earlier about royal prerogatives, dramatized by the pomp and ceremony attending upon the monarch. Also in view, at least for the Framers, was the insistence by writers such as Montesquieu, several times referred to in the Federal Convention and many times referred to during the Ratification Campaign, that only a monarchical form of government could rule a large country properly.

The determination in the early days of the Republic to keep the President under control may be seen in the way he is spoken of. Thus, in the arguments reported for *Marbury* v. *Madison* in 1803, the former President can be several times identified simply as "Mr. Adams."[86] It is also instructive that the Executive Article is the second article in the Constitution, not the first, and that it is far shorter than the first.

In any event, it is not good either for the President or for the Country to make as much of the President as we now do, no matter who he may happen to be. A dispatch from an American columnist in Paris strikes a healthy note in opposition to the symphony of adulation with which Presidents tend to be besieged today. The column, "Why Treat Presidents Like Gods?",[87] begins as follows:

When the President of the United States travels abroad, his tasters precede him, trying the food he is to eat, overseeing the preparation of the banquets he will attend. At the dinner given by West Germa-

121

ny's President in Bonn on May 4, American security men told German officials where they could, and could not, move about. The President of France was blocked in his car for 20 minutes because the Secret Service would not move President Reagan's back-up car. What does this remind you of?

The Founding Fathers considered setting up a monarchy but decided, in all gravity, not to do so. George Washington refused a crown. He was too modest, or merely before his time. Today, in fact but not in name, the United States has a king (or emperor), surrounded by pomp, protocol and protection.[88]

Consider, by way of contrast, these observations:

In the meantime, the President of the Swiss Federation, not a global power but not an inconsiderable one either, jostles with other guests to get his coat from the cloakroom at concerts. The President of the French Republic takes his friends to dinner in restaurants, and leaves the quality of his food to the chef.[89]

And now, back to the United States:

It wasn't so long ago that such things happened in Washington—in republican, pre-imperial Washington. Ah, the reader may say, but times today are different. They are, but not that much.

There are terrorists today, but there were terrorists yesterday, and the great and murderous American Nut, who shoots famous people to give a little meaning to his life, has always been with us.[90]

It is instructive to be reminded:

There is an intelligent and experienced Vice President. There is a line of succession. There are, to be blunt, plenty more where this one came from. The halls of Congress and the statehouses are crowded with people who want desperately to be President—and have the qualifications, such as they are. A new election comes along every four years.[91]

We should take to heart the casual way the Swiss President is treated and the humane way the French President conducts his private life, however dangerous this can be from time to time. Is there not something demeaning to a republican people to make what we now do of our Presidents and of their families and other intimates? Furthermore, is it salutary to make as much as we do of the preser-

122

vation of the life of any man? What does that teach the rest of us?

However important it may be to notice that the powers of the President are far more limited than they often seem, he does have power enough, because of the way we now kowtow to the Presidency, to have a corrupting influence in a Republic. Among the consequences of our unbecoming obsequiousness, which the mass media "naturally" exploit, is that we are diverted both from serious politics and from a proper reading of the Constitution.

It is, after all, a Constitution pursuant to which the President can do no more than recommend to the *consideration* of Congress "such Measures as he shall judge necessary and expedient." This is something that we as citizens are, in accordance with the First Amendment, also entitled to do. The measures we are free to recommend include those that could help restore the Presidency to proper proportions, even as we resist the temptation to harass our Presidents when they run into the trouble they all too often deserve.

We can begin to set things right by leaving Presidents pretty much on their own, with no more than a reasonable pension, once their terms are finished. To consider the Presidency virtually a "Title of Nobility" is subversive of republican virtue and encourages both misreadings of the Constitution and misconduct by men eager to serve the President and thereby themselves. "We the People" are not well served when this happens.

10. Article III, Sections 1 & 2

I

I have argued, in discussing Article II, that the President has been made more of in our political system than the Constitution expects. Similarly, in what I say about Article III, I will be arguing that the Judiciary has been made too much of. And yet I will also argue that the Judiciary is not made enough of.

The Judiciary has been made too much of in that it is generally assumed that the National Courts are entitled and obliged to review acts of Congress for their Constitutionality. I have already touched upon this, especially when I discussed the veto power of the President in Lecture No. 4. I shall return to this supposed power of judicial review in my next lecture, a power first exercised by the Supreme Court (it is usually said) in an 1803 case[92] that saw the Court interpret the provisions in Section 2 of Article III for the original jurisdiction and the appellate jurisdiction of the Supreme Court (about which provisions, too, I will have something to say later).

It is in my next lecture, then, that I will be arguing that the Judiciary has been made too much of in certain respects. On this occasion, however, I argue that the Judiciary has not been made enough of—and this is with respect to the proper powers of the National Courts in determining and developing the common law in this Country. Before we look at this problem, however, we should examine Sections 1 and 2 of Article III.

This lecture, and the next one, will be the most complex in this Commentary. This is appropriate, indeed even instructive, considering the subject matter. Everyone recognizes that judges are called upon for a more technical—a less political and hence a less accessible—learning than either legislators or executives. It is not surprising, therefore, that the public tends to defer to judges as learned, whereas they consider, if not even look down upon, legislators as very much like themselves. And so, when a Jack Cade runs wild in Shakespeare's 2 *Henry VI*, his attack upon all learning is dramatized by the proposal that his mob kill the lawyers.

II

The existence of "one supreme Court" is recognized at the outset of Article III, with other courts being left to Congress to "ordain and establish." Thus, Congress is to do for the judicial system of the United States what the American people do for the Constitution itself: "ordain and establish." One is reminded also of the various Executive departments that Congress is responsible for establishing. It should be noticed, as still another instance of legislative supremacy under the Constitution, that the Supreme Court is shaped in decisive respects by Congress, including various aspects of its activities. Even the size of the Supreme Court is determined by Congress, a size that Congress may change whenever it chooses. (Congress has not chosen to do so for more than a century.)

The considerable subordination of the National Courts to Congressional regulation is offset by providing protection for judges that is not available for any other public servants under the Constitution. There is, in effect, lifetime tenure, as well as the provision that one's compensation may be increased but not diminished while one is in office. Such protection must have seemed natural to the Framers, familiar as they were with the prerogatives of the British judges of their day.

British judges seem to have been highly regarded, for the most part. Americans evidently hoped that their judges would be comparable not only in the security they would enjoy but also in the wisdom and the integrity that that security would permit them to exhibit without fear of retaliation.

The National Courts—both the "one supreme Court" established by the Constitution and the various "inferior Courts" that may be established by the Congress—have vested in them the "judicial Power of the United States." It seems that all of such power is vested in these Courts, but it may depend upon Congress to determine precisely how that judicial power should be exercised.

III

Section 2 of Article III tells us what the judicial power of the United States extends to. Various kinds of "Cases" and "Controversies" are listed.[93]

It is not hard to figure out why the things listed here should be declared to be subject to the jurisdiction of the National Courts. First, there are the strictly national matters—those matters that arise "under this Constitution, the Laws of the United States, and Treaties made, or which shall be made, under their Authority." It should be obvious that these are matters with which the Courts of the General Government should probably be entrusted.

Second, there are the matters that bear upon the conduct of foreign relations by the General Government. These may be seen not only in the treaties already referred to, but also in the "Cases affecting Ambassadors, other public Ministers and Consuls" and in "Cases of admiralty and maritime Jurisdiction," as well as simply in "Controversies to which the United States shall be a Party." These are matters that no State courts should be permitted to control completely if there is to be a truly national government.

Third, there are the matters involving differences between States, either directly or indirectly (with citizens of one State in opposition to another State or to citizens thereof). One can see, upon consulting the Articles of Confederation, how such differences between States or between the citizens of diverse States were anticipated. Elaborate procedures are spelled out in Section IX of the Articles for establishing a fair tribunal in each such instance. This was because no permanent national court system was established by the framers of the Articles of Confederation, who seem to have relied for the most part upon State courts to continue to take care of most of the judicial business of the Country.

Such then are the matters to which the "judicial Power of the United States" shall extend, matters that seemed to the Framers of the Constitution better dealt with in the National Courts than in the courts of the several States. This observation is consistent with the argument made throughout this Commentary that the Constitution can be seen to make sense. There are plausible reasons why it is put together the way it is.

IV

Should we say that this "judicial Power of the United States" not only must be vested in the National Courts but also that it must be fully vested in those courts? The Constitution does sound that way, and this would mean that at least the Supreme Court should have some access to all cases of the kinds described in Section 2 of Article III. Whether any other National Courts would ever be involved would depend upon whether they had been established by Congress and on what terms. In any event, is there not a limit to what Congress is entitled to do in keeping certain kinds of cases from being within the ultimate control of the National Courts?

There was some talk in the Federal Convention and in the First Congress about having the General Government rely entirely upon State trial courts for routine litigation, as the Articles of Confederation government had done, rather than having Congress establish trial courts of its own. Certainly, it would be easier for the General Government to rely upon the States to take care of much of the judicial business of the United States than it would be for that government to rely upon the States for either legislative or executive duties on behalf of the United States. Exclusive reliance upon State trial courts would face the problem, however, that such courts need not have the tenure and compensation guarantees that the Constitution evidently considers desirable, if not necessary, for proper judicial conduct in exercising the "judicial Power of the United States."

It did seem to be understood in 1787 that a competent judge, at least in the English-speaking world, was bound by a generally known set of rules, principles and precedents wherever he sat. It seems also to have been understood that a supreme court would be needed to keep in line all the inferior courts in this Country, whether State or National, at least to the extent that such courts dealt with the laws of the United States.

Some supervisory power by the National Courts over State courts makes sense because even routine State-court proceedings can raise, sometimes unexpectedly, questions that depend upon a proper understanding of the Constitution, statutes, or treaties of the United States. A power of reviewing State-court decisions in such matters seems to be needed in the National Courts if the judicial power of the United States is to be applied consistently. This suggests that all the kinds of cases and controversies to which the judicial power of the United States extends should be susceptible to supervisory control, one way or another, by the National Courts. It may be the duty of Congress, then, to keep all such cases *within the reach* of the National Courts, allowing those courts discretion as to what they will handle and how. (I return to these matters in Lecture No. 11.)

V

A critical question remains down to our day and will extend beyond it: How is the common law to be developed in the United States? The common law is the body of customary law that stretches back for several hundred years in Anglo-American jurisprudence, having found expression, for the most part, in the judgments and opinions of generation after generation of judges. It is the common law that used to govern many, perhaps most, of the everyday relations of people to one another in this Country. Even with the growth in reliance upon statutory law and regulations among us, the underlying common law is still of considerable importance. Were common-law disputes intended to be included within the provision of "all Cases, in Law and Equity, arising under this Constitution"? The most likely way common-law disputes would arise in the National Courts would be in the diversity-of-citizenship controversies provided for in Section 2 of Article III. The decisive question here is not whether the United States Supreme Court is to exercise continuing, direct, and deliberate control over common-law developments in State and other courts in this Country. Rather, the decisive question here is this: Where are the National Courts to look for the rule in the cases that do happen to come before them in which common-law determinations must be made?

The answer to this question was, from the earliest days of the Republic[94] until a half-century ago,[95] that the National Courts do what all courts in the English-speaking world should do when confronted with a common-law issue. The traditional teaching had been that a court should, with due deference to the rulings of superior courts, use its best judgment to determine what the common law is. (The lower the court, the more deference it is expected to exhibit.) In short, the judges in the National Courts, including the Supreme Court, were counted upon to be judges, doing what centuries of common-law judges had done.

The traditional approach tended to encourage and permit a national uniformity with respect to the common law, with the Supreme Court leading the way. At the very least, Supreme Court precedents would appear to judges in all the States as authority not to be lightly disregarded. It is here, however, that the Judiciary of the United States has been made far less of than it should have been. Since 1938 it has become fashionable to believe that the National Courts should exercise no independent judgment with respect to any common-law determinations they may make in diversity cases. Rather, they are to look to the rule that happens to have been laid down by State courts in the State considered to be "controlling" in any particular case that has found its way into the federal system.[96]

State Courts, when they come to make common-law determinations, are not similarly bound, however. They are not even bound by their own precedents. Rather, they are free, in their efforts to do justice, to try to arrive at the best judgment possible in the circumstances. Only the National Courts, including the Supreme Court, are now precluded from doing what common-law courts have always done, and what the National Courts themselves tried to do during the first century and a half under the Constitution. Simply put, the National Courts are now precluded from being fully courts of justice. They are unable to exercise in its amplitude that "judicial Power of the United States" with which Article III is concerned.

VI

The depreciation of the Supreme Court's role in common-law cases may be related to a general failure to appreciate how wide the Congressional power is, especially with respect to commerce.

Commerce and commercial relations are matters with which much of the common law is concerned, in the form of the law of contracts, sales, and negotiable instruments, the law of property, and the law of torts.

One can even suspect that the depreciation of the powers of the Supreme Court as a common-law court is in large part due to efforts on the part of Southern interests who were concerned about the possibility of Congressional interference with local regulation of slavery. Those efforts included a Southern insistence upon narrowing the commerce power of Congress, thereby making it more likely that the General Government would not interfere with how Southern States dealt with their threatening and threatened institution of slavery.

If, on the other hand, a broad common-law power is recognized in the National Courts, this means that there is likely to be a legislature, preferably a coordinate legislature (that is, Congress), able to deal with (and regulate and, if need be, correct) the matters that common-law courts deal with. Courts have never been considered entirely on their own with respect to such matters. It is considered anomalous by students of the common law to have a court with great common-law powers without a concurrent legislature with some authority over the same subject matter. And so it has been routinely recognized, in the United States as in Great Britain, that legislatures can alter the rules that common-law courts lay down, however much justice requires that courts should be left alone in particular cases, once judgment has been rendered between parties. One consequence of, if not a reason for, denying extensive common-law powers to the National Courts was to make less evident the broad legislative powers of Congress, especially with respect to commerce. But this is one country economically, and the common law, especially with respect to the law of contracts, sales, and negotiable instruments, should reflect that fact. The accepted Constitutional interpretation has come around somewhat to this view, recognizing as it does a virtually unlimited commerce power in Congress, however confusing the way this recognition has developed might have been.

By the time the National Courts were stripped of their long-standing and broad common-law powers, the Supreme Court had begun to recognize a broad commerce power in Congress. But the connection between the commerce power in Congress and the common-law power in the National Courts had long since been lost sight of. Besides, the more sophisticated American scholars and judges had been converted to a jurisprudential doctrine that explains common-law rulings not as the products of reasoning with a view to justice, but rather as merely the exercise of sovereign power, and the States could be looked to as sufficient repositories of such power.

One strange thing about all this is that the principal judicial spokesman for this development was a thrice-wounded Union veteran of the Civil War who evidently did not recognize the extent to which he was in effect advancing Southern "States' Rights" doctrine at the expense of national unity, in this case a unity dedicated to a rational system of law grounded in nature (which is, after all, what the common law stands for).[97]

VII

The Supreme Court, when it switched in 1938, saw itself as being realistic about what courts really do. In addition, it further justified the new approach, which required the National Courts to defer for the most part to State courts' common-law determinations, by arguing that the old approach permitted plaintiffs to "shop" for friendly forums by resorting to the National Courts when the law in the State courts they would otherwise have to submit to seemed unreceptive to their claims.

Whether "forum shopping" has truly been curtailed or only made more sophisticated is a complex question. One thing is certain: the National Courts, usually staffed by the better judges in this Country, are no longer to use their own best judgment, and their learning, in making the common-law determinations they are obliged to make. Instead, they are merely to decide two subordinate questions, which require only more or less mechanical responses on their part: What State's common law is controlling in this case? What does that State's common law say on such a matter, as that law is recorded in the official reports? This means that the common law, as applied by the National Courts, can no longer be readily adapted to circumstances, although adaptability has always been one of the virtues of the common law. Rather, the National Courts are bound by what happens then to be the recorded State doctrine, no matter how unreasonable, or difficult to justify, that doctrine may have become and no matter how vulnerable that recorded doctrine may be in that very State the next time the Supreme Court of that State is given an opportunity to reconsider it. This, at least, was the way the Supreme Court laid down the contemporary approach in 1938.

Critical to this approach seems to be the assumption that one body of State common law is just as good as another body of State common law, at least so far as the National Courts should be concerned. This approach assumes that marked and permanent divergences in the *common* law make sense. It teaches in effect that law is primarily the emanation of some will (or sovereign) rather than a dictate of reason (or nature). We thereby are likely to lose sight of the fact that a standard of right and wrong is something all are somehow aware of or may be guided by.

Fundamental here, in this discussion of the common-law role of the National Courts, is not a historical question or even any question about the original intention of the Framers. Rather, it is a question about the very nature of law and how justice is to be arrived at by courts working on their own, somewhat independently of legislatures. It is a question about the way that reason and nature may be looked to in establishing justice, something that common-law courts have always been thought of as most adept in doing, and doing in such a way as to take due account of the opinions, expectations, and limitations of the people they serve. Vital to the common-law approach is the reliance upon argument in assessing judicial attempts to apply long-established principles to changing circumstances.

The current situation is especially odd, as I have indicated, in that State courts, when they come to consider their own common-law rulings, usually try to draw upon the best opinions available to them. This is consistent with the way common-law judges work. Since everyone knows that people may differ when they try to employ reason in determining the just rule in a particular kind of situation, there is much to be said for having superior courts with the power to choose among the determinations of various inferior courts. There has to be in a country, it is reasonable to conclude, one authoritative court that is to guide the general common-law development, especially with respect to matters, such as commercial law, upon which the entire country depends. Such a court should itself be subject to criticism by scholars and by other judges and to correction by a legislature ultimately controlled by the people. The current doctrine, on the other hand, leaves too much scope to chance in the development and application of the common law in the United States.

It may well be, of course, that a national common law is again developing in various fields, at least in part because of certain necessities and with the guidance of Congressional legislation. But the most important aspect of the current approach, at least for the student of our institutions, is that it tends to teach us the wrong lessons about the very nature of justice and about the relation of justice to law, just as it helps conceal from view the achievements and the aspirations of common-law practitioners.

VIII

We return to historical considerations when we notice that it would have been thought peculiar by the Framers that diverse manifestations of the common law on any particular issue could endure within the Country. They would have assumed that all judges would try to do the same thing, with the United States Supreme Court having a particularly influential say as to what the law should be, a say that would tend to smooth out the discrepancies that develop between courts from time to time. Thus, in the Articles of Confederation, a common-law jurisdiction was assumed to be routine for American courts, with the various State and other tribunals doing more or less the same thing, even though there was no high court to provide the required guidance for the entire Country.

The Framers would have wondered how the United States Supreme Court could truly be considered supreme if it should have to be subordinated, in a distinctively judicial activity, to the precedents of the courts of the various States. On the other hand, setting up courts and determining their jurisdictions need not have been considered a judicial function, but rather a legislative function. It is important thus to emphasize the difference between, first, *what* the Supreme Court can pass upon (including the common law) and, second, *when* or *how* the Supreme Court can pass upon it (which may depend upon legislative guidance). Or, put another way, the Supreme Court should have ultimate judicial authority over what the common law in this Country is to be, even though it may not have ultimate authority over which courts may handle which common-law (or any other) issues from time to time. Of course, the Supreme Court cannot handle more than a very small part of the litigation in the Country, but it *can* make the substantial statements about the law, whether interpreting acts of Congress or expounding the common law, which every court in the Country should be urged and inclined to draw upon as much as possible. Such deference is neither desired nor likely if it should generally come to be believed that law is little more than an act of power or will, not a dictate of reason on the part of someone authorized thus to speak for the community.

IX

I have suggested that it is impossible to appreciate fully the Supreme Court for what it was intended to be if its common-law powers and duties are not recognized. But then, it is impossible to understand the United States Constitution itself if its considerable dependence upon the common law is not recognized, a dependence so deep and so extensive as to make it seem only natural that the Supreme Court should be regarded as a vital part of the common-law system in this Country.

The common law is again and again taken for granted in the Constitution. Many of the terms used (including *citizen, inhabitant, treason, felony,* and *breach of the peace*) have been shaped by centuries of the common law. Many of the rights referred to, and guaranteed, by the Constitution and later by the Bill of Rights depend for their detailed application upon the common law, even when they have been modified by statute (including the right to the writ of habeas corpus and the right to trial by jury). Consider as well how much the common law is drawn upon in the Constitutional assurance given as to "Privileges and Immunities." The rule of law is taken for granted throughout the Constitution, not only in the restrictions with respect to bills of attainder and ex post facto laws, but also in the very dependence upon legislation—a rule of law that centuries of the common law had taught the English-speaking peoples to expect and to make proper use of.

One does not need to know anything about what happened in the Federal Convention of 1787, where the common law was again and again relied upon and where the authority of William Blackstone, as the great eighteenth-century expositor of the common law, could be routinely invoked, in order to conclude that the common law is vital to our Constitutional system. (The considerable recourse to Blackstone is evident in what was done in the Convention, even though it is not explicitly recorded in Madison's *Notes*. It is well to be reminded from time to time that much is obviously left out not only of those *Notes* but also of the records of the State Ratification Conventions.) Nor does one need to look into the doings of Congress, both under the Articles of Confederation and under the Constitution of 1787 (such doings as the Northwest Ordinance enacted by the Confederation Congress and the Bill of Rights drafted in the First Congress), to see that the common law was continually taken for granted. The Constitution itself stands as a monument to the common law, built as it is upon it.

A common-law system that is so deeply rooted as to be generally accepted can reaffirm the traditional teaching that reason and a sense of natural justice should be looked to for guidance in courts of law. A proper opinion about the common law, and about the duties and powers of the National Courts with respect to the common law, stands as a bulwark against subversion of our institutions by positivism, relativism, and legal realism, if not even against a mindless fascination with power for its own sake.

The most serious complaint to be made against the United States Supreme Court, therefore, is not that it has been too "activist," but rather that it has not been active enough in this respect. That is, the Supreme Court has not been fully aware of what it can and should mean under the Constitution for a court to be a court. It has been kept from its full realization as a court, and as a national teacher of what law is, by its diversion into that career as a superlegislature which easily follows from making much of a general power of judicial review, something which I shall examine further (along with the common law) in my next lecture.

11. Article III, Sections 2 & 3

I

For more than a century the United States Supreme Court has conducted itself as a superlegislature or, at least, as a third or fourth branch of the national legislature. This means that the Court, as well as thousands of lawyers and judges, must spend considerable time and energy reviewing Constitutionality questions, which are almost always decided in favor of what has been done by Congress.

Among the Constitutional questions the Supreme Court has decided is one that has, as we have seen, made it act less as a court than it should, for it has surrendered its power and forsaken its duty to serve as the ultimate judicial supervisor of the common law in the United States. Instead, the Supreme Court since 1938 has considered itself bound, when it has had to decide common-law questions, to take its guidance from one State legal system or another. The common law, it is well to be reminded, is that body of largely customary law, usually left to judges to declare, which governs many, if not most, of the everyday legal relations between people.

The States are now relied upon by the Supreme Court to develop the common law. Much is to be said for the States and for federalism, of course, and I will do some of that saying in my remaining lectures.[98] Since the common law is a complex subject, and one that has to be drawn upon repeatedly in interpreting Article III of the Constitution in this lecture, it should be useful for me to say even more about it than I already have.

The States simply cannot be depended upon to develop a proper common law or efficient commercial codes for the Country at large. What the State courts can do they are doing. They work things out the best they can, but with irreconcilable majority and minority rules developing among them on various subjects.

It is a matter of chance, it sometimes seems, when a satisfactory general rule emerges in this fashion. The General Government gets into the process somewhat, by legislation keyed to the commerce power or to the monetary power, but such hit-or-miss participation cannot substitute for the steady common-law and uniform-code contributions that the National Courts and Congress could make.

The Supreme Court may believe that it has more than enough business that the States cannot at all take care of, and so it is well rid of any effort to supervise the common law and the uniform codes that partially replace the common law. But the Court may have given up, through its 1938 abdication, one of its most useful activities. No one else can act here for the Country at large.

It is often important with respect to the common law that there be a generally known rule, not necessarily the best possible rule, especially if nationwide commercial developments are to be advanced. It is even more reassuring when it is understood that the generally known rule is also likely to be, because of the competence of the highest reviewing court, a quite good (perhaps even the best possible) rule in the circumstances.

The approach pursuant to which the Supreme Court now conducts itself tends to confirm the proposition that the common law (like the Constitution?) is what the judges say it is, rather than that reasoned consensus about justice that is continually to be searched for and reexamined in varying circumstances. Thus, I have argued, the most serious problem with the current approach is what it teaches us about what law is and is not.

II

The common law depends upon arguments and upon assessing what has been said and done. It requires, because of faulty reasoning by some judges and because of changing conditions, repeated reconsideration of received opinion. In a common-law system (including now the uniform codes), things work themselves out over decades; reason and a sense of natural justice tend to assert themselves. One truly great power that the National Courts should exercise as common-law courts is that of shaping the general moral sense of the Country, and in a relatively uncontroversial manner.

The common law is a way of applying, case-by-case, the enduring standards of the community, and in such a way as to bring the community along, even as reforms are being made. It is salutary to emphasize here that common-law judges discover the law; they do not simply make it. Reason looks to nature (instead of will looking to desire) in declaring the rule that is to be followed.

The common law, I have also suggested, is very much taken for granted by the Constitution, not least with respect to the "judicial Power of the United States." The common law that is taken for granted is a vital common law, not something either fossilized or fragmented—that is, either frozen as of 1776–1789 or dependent upon the diverse rulings of various "sovereign" States.

The common law presupposes, then, some court that can provide guidance for all the judges in the Country, and it is difficult to see how that can be done by any court but the United States Supreme Court. It also presupposes—and this recognition, at a time when efforts were being made to keep national power to the minimum, might have contributed to the original subversion of the common-law function of the National Courts—it presupposes a legislature able to keep common-law courts in line, to guide them and to correct aberrations or to lay out changes in course that would be too abrupt or too extensive for any common-law court to make. We can thus see, once again, the ultimate superiority intended for Congress in our Constitutional system.

Whether the National Courts exercise a common-law power, those courts have their work largely determined by the legislative activity of Congress—by the directives and programs in the statute books. The judicial function of the National Courts includes their interpretation and application of the laws Congress makes and of the regulations (or so-called laws) executive agencies make. Much of this must be routine and tedious, and yet that is most of what the National Courts are now bound to do. I suspect, therefore, that these judges would be enlivened if the National Courts had old-fashioned common-law questions put to them routinely to consider properly, thereby linking them with great common-law judges across the centuries.

III

The laws of Congress, we have observed, extend to the creation of most of the National Courts, to the determination of the size of such courts (as well as the size of the Supreme Court), and to the provision of salaries, facilities, and support services.

Even more important, Congress can determine what the jurisdiction is of the many courts that it provides for. The rule-making power with respect to judicial activity is, in principle, legislative; it must rest ultimately with the legislature, however much a legislature may delegate this power to courts from time to time.

One Article III limitation is placed upon Congress here, and that is with respect to the original jurisdiction conferred by the Constitution upon the Supreme Court. The original jurisdiction seems to be immutable, at least in that nothing can be removed from the Supreme Court's original jurisdiction that the Constitution has placed there.

But the Constitution indicates that the appellate jurisdiction of the Supreme Court can be adjusted by Congress, for the allocation in Article III is made subject to "such Exceptions, and under such Regulations as the Congress shall make." We must now examine this provision, for it is in its interpretation and application that we encounter the first instance in which part of an act of Congress was declared unconstitutional by the United States Supreme Court. This was in the famous 1803 case of *Marbury* v. *Madison*.[99]

IV

We need not concern ourselves with the facts of *Marbury*.[100] It suffices to notice that William Marbury brought suit in the Supreme Court in order to secure the post he believed himself entitled to as a Justice of the Peace in the District of Columbia. Among the questions the Supreme Court addressed was whether Congress had been Constitutionally empowered to do what it was said had been done by Congress, the addition to the original jurisdiction of the

Supreme Court of a right to hear, and to issue a mandamus in, such a case as Marbury had brought.

According to the Supreme Court in *Marbury*, the First Congress had, in the Judiciary Act of 1789,[101] moved a class of cases from the appellate to the original jurisdiction of the Supreme Court, and this, the Court insisted, Congress should not have done. Critical to the Court's conclusion was the argument that if Congress could thus move something out of the appellate and into the original jurisdiction of the Supreme Court, there would have been no purpose in the original Constitutional allocation.

But is this so? Could not the initial allocation of appellate jurisdiction in Article III have been considered a provisional arrangement, just as there are other provisional arrangements in the Constitution? There is good reason for such provisional arrangements. The Framers wanted the system to be able to start running from the outset, and this was to be true for the Supreme Court as well, once it was set up by Congress and its members had been selected.[102]

So from the outset, it would have been useful to know what the Supreme Court's jurisdiction was, both original and appellate. Then, as experience suggested and time permitted, Congress could rearrange the initially allocated appellate jurisdiction, which means that it could put some of it in the original jurisdiction of the Supreme Court, and it could do so in such detail as the Framers might have thought premature or otherwise inappropriate for the Constitution itself to provide.

It is not hard to figure out why certain kinds of cases should always be in the original jurisdiction of the Supreme Court. But was there any reason why other kinds of cases could not be added to (and thereafter removed from) the original jurisdiction, as experience and reflection suggested? The Supreme Court never faced up to this argument in its insistence that the Congress should not have done what it did in the Judiciary Act of 1789.

Not only did the Court insist that Congress should not have done this, but it also ruled that Congress could never do this, that what it had done was unconstitutional and hence void. And thus judicial review of acts of Congress (and of acts of the President?) had its first effective exercise.

V

Among the serious consequences of the position taken by the Supreme Court in *Marbury* v. *Madison* is one that does not seem to be generally appreciated, for the *Marbury* ruling in effect concedes that the "Exceptions" power means that Congress can keep altogether out of the jurisdiction of the Supreme Court, both appellate and original, any of the variety of cases referred to in the appellate-jurisdiction provision. Once the Court insisted that excepting a case from the appellate jurisdiction of the Supreme Court could never mean adding it to the original jurisdiction of the Supreme Court, then it tacitly conceded that it must mean (if "excepting" is to mean anything) that cases may be altogether removed by Congress from the jurisdiction of the Supreme Court.

Yet, one might wonder, should not the "judicial Power of the United States" always be within the reach of, and hence subject to supervision by, the United States Supreme Court? This bears upon a controversy that flares up from time to time: Can any of the kinds of cases listed in Section 2 of Article III be kept away from the Supreme Court altogether? The authorities often say that they can be. But is not this improper, being against the spirit of the Constitution, as would be extinguishing the Court itself by making no replacements to it as its members retire or die?

Even without judicial review of acts of Congress, there are vital cases that should always be within the purview of the Supreme Court, including the assessment for Constitutionality of various State actions, something that seems to be anticipated by the Constitution and that the Judiciary Act of 1789 explicitly recognizes. It is revealing, therefore, that in the very case in which the Supreme Court insisted upon its power of judicial review over acts of Congress, it also tacitly recognized that Congress can routinely remove from review by the Court any cases within its appellate jurisdiction that might result in declarations of the unconstitutionality of State actions as well as of acts of Congress. This, alone, should make one wonder about how much sense judicial review of Congressional enactments makes in our system.

Judicial review, fully to make sense, must repudiate in principle the holding of the Supreme Court in the very case in which it was first exercised to declare an act of Congress unconstitutional. Must not all of the kinds of cases listed in Section 2 of Article III remain within the reach of the Supreme Court if there is to be a practical check upon unconstitutional legislation by the National Courts? But then, I have suggested, the Supreme Court may simply have distorted the Constitution (because of partisan considerations?), and this would mean that the "judicial Power of the United States" (whatever it includes) cannot properly be impaired (however it may be rearranged) by Congress.

To redeem the Court thus, by correcting its reading of the Constitution, obliges us to wonder why we want judicial review in the first place. It is not in order to get still another opinion about Constitutionality, but rather to get an authoritatively correct opinion. Yet in the first notorious instance in which the power of judicial review was exercised adversely to Congress, the Supreme Court might well have been wrong, or at least not clearly right, in its reading of the Constitution—with mischievous implications for the safety of the Court itself.

After *Marbury* v. *Madison*, the Supreme Court did not venture for a half-century to declare another act of Congress unconstitutional. This suggests that there must have been something special about the 1803 *Marbury* case, so special that any claim by the Court to the general power of judicial review remained under a cloud. The Court may even have been trying in *Marbury* to protect its prerogatives or to insist upon procedural proprieties, which might be proper, however limited, exercises of judicial review. When the Court did venture, a second time, to declare an act of Congress unconstitutional, it so put the Country in jeopardy that it could very well have, perhaps should have, finished off the institution of judicial review, for its second notorious venture into judicial review was the *Dred Scott* case of 1857.[103] In that case the Court ruled in effect that Congress had no power to prohibit the spread of slavery into the Territories of the United States, even though the Confederation Congress had done precisely that in its Northwest Ordinance of 1787, an act deliberately ratified in 1789 by the First Congress.[104]

The *Dred Scott* case reminds us that whenever the Congress and the Supreme Court have differed on those great matters of Constitutional interpretation that have assumed crisis proportions in this Country, the Congress has been correct. The two most conspicu-

Current Check-Outs summary for Skerbec,
    Mon Nov 28 10:46:31 EST 2011

BARCODE: 31963001679713
TITLE: Judicial power and the Constituti
DUE DATE: Dec 17 2011
STATUS:

BARCODE: 31963001079526
TITLE: The Supreme Court : a citizen's g
DUE DATE: Dec 17 2011
STATUS:

BARCODE: 31963001194515
TITLE: The Constitution of 1787 : a comm
DUE DATE: Dec 17 2011
STATUS:

BARCODE: 31963003043322
TITLE: The politically incorrect guide t
DUE DATE: Dec 17 2011
STATUS:

ous instances have been the *Dred Scott* case and the early New Deal cases.[105] The New Deal cases found the Court insisting, in effect, that Congress had no substantial power to attempt to bring the national economy out of a great depression. It is hardly an argument for judicial review to say that the Court can be relied upon when relatively minor Constitutional questions are before it but that it can cripple the Country when truly major questions arise.

We can detect, even in such an accidental case as *Marbury* v. *Madison*, the effects of political passions upon the Court. It is not equipped to deal effectively with such passions, especially in confrontations with Congress. Indeed, depending upon the times, such passions may be intensified, if not created, by an improvident exercise of judicial review.

VI

Difficulties with judicial review seem to have been anticipated by the Federal Convention of 1787, at least sufficiently so that the Framers clearly rejected on more than one occasion attempts to provide for something like judicial review of acts of Congress.[106] Certainly, it is not provided for in the Constitution, whereas the veto power of the President is spelled out in detail. The President can consider Constitutionality when he reviews a bill presented to him by Congress, but Congress is left free to override Presidential disapproval, however he might have explained it in the message he sent Congress along with his disapproval. We have seen that there are many questions about how the institution of judicial review should operate, questions that would surely have been anticipated if the institution had been intended. Logic, some say, demands judicial review, but logic also seems to require as much guidance in the Constitution for the exercise of judicial review as is provided there for the exercise of other major powers.

Besides, the slightest acquaintance with the British Constitution, as drawn upon for example in Blackstone's *Commentaries*,[107] would have reminded the Framers that the Legislature is by nature supreme—not any court, nor the executive alone, whatever its part in the legislative process may be—and thus the Framers would have known that if something other than legislative supremacy had been intended, it should have been provided for unequivocally

143

by the Constitution. In the most technical sense, then, the judgments that the Supreme Court issues in exercising judicial review may be little more than "advisory opinions," something, by the way, that the Court says it may not properly issue. These judgments have been, in effect, advisory opinions to which both Congress and the President have not imprudently acquiesced.

VII

What, then, should be done about all this? Should judicial review be accepted now as an accomplished fact, even as the Court makes less and less use of it? Because much has been organized around this institution, including habits and expectations not only in the people at large but also in the Congress and in the Executive branch, we should proceed with caution in changing what we now have, just as we should with the Electoral College. Although it may well be a matter of chance that the Supreme Court exercises the power of judicial review and that Congress and the Executive acquiesce to it, we must still wonder whether it is now a good thing and, if so, in what respects.

The Framers might have conceded such a power of review to the Supreme Court to protect its own prerogatives, just as Congress and the President can protect their respective prerogatives. Blackstone recognized, for instance, that each part of Parliament may be able to act alone "in matters relating to [its] own privileges."[108] Perhaps the Court saw itself as acting defensively in *Marbury* v. *Madison*, even though it might have made itself vulnerable to being stripped altogether of various parts of its appellate jurisdiction whenever Congress chooses to do so. It thus made itself vulnerable even as it claimed what was, in Anglo-American jurisprudence and constitutional history, almost unprecedented powers of judicial review.

The Framers might also have conceded that the National Courts need not accept as law any purported statute that is not made pursuant to the legislative process prescribed by the Constitution. Furthermore, as we have seen, courts as courts should insist upon due process in all proceedings they participate in; such insistence need not depend upon the Fifth or the Fourteenth Amendments.

In addition, the National Courts can interpret laws enacted by

Congress as if they conformed to the Constitution as generally understood. If the Supreme Court draws in this way upon the Constitution in interpreting and applying a law, Congress will naturally be reluctant to contradict the Court by insisting that it intended something "unconstitutional" in the law under consideration.

Our principal concern, though, should not be with any possible Congressional refusal to respect the Court's judgment but rather with Congress's willingness, even eagerness, to depend upon the Court. After all, Congress would usually prefer to do the popular, and politic, thing, leaving to others the hard Constitutional decisions. But that is a bad habit for us to permit legislators to fall into, since most things Congress does cannot easily, if at all, be subjected to judicial review. For better and for worse, we have to rely upon Congress to be faithful to its charge.[109]

Besides, another dubious feature of a reliance upon judicial review is that Constitutional amendments seem to be required to correct judicial errors, not merely an overruling by a supermajority of the legislature, as in the case of Presidential vetoes. If the Supreme Court should be mistaken in a case of great national interest, the confidence of people as to the principles of right and wrong can be undermined. Particularly pernicious can be the opinion that the Constitution is what judges say it is, for it is all too often clear that what the judges say is not good. Moreover, if the Constitution is taken to be only whatever the judges say it is, what respectable basis can there ever be for asking judges to reverse themselves?

People want to believe that the Constitution is something by which even judges are bound, and judges will continue to be respected so long as they are believed to be speaking knowledgeably about what the Constitution says.

VIII

The trial-by-jury guarantee in Section 2 of Article III provides another important check that courts were intended to have upon misconduct by other branches of the General Government. The courts can insist that judicial proceedings be conducted according to rules laid down in the common law and by the Constitution.

We see even here, however, the supervisory power of Congress. For example, it alone can determine where criminal trials are to be held when "the said Crimes" have not been "committed within any State." Also, the common law has to be looked to for guidance in determining what is required for a proper trial by jury.

Trial by jury reflects substantial popular control over judges. Thus, day in and day out, in the criminal courts of the Country, no judge can convict by himself a defendant charged with a felony, unless the defendant waives a jury trial. In civil matters as well, considerable power is left to juries, a power ratified by the Seventh Amendment to the Constitution for common-law suits in the National Courts. (This amendment ratifies also the integrity of these Courts as common-law courts.)

IX

An even more dramatic limitation placed upon the National Courts, as well as upon Congress, appears in the final section of Article III, which is devoted to "Treason against the United States." It seems to be provided that one can commit such treason only by engaging in a rebellion against the United States or by aiding its enemies, which suggests that a declared war must be in progress with certified enemies.[110]

The treason provision might have been put where it is, rather than in the Legislative Article, because historically the most severe, even barbaric, abuses and condemnations of supposed traitors seem to have been at the hands of judges. So Congress, and definitely not the Courts, is left with "Power to declare the Punishment of Treason."

Placing the treason provision in the Judicial Article may recognize in still another way the common-law power of the National Courts in that common-law crimes seem to be taken for granted by the Constitution. Is it assumed in Section 3 of Article III that the crime of treason already exists, so much so that it has to be restricted in its coverage? In any case, Article III concludes by checking judges and others with respect to treason.

We have observed that the last provision directed primarily at Congress in Article I (in Section 9) is devoted to keeping citizens of the United States from acquiring titles of nobility or any related gifts and honors either from the United States or from "any King,

Prince, or foreign State." We have also observed that the last word with respect to the President in Article II is devoted to the impeachment of the President and others. We now observe that the last word with respect to the National Courts in Article III is devoted to the prohibition of any "Attainder of Treason [that] shall work Corruption of Blood, or Forfeiture except during the Life of the Person attainted."

In all three instances of "the last word," I suggest, the same concern (or principle) is being addressed (or invoked)—the dedication to equality upon which the American regime so much depends. Thus, there can be no titles of nobility (Article I). Thus, also, even the President himself may be brought to account before the law (Article II). Thus, as well, just as there are to be no titles of nobility, there are to be no titles of disability, that is, no hereditary punishment or deprivation (Article III).

We can see, even from the way the last word is framed with respect to the establishment of each of the three branches of the General Government, that equality before the law is what the American regime very much depends upon. I have many times referred to the importance among us of the dedication to equality. This points up the anomaly of the institution of slavery in the United States from the very beginning, something that I will consider in more detail when I examine the place of the States in the Constitutional system.

But, I should at once add here, the dedication to equality is restrained in the Constitution. The fact that we have judges placed in privileged positions reflects our insistence that ignorance and vice be subjugated, whatever the Jack Cades of the world may happen to believe. Or, as Thomas Jefferson said about the judiciary in a letter of March 15, 1789, to James Madison, "This is a body, which if rendered independent & kept strictly to their own department, merits great confidence for their learning & integrity."[111]

Another compromise of sorts with equality may be seen in something else I have depended upon throughout this Commentary, the care and competence with which the Constitution itself is drafted. Not every possible interpretation that may be conjured up about the Constitution is sound. Some interpreters are surely better than others at reading the Constitution. On the other hand, a respect for equality may be seen in the general understanding that the Constitution is available to everyone to draw upon, to examine, and to invoke.

Furthermore, does not the symmetry of having the last word with respect to the Congress, to the President, and to the Courts in the first three articles of the Constitution return in each case to that principle of equality drawn upon in the "We the People" language of the Preamble—does not this remarkable symmetry exhibit a thoughtful draftsman at work in the way the entire Constitution is put together? Should not this too encourage us to take the Constitution seriously as we try to discover, one by one, but especially all together, what is, and is not, provided for and why?

12. The State Constitutions in 1787

I

I have examined thus far in this Commentary the first three articles of the Constitution of 1787, those articles that provide for the Legislative, Executive and Judicial departments or branches of the General Government. In the next four lectures of this series, I shall look at Articles IV, V, VI, and VII, those articles in which the States of the Union figure prominently.

Before we turn to the States, which we have already touched upon from time to time, as when we looked at the restrictions upon them found in Section 10 of Article I, we should notice the constitutional arrangements in the States at the time the Federal Convention met in Philadelphia in 1787.

The United States is generally considered to have come into being, as an independent Country, on July 4, 1776. This, we have noted, is reflected in the way that official documents are identified down to our day. We completed on July 4, 1986, the two hundred and tenth year of the Independence of the United States. It was not until the twelfth year "of the Independence of the United States" that the Constitution we now have was prepared.

There were, of course, significant constitutional developments on this Continent, not only before September 17, 1787, the day the Constitution was completed by its Framers, but also before July 4, 1776. The thirteen Colonies, later to become States, wrote constitutions of their own well before the United States did. No doubt, the interest we now have in early Colonial and State constitutional developments depends, in large part, upon what happened in 1776 and after 1787, but we cannot hope to understand what we have now and have had for two centuries if we are not aware of what contributed to the evolution that culminated in the deliberations that produced the Constitution of 1787.

II

Constitutional government was very much taken for granted by British Americans for two centuries before Independence. Virginia, for instance, could look back for its founding to a grant to Sir Walter Raleigh in 1584, and thereafter to a charter of 1606; that is, it could look back to the time of Shakespeare for its formal origins. By the 1776–1787 period, North Americans had become practiced in reliance upon written constitutional instruments, and not only in their disputes with the British government.

They were accustomed as well to the rights, duties, and expectations of Englishmen under the British Constitution, written and unwritten. Thus the Declaration of Independence, in which Great Britain is roundly condemned, is itself firmly grounded in the British Constitution and its common-law system, as well as in the natural rights of mankind. The same combination is evident in many of the original State constitutions. The British Constitution may be seen as well even in the ways the Americans organized themselves, in conventions and other assemblies, as they maneuvered, State by State and yet as one people, to arrange and to justify what they were doing in setting out on their own.

These maneuverings included many resolutions and actions in the various Colonies, with Virginia and Massachusetts quite prominent in early resistance to British authority. Congress, too, had been active long before it issued its decisive statement on July 4, 1776. From 1774 on, one Continental Congress after another (that is, the Congress for the British Colonies on the North American Continent) spoke repeatedly for the Colonies and later the States.

Useful collections of documents are available that illuminate the doings of the pre-1776 Congresses. I need mention, by way of illustration, only a few of the episodes that set the stage for 1776 and 1787.[112]

A convenient place to start is with the Resolutions of the Stamp Act Congress, October 19, 1765, in which the Colonists insisted that they should not be taxed without proper representation and that they were entitled to trial by jury as well as to the right to petition for redress of grievances. They further pointed out that they could not be properly represented in the British Parliament, maintaining that if they were to be taxed, it had to be by their own legislatures on this side of the Atlantic.

The Declarations and Resolves of the Continental Congress, October 14, 1774, condemned various acts of Parliament as "impolitic, unjust, and cruel, as well as unconstitutional, and most dangerous and destructive of American rights." The Colonists thus insisted upon their rights as Englishmen, especially those rights assured by the common law. Their own charters and the statutes of England, some of them incorporating and extending the common law, were also invoked on this as on many other occasions.

These Declarations and Resolves were followed up a week later, October 20, 1774, with the announcement by the Continental Congress, in "The Association," that the Colonists would neither import nor consume British goods. The British government did not take lightly these various manifestations of Colonial resistance. That government then made what turned out to be a serious blunder, a recourse to arms.

The Americans could thereupon take a righteous defensive posture, as may be seen in their Declaration of the Causes and Necessities of Taking Up Arms, of July 6, 1775. They described themselves as a "Congress of delegates from the United Colonies," and they challenged what they took to be Parliament's claim to be entitled to "make laws to bind [them] in all cases whatever," even though no member of Parliament was chosen by them. They insisted that they did not mean to dissolve the union between Great Britain and the United Colonies. "Necessity has not yet driven us to that desperate measure," they reported. This was their way of warning that they might well be on the verge of so serious a step, a step they hoped would be guided, if they were driven to it, by the Divinity that they several times invoked. Two days later, July 8, 1775, a petition of grievances and requests was sent to the King from the Continental Congress.

The following year the Continental Congress reported that "no answer whatever to the humble petitions of the colonies for redress of grievances and reconciliation with Great Britain [had] been or [was] likely to be given." Still, it was vital to the way the Colonists regarded themselves and hence their cause that they make repeated attempts to explain themselves and that they work through what we call channels. Such reliance upon both argument and established processes reflects respect for constitutionalism and the rule of law. In this way, they were not only invoking the rights of humanity but were also challenging the British with key principles from their own great tradition. The British were thus challenged by the best of themselves, and in such a way that, in the long run, they could lose only by "winning." A British military victory in North America, riding roughshod over constitutional principles and over fellow citizens, might well have threatened the rule of law and hence English liberties even at home.

III

And so things moved inexorably, it now seems, to the decisive step on July 4, 1776. Two months before the Declaration of Independence, in mid-May of 1776, the Continental Congress recommended the formation of appropriate governments in the various Colonies:

Whereas, His Britannic Majesty, in conjunction with the Lords and Commons of Great Britain, has, by a late Act of Parliament, excluded the inhabitants of these United Colonies from the protection of his Crown; and whereas, no answer whatever to the humble petitions of the colonies for redress of grievances and reconciliation with Great Britain has been or is likely to be given; but the whole force of that kingdom, aided by foreign mercenaries, is to be exerted for the destruction of the good people of these colonies; and whereas, it appears absolutely irreconcileable to reason and good conscience for the people of these colonies now to take the oaths and affirmations necessary for the support of any government under the Crown of Great Britain, and it is necessary that every kind of authority under the said Crown should be totally suppressed, and all the powers of government exerted, under the authority of the people of these colonies, for the preservation of internal peace, virtue, and good order, as well as for the defence of their lives, liberties, and properties against the hostile invasions and cruel depredations of their enemies; therefore

Resolved, That it be recommended to the respective Assemblies and

Conventions of the United Colonies, where no government sufficient to the exigencies of their affairs have been hitherto established,
to adopt such a government as shall, in the opinion of the representatives of the people, best conduce to the happiness and safety of
their constituents in particular, and America in general.

The resolution set forth here, the final half-dozen lines of this
pronouncement, preceded in time its considerably longer preamble. The resolution, which is said to have been the work primarily
of John Adams, was passed on May 10, 1776; its preamble, on
May 15, 1776. The preamble, in its mustering of grievances against
"His Britannic Majesty," anticipates the authoritative constitutional position set forth two months later in the Declaration of Independence.

We notice that this preamble assumes that a proper concern of
government is to preserve "internal peace, virtue, and good order," along with the defense of "lives, liberties, and properties."
We also notice that the Colonial governments are obliged to look
out not only for the happiness and safety of their respective constituents, but also for the happiness and safety of "America in general." It would seem that the legitimate powers of government are
comprehensive and that there is a recognizable national community from the outset, and hence a general interest to take account
of along with particular local interests.

We have observed that the May 15th preamble, or explanation,
followed the May 10th resolution, or action. That was true of
many constitutional and political developments in that period. Often the explanation, or formal authority, followed the actions
taken. Even so, the actions were not complete—they were not sufficiently grounded—until the Declaration of Independence could
present the authoritative explanation of what they were doing.

IV

The May 1776 recommendation of the Continental Congress
was taken to refer to the need for the development of written constitutions in various of the Colonies. The Congress made this suggestion despite the fact that it had no written constitution of its
own at that very time, nor would it have any, technically speak-

ing, for five more years. The American people—the more or less United Colonies and, later, the United States—did many remarkable things (perhaps the most decisive things in the history of this Country) without any written national constitution, through a twenty-year period, from about 1760 to 1781 (the year in which the Articles of Confederation were at last fully ratified). There had been a general understanding about how their Congresses might proceed (including the somewhat dubious arrangement whereby each Colony had one vote), as they addressed themselves to awesome questions about independence, war and peace, and the finances of the Country, as well as to the day-to-day tasks of raising and equipping armed forces, appointing and supervising officers and diplomats, and generally conducting the military and international efforts of the Country. Perhaps no foreign policy or war policy in the Nation's history has been as successful as the policies formulated and administered by Congress in the 1770s and the 1780s, and all this with no independent Executive.

Although they had no written constitution to guide them, the original delegates to the Continental Congress knew both how to conduct themselves and what to expect from one another. They certainly knew how to organize themselves to make good use of their somewhat limited powers, and the same can be said of the Federal Convention, which met in Philadelphia in 1787. But then, in thus conducting themselves, they were in the best tradition of the British Constitution, which is, for the most part, not written.

Still, the delegates believed it prudent in their circumstances that, whatever the status of a national constitution, the Colonies should look to their forms of government, and this the Continental Congress advised them to do in May 1776.

V

The Congress made this suggestion to the Colonies although the Colonies (like the Congress) had also been doing things critical to the national effort without the written constitutions that now seemed to be called for, and they had been doing what they had done in defiance of British laws and Constitution, both written and unwritten.

Among the things the Colonies had been able to do was to supply delegates and resources to the Continental Congress. Colonial legislatures and conventions, or other associations, had been organized, sometimes pursuant to royal or other charters and grants and sometimes without or in opposition to such authority. The people of the various Colonies seemed to have a general understanding about what they could do, and this they did. They also recognized that, by and large, competent people in each Colony were conducting their own domestic affairs, confidently drawing upon the two centuries of experience in virtual self-government that was due, in large part, to their great distance from Europe.

The amazing thing is not that the Colonies, and later the States, could work as well as they did with no written constitutions or with rudimentary constitutions. After all, Great Britain also operated thus, or so it seemed. Rather, the amazing thing is that the British government did not recognize in time how competent the American people had become. No doubt, the lessons learned by Great Britain in dealing with the Americans later served them in good stead when they came to deal in turn with independence-minded Canadians, Australians, and New Zealanders (but not with the Irish, the Indians and the South Africans?).

Although the State constitutions may not have been absolutely necessary in order for the States to be able to continue to do the work the Colonies had begun, they did prove critical in shaping the national constitution. The States are very much taken for granted in the Constitution of 1787; the existence of States, their names, their boundaries, their relative sizes, and their relations to one another are drawn upon. Various State institutions, including State constitutions, are also taken for granted, such as their modes for determining suffrage, their election machinery, their provisions for citizenship, their militia, and the dominance within State governments of their legislatures.

The availability of many State constitutional provisions for consideration, adoption, refinement, and rearrangement in the shaping of the Constitution of the United States was critical as well. Even more significant was that overall approach of the Framers which led them to use the State provisions they did in shaping a National Constitution in 1787. We can see here, as elsewhere in this Commentary, a confident political (if not even natural) use of "history."

VI

Virtually all of the thirteen Colonies/States responded to the May 1776 recommendation by the Continental Congress that they look to their forms of government. In so doing, did they not confirm the superintending authority of Congress? At no time, so far as we can tell, did the separate Colonies do much completely on their own in declaring themselves independent or in establishing new forms of government. All this is related to the insistence by Abraham Lincoln that the Union preceded both the States and the Constitution.

And so there are repeated recognitions (often implicit, sometimes explicit) of the supremacy of the Continental Congress and thereafter the Confederation Congress, or the Government of the United States, in its proper sphere. Furthermore, so long as the Colonies depended upon their Colonial charters and grants, they tacitly recognized the superiority of the British government in its proper sphere.

Much was carried over from the past in the Colonial/State constitutions. For example, the Pennsylvania Constitution provided that "trials shall be by jury as heretofore." Attempts were made to reduce to writing the people's rights and various governmental arrangements, but different things were recalled or emphasized in various States, depending upon their circumstances and experiences.[113]

There was never a completely new beginning. Provision for getting things moving under the revised dispensation was usually made, with considerable reliance upon already existing intra-State divisions, local officialdom and practices, and upon accepted property allocations. A proper study of State constitutions should include a review of the predecessor charters, grants and constitutions. Even so, a brief examination here of the State constitutions that were in force at the time the Federal Convention sat in 1787 can be instructive.

VII

The two oldest State Constitutions in place in 1787 were those of Connecticut and Rhode Island, those States having continued to use, with modifications, their longstanding charters of 1662 and 1663, respectively.[114] Connecticut had, in 1776, prepared itself a short Constitution that confirmed its 1662 charter with appropriate adjustments and with the guarantee of a few rights. Rhode Island made adjustments in the preamble of its 1663 charter. These two States were evidently content to continue with these revamped charters, which constitutions they would use until 1818 and 1842, respectively.

Even though these two States did not have modern constitutions, but rather relied upon documents more than a century old, they were still able to conduct themselves much as the others did. True, Rhode Island stayed out of the Federal Convention in 1787 and was quite late in ratifying the Constitution. But North Carolina, too, was quite late in ratifying, even though it had been represented in the Convention. Connecticut, on the other hand, was active in the Convention and was quick to ratify the Constitution.

The situations in Connecticut and Rhode Island remind us of something to be found in all of the States: there was continuity with more than a century of experience and thought with respect to government and the rights of Englishmen. We are again reminded of the entire body of law, written and unwritten (including the common law), that was taken for granted in all of the States and that was taken for granted as well in the general constitutional understanding. We are also reminded that these State governments generally conducted themselves the same way toward their citizens whether they had explicit bills of rights or whether this or that particular right was included in such bills. Certainly, it was difficult, if not impossible, to determine on the basis of what was said or done by any delegate in the Federal Convention what his State Constitution was like or what its bill of rights, if any, included unless he mentioned it. Connecticut, for example, was regarded as one of the more democratic States, despite its quite old-fashioned constitution.

It is useful, before we consider briefly the other eleven State constitutions of 1787, to stress a point I have been making in this Commentary about the British and American Constitutions. For the British, more of their Constitution is written than we usually recognize, for it includes such celebrated parts as Magna Carta, the Petition of Right, and the Habeas Corpus Act. On the other hand, for Americans, more of their Constitution is unwritten than we recognize, for it includes reliance upon such things as an accepted mode of interpretation, the common law, and an understanding of what and where the States are. As one examines the State constitutions in the 1776–1787 period, one can see how much was implicit in them and in the Articles of Confederation as well.

Americans have generally had recourse to constitutions with a larger proportion of written elements than have the British. This may be, in part, because America has been less homogeneous than England in its population and circumstances and hence needed to have things spelled out more for there to be a reliable consensus. Related to this is the fact that the Americans have had to move faster than the British. One may not need to spell out as many things, or reduce them to writing, if one's constitution is the product of slow growth and adaptation. The parts of the British Constitution that are written, such as Magna Carta and the Petititon of Right, tend to be associated with crises in English constitutional development.

The continuous American crisis from the 1760s on may help account for the widespread recourse in this Country to written State and National constitutions, something that may be seen as well in that most august constitutional document, the Declaration of Independence.

VIII

We have accounted for the two oldest State Constitutions as of 1787, the revamped charters of Connecticut and Rhode Island to which these Colonies/States had recourse in response to the May 1776 recommendation of the Continental Congress to the Colonies.

Nine of the other State Constitutions in place in 1787 were prepared during the 1776–1778 period. These were, in the order in which they were completed, Virginia (June 29, 1776); New Jersey (July 3, 1776); Delaware (September 21, 1776); Pennsylvania (September 28, 1776); Maryland (November 11, 1776); North Carolina (December 18, 1776); Georgia (February 3, 1777); New York (April 20, 1777); and South Carolina (March 19, 1778).

Two of these nine Constitutions, those of Virginia and of New

Jersey, were completed before the July 4th Declaration of Independence by the Continental Congress. All of them can be considered responses, at least in part, to the May 1776 recommendation by the Continental Congress that the forms of government of the Colonies be looked to. One of these constitutions, that of South Carolina in 1778, had been preceded by another constitution, that of March 26, 1776. Several of these constitutions leave the way open to a possible reconciliation with Great Britain. The earlier they are, the more likely they are to do so.

The two remaining constitutions in place in 1787 were those of Massachusetts (March 2, 1780) and New Hampshire (June 2, 1784). New Hampshire had had a much earlier constitution, one of January 5, 1776, which had not waited upon the May 1776 recommendation by the Continental Congress but which, like the 1776 South Carolina constitution, seems to have been prepared in response to an earlier recommendation by the Continental Congress.[115]

Virginia, with the oldest of the "modern" constitutions in place in 1787, is considered to have led the way into constitution-making, just as it was to do in the Federal Convention. It was especially influential because of its bill of rights, which was adopted on June 13, 1776, six weeks before the Virginia constitution was adopted.[116] The 1777 constitution of New York has been praised as one of the best-written State constitutions available before 1787, second only perhaps to the 1780 Massachusetts Constitution. Yet the New York Constitution was written by a convention very much on the run because of the events of the war.

Each of the thirteen constitutions has its distinctive features. The older they are, the shorter they are apt to be, even shorter than the Constitution of the United States was to be. The longer ones, ranging from two to three times the length of the Constitution of the United States, are found among the later constitutions—those of New York, Maryland, New Hampshire, and Massachusetts, in ascending order of length.

There were, despite their differences, significant affinities among the constitutions made from 1776 on. They are, first of all, very much American constitutions. By this time, of course, English only is used in such documents, not Latin, as in an occasional early instrument. More important, all of the States had been formed in some ways by the constitutional crises of the preceding decade.

No doubt, some of the later constitution-writers were aware of what had happened in other States. Throughout, it was the American people, a people made more nearly homogeneous politically by the perceived oppressiveness of the British government than they might otherwise have been, who moved in and out of, and through, these State constitutions. The differences in their constitutions reflected their varied circumstances, something which should be evident in the abundant quotations in Lecture No. 15.

And so experimentation continued as the Americans made their way, in effect and without fully realizing it, to Philadelphia in 1787.

IX

There are several additional features of the State constitutions written from 1776 on that we should notice. Perhaps most dramatic for us, aside from the massive fact that these were constitutions ordained and established by the authority of the American people, State by State, is that so much of the language now familiar to us from the Constitution of 1787 may be found in the pre-1787 State constitutions. We can also see various institutions and processes tried out in one constitution or another before being refined into the form we now have in the Constitution of 1787. We can see as well arrangements that have been rejected after having been tried in one or another State constitution. Pennsylvania, perhaps somewhat under the influence of Benjamin Franklin, the President of its State constitutional convention of 1776, provided a fertile testing ground for experiments that few others wanted to have much to do with thereafter—particularly its reliance upon a plural executive, a unicameral legislature, and a requirement that most bills could not become law until the convening of the legislature after the one in which the bills were first introduced.

We have already noticed that State governments continued doing pretty much what they had been doing, whether they kept, in modified form, their ancient charters or devised quite "modern" constitutions. It seemed to be taken for granted in all of the State constitutions in force in 1787 that the State legislatures had plenary powers, being entitled, perhaps even obliged, to concern themselves with virtually all aspects of the lives of their people, including their morals and their education. Those State governments were able to do whatever government naturally does, subject of course to the limitations that may have been long recognized in British constitutional law, including common-law and natural-right principles, or that may have recently been provided for in declarations of rights.

X

These State constitutions say relatively little about the powers of the State governments. But they display a lively concern, just as does the Constitution of the United States, with arranging relations among the three branches of government and for getting and keeping "the machinery of government" working. Considerable detail is provided about how various officers of government are to be chosen, what the age, residence, property, and other qualifications of such officers and of their electors are to be, how legislative bodies and other government activities are to be organized, how legislative seats are to be apportioned, and what is to constitute a quorum in legislative bodies. These are immediate, practical concerns that have to be settled one way or another. No doubt much that had happened in recent decades helped determine how these matters were to be provided for, what precautions should be taken (for example, against executive interference with legislative processes), and how the people are to be kept informed of what goes on in government (with provision for ready public access to legislative journals in which, for example, the *Yeas* and *Nays* of legislators are recorded).

The striking diversity in suffrage qualifications from State to State helps account for the decision of the Federal Convention to leave this matter to determinations in the several States, even when national officers are being chosen. To have proceeded otherwise would have risked considerable, and probably unproductive, political disturbances in those States.

Although the people were obviously in control, it was considered necessary, or at least desirable, to leave it to the people, State by State, to determine precisely who would be able to speak for the people. Rule by the people is evident from the beginning. It can

161

even be said that there was implicit in the Americans' approach to things not only universal adult suffrage, but perhaps also the eventual elimination of slavery. The last two State constitutions adopted before 1787, Massachusetts and New Hampshire, shared a feature that was to prove critical for the Constitution of the United States: these were the only two State constitutions before 1787 that were submitted to the people in their respective States for ratification.

This movement toward ratification by the people found its culmination in those arrangements made in the Constitution of 1787 that permitted the Framers of the Constitution to open the Preamble with "We the People of the United States." This introduction was different from that of the Articles of Confederation, which presented that constitution as having been agreed to by the delegates of the thirteen States named there, not simply by the people of one united Country.

XI

Many of the provisions in the State constitutions assumed ultimate control by the people. Various of the elements in their bills of rights, which proved important sources for the first ten amendments to the Constitution of the United States, recognized the rights of the people, such as the rights to trial by jury, to habeas corpus, to the common law itself, to due process, and to property. These State constitutions emphasized the importance of annual elections, representative government, and majority rule, all of which reflect deference to the people. The people were further enhanced in their control by the disparagement of hereditary privileges and by the elimination of primogeniture, as well as by an insistence upon the liberty of the press.

Control by the people was probably reflected as well in the assumption in the pre-1787 State constitutions that the legislative branch of government was to be dominant. Legislative supremacy was also apparent, I have suggested, in constitution-framing itself, because what the writers of constitutions do—and do in an authoritative way—is what legislatures do: they lay down the law. (Of what significance is it that virtually all of the governing that was done for the Country as a whole for the decade before 1787 was by the Confederation Congress, which, as we have seen, not only legislated but also made appointments, supervised military operations, and conducted foreign relations? The Articles of Confederation provided as well that Congress would be "the last resort on appeal in all disputes and differences" between States.)

When one looks at the legislatures of the States before 1787, one finds that the dominant house of the legislature was usually the more numerous branch. That house typically had the first say, and sometimes the only say, about revenue bills. Sometimes it also chose the other house, perhaps from among its members.

There were occasional affirmations that there should be distinct branches, or departments, of government. That was believed to be consistent with the legislative power to choose the governor, which was often provided for, to choose and otherwise to provide for judges, and to impeach all officers. Usually there was no veto power given the governor; certainly, there was no hint of any power of judicial review in the courts. The executive became more important in the later State constitutions and in the Constitution of the United States. But the dominance of the legislature, which was considered the branch of government closest to, and more directly subject to control by, the people, was never lost sight of, especially as precautions were repeatedly taken against military usurpation, which was associated with executive power. The ultimate power of the people was further reflected in one vital power or right retained by the people, the power or right of revolution that was several times referred to in the State constitutions and that was vigorously exercised by the American people from 1776 on, if not even before.

The people, in turn, were held in check by their informed recognition of the natural rights of mankind and by their pious submission to the judgment of God. Whatever a few here and there might have said or meant about "the separation of church and state," it is difficult, perhaps impossible, to read the pre-1787 constitutional documents without recognizing the widespread and evidently deeply felt reliance by Americans, in public life as well as in private, upon Divinity. This reliance, as we will see in Lecture No. 15, was reflected in the considerable recourse to oaths of various kinds, oaths that often included affirmations of specified religious opinions. Such reliance was usually accompanied by the general desire for religious toleration, a desire that was intensified by the recognition that there was considerable religious diversity in the Country at large and hence among citizens who moved around from one State to another. This desire for toleration, which is enshrined in the First Amendment, was considered consistent with continuing official reliance upon, and even public financial support of, religious institutions in the various States.

Indeed, it probably was generally believed in 1787 that a Godless people cannot long be trusted to be self-governing.

XII

We have noticed several times that the United States was technically without a written constitution during much of the Revolutionary Period. Although the Articles of Confederation were written by a committee of the Continental Congress in 1776 and adopted by that Congress in 1777, they were not fully ratified until 1781.

But Congress began its work before Independence and continued until it was replaced by the legislature provided for by the Constitution of 1787. Congress could do what it did, and could be accepted in doing what it did, because people generally relied upon the same kind of understanding of what government should do as may be seen in the States, where governments could carry on equally well with or without written constitutions. Do we not see here, in effect, the largely unwritten British constitutional system still guiding the American people, with the Continental and Confederation Congresses being allowed by the States the narrowest range of powers conceded by Americans to the British government?

We are thus reminded that we should not make too much of written constitutions, especially when a people's character and habits are sound. And we can wonder: To what extent, and in what way, was it assumed among the Americans of 1787 that the Union *is*, that the United States should, and will, continue to exist, that the States are dependent upon the people of the Union, and that the American people will, one way or another, govern themselves? Much is made of "perpetual Union" in the Articles of Confederation of 1777, which leads into the "more perfect Union" in the Constitution of 1787.

With or without written constitutions, State or National, Americans did govern themselves and could have been expected to continue doing so indefinitely. After all, as we have noticed, this people, without written constitutions, made and successfully executed perhaps the most important policies ever developed by the United States. We should also notice that various other peoples, even when they have copied the American Constitution of 1787, have not been able to do very well governing themselves.

To speak, then, of unwritten constitutions as I have throughout this Commentary is still another way of talking about the political habits and enduring character of a people.

XIII

The Federal Convention of 1787 drew upon the existing State constitutions and upon much more, including the remarkable British constitutional heritage shared by the Americans. That Convention reshaped the national constitution for an even better attempt at self-government by the Country as a whole. Perhaps the written Constitution of 1787 was needed primarily to restore to the national legislature the plenary powers over those matters of obvious national concern, such as taxation, commerce, peace, and war, that had been imprudently denied under the Articles of Confederation. Those Articles and their troubled implementation show the effects of an unhealthy suspicion of all central government, in part because of the then-recent unhappy experience of Americans with the British government.

The Constitution of 1787 both responded to what had gone before, by drawing upon it or departing from it, and ratified, or reinforced, what was already being done. The written Constitution of 1787 made explicit the general constitutional framework within which the States would continue to work, including new States that would have to be properly shaped for admission to the Union. The Constitution of 1787 provided Americans overnight, so to speak, the general constitutional framework that the British had had centuries to develop for themselves and within which Colonial charters, grants, and other political and judicial arrangements had found places.

Particularly significant for the Framers who concluded their work on September 17, 1787, was, we all know, the Declaration of Independence proclaimed on July 4, 1776. We can see in that Declaration the authoritative invocation of the relevant constitutional heritage and of the guiding principles upon which the American people were to draw in framing both their State constitutions and their Constitution of 1787.

Fundamental to all these developments, it is salutary to repeat, is the recognition that the American people, in the very framing of founding instruments for better governing themselves, exercised in its highest form the art of legislation.

13. Article IV

I

The Constitution of 1787 becomes, in a manner of speaking, more self-conscious after having provided for the General Government of the United States in Articles I, II, and III.

In Article IV, the Constitution can turn to the place of the States in the Union and to the relations of the States to one another. Although the States are made use of, dealt with, and restrained in various ways in the first three articles of the Constitution, just as they are in the last three articles, it is in the central one of the seven articles of the Constitution of 1787 that the States are primarily, or at least substantially, dealt with. Much, then, turns around Article IV, an article in which the federalism of the regime is both recognized and disciplined.

There are four sections in Article IV, all of which can be said to regulate one "movement" or another. Section 1, with its Full Faith and Credit provision, is concerned with the movements from one State to another of "the public Acts, Records, and judicial Proceedings" of States. Section 2 is concerned with the movements, legitimate and illegitimate, of persons from one State to another. Section 3, with its provisions for new States and for the governance of Territories, is concerned with the movements of various parts of the Country from one status to another, that is, from Territory to State. Section 4 is concerned with those movements within States that bear upon domestic tranquility and their form of government.

The matters dealt with in Article IV need not directly affect the activities of the General Government. However, the relations between, and the activities of, States bear upon the prosperity and tranquility of the Country and can otherwise affect the character and the expectations of the people upon whom the General Government depends. How republican the General Government can be may depend, at least in part, upon the form of government in "every State in this Union."

II

The Full Faith and Credit requirement in Section 1 ministers to an obvious need, since there must be some rule as to how States are to regard one another's records and judicial proceedings. Otherwise, it would be uncertain what the effect is in all other States of the findings and determinations of any particular State, especially when those who are ruled against in one State take themselves and their property to another State.

In Section 1, the powers of all States are so supervised as to enhance the dignity and effectiveness of official proceedings wherever they originate. Are not the conditions guaranteed those which would make it more likely that the determinations in any particular State will be much like the determinations in like circumstances in all other States? Such uniformity makes it more attractive than it might otherwise be for Americans generally to rely upon what happens in any particular State.

That such a provision is needed if any enduring Union is to be secured is reflected in the fact that even the Articles of Confederation, with its considerably looser relations among States, had a comparable provision (also in its fourth article):

> Full faith and credit shall be given in each of these states to the records, acts and judicial proceedings of the courts and magistrates of every other state.

The Constitution of 1787 adds to this kind of provision the grant of power to Congress to "prescribe the Manner" in which such things are to be proved, "and the Effect thereof." This reminds us, still another time, of the general supervisory powers that Congress is intended to have under the Constitution of 1787. Someone should be able to say, in an authoritative manner, how the States are to receive and respond to what is submitted to them as the official actions of other States, particularly the actions in the courts of other States. There are more and less desirable ways of proving what has been done elsewhere, and Congress may choose among them.

A reliable uniformity in responses is to be sought. Notice the restriction placed upon Congress: it must lay down its rules "by general Laws." This restriction seems to be intended to keep Congress from meddling in particular cases, reminding us of the understanding in a proper constitutionalism that the legislative power, however dominant it properly is, should not be permitted to interfere with the disposition of particular cases by the judiciary.

The arrangement in Section 1, with Congress empowered to lay down rules for handling relations between States, reminds us of the arrangement in Section 2 of Article III, where it is provided that the "judicial Power of the United States" shall extend to "Controversies between two or more States." Amicable and productive relations among "sovereign" States, just as among "sovereign" citizens, are much more likely when there is a sensible government to supervise those relations.

III

Section 1 provides, we have seen, for how various official doings of one State should be received and treated in other States. Section 2 continues with the concern of Section 1 by providing for how persons from one State are to be received and treated in other States.

Three categories of visitors are anticipated: persons traveling in ordinary circumstances from one State to another, persons "flee-[ing] from Justice" in one State to another, and persons "held to Service or Labour in one State" who escape to another.

The ordinary traveler, if a citizen of the United States, is entitled to be treated, in whatever State he happens to be, the same way any citizen who resides permanently in that State is entitled to be treated in like circumstances. He is protected in effect both by the rule of law and by the reluctance of the local people to deprive themselves of "Privileges and Immunities" that they would have to give up to be able to deprive the visitor.

The rationale of the Privileges and Immunities Guarantee in Section 2 of Article IV is indicated by the comparable provision in

Article IV of the Articles of Confederation:

The better to secure and perpetuate mutual friendship and intercourse among the people of the different states in this union, the free
inhabitants of each of these states, paupers, vagabonds and fugitives from justice excepted, shall be entitled to all privileges and immunities of free citizens in the several states; and the people of each
state shall have free ingress and regress to and from any other state,
and shall enjoy therein all the privileges of trade and commerce,
subject to the same duties, impositions and restrictions as the inhabitants thereof respectively, provided that such restriction shall not
extend so far as to prevent the removal of property imported into
any state, to any other state, of which the Owner is an inhabitant.

We need not determine on this occasion what the precise purpose
and effect may be of the differences in wording between these two
provisions. Is it not likely that much the same concern is exhibited
in both the Articles of Confederation and the Constitution of 1787,
a concern particularly important because of what was known and
what was expected about the considerable mobility of Americans?

We notice that there is in this Articles of Confederation provision an explicit exception for "fugitives from justice," something
that the Constitution reserves for the second paragraph of Section
2, where there is what we know as the extradition, or interstate
rendition, duty prescribed for the State into which a fugitive has
fled. This extradition duty may be considered a special case of that
general respect for the legal integrity of one State which another
State is expected to exhibit.

The respect required for legal arrangements elsewhere is carried
one step further when the persons who come from another State
are not fleeing from justice, but rather are escaping from the service or labor required of them. Without such required respect, the
borders between States and the relations among States are likely to
become quite troubled. (I return to the Fugitive Slave Clause in
Section VI of this lecture.)

What are the powers of Congress here? May Congress "prescribe the Manner" in which the three provisions in Section 2 are to
be carried out? Such a power is explicitly granted Congress in Section 1. Does the absence of such a grant in Section 2 suggest that
Congress is not empowered to act here, that these matters are to be
left primarily to State officials guided by their oaths? And, one

may further wonder, are the National Courts available to help secure compliance with the various restrictions upon States found in Section 2 of Article IV?

We move in Section 2 of Article IV from the rights of visitors to the disabilities of visitors—and hence to the rights or at least the powers of those whom the visitors are trying to avoid in the States from which they have fled.

IV

Once various critical relations among States are addressed in the first two sections of Article IV, an even more critical relation must be addressed: What States are provided for in Article IV?

It is several times indicated elsewhere in the Constitution what constitutes the States that are referred to throughout. The House-of-Representatives allocations in Section 2 of Article I indicate that thirteen States are anticipated as the original contingent, subject to their ratification of the Constitution. Provision is made in Section 3 of Article IV for additional States, for the "movement" of Territories of the United States into fully empowered States of the United States. These States can expect to have their official doings treated the way the official doings of the original States are treated.

Precautions are taken to protect States already established, lest parts of them be removed or their separateness be destroyed without their consent. Notice that here, too, there is an emphasis upon the legislative branch of government, for these arrangements and rearrangements with respect to the States are emphatically said to depend upon decisions by Congress and "the Legislatures of the States concerned." There is no reference here to "the executive Authority." That had been relied upon in the extradition provision in Section 2 where the execution of laws is dealt with. Is it not important that Congress should dominate the decisions about additional States, since the very composition of Congress may be considerably affected by such decisions? I do not mean to suggest, however, that the President may not attempt to exercise here the powers of review he generally exercises when any bill or resolution is passed by Congress.

It makes sense, then, that the General Government should have the powers it does with respect to the Territories, especially since

Territories may eventually become States. By the time the Constitution of 1787 was written, Americans had seen, in the Northwest Ordinance, the sort of thing Congress was expected to do both in governing a Territory and in preparing the way for the creation of new States and their admission to the Union.

A massive fact has been taken for granted, it would seem, if not in the Constitution itself, at least in how it has been interpreted and applied from the outset: there are not to be, on the North American continent, any permanent second-class territories controlled by the United States. This is anticipated by the Northwest Ordinance and is consistent with the assumption, drawn upon in Section 1 of Article IV, that Americans can expect to be treated like Americans wherever they go in their Country.

Nothing is said here or elsewhere, explicitly, about whether any States, once in the Union, may leave on their own. The reference in the Preamble to "a more perfect Union" suggests a permanent association. So may the detailed provision in Article V for amendments, which suggests that there may be no other way, aside from a legitimate recourse to the right of revolution, to make massive constitutional changes in a short time.

V

We find in the final section of Article IV three duties prescribed for the Government of the United States, duties that must be performed if the States provided for throughout this article are to be appropriate for this Union. Protection is provided for republican institutions from subversive changes, for the territory of a State from external attacks, and for the life of a State from internal disturbances.

All this bears upon the relations among States and upon the character of the Union. If, as we have seen in Articles I and II, State election arrangements are relied upon in the choices of members of Congress and in the choice of a President, then the States should be of a character appropriate for a republican Union. The Government of the United States has a duty, on its own initiative, to judge that character. On the other hand, the States judge whether any particular manifestation of "domestic Violence" requires intervention by the United States. The General Government may act on the basis of the Republican Form of Government Guarantee, independently of any State request, for still another reason: if republican government has been subverted in a State, that State may have no legislature whose opinion must be awaited or need be respected by the United States.

The question remains as to what is meant by "a Republican Form of Government." The variety of the State constitutions, as of 1787, suggests how flexible republicanism was taken to be. The United States Constitution of 1787 was probably regarded as an exemplary manifestation of republican government. That constitution helped shape nineteenth-century State constitutions, including the development of the requirement that a written instrument be part of the system of constitutional government in every State.

It is easy to dismiss the Republican Form of Government Guarantee as vague and hence inconsequential. Must not the standards for republicanism remain flexible, lest reliance upon technical compliance mask a spirit that is unrepublican? Still, various things are assumed: monarchy and hereditary aristocracy are ruled out; elections are to be genuinely free, not charades; and the people are ultimately to be in control, which implies that they should be at liberty to discuss public affairs fully.[117] Questions can be raised about such things as bicameralism in the legislature and the degree of separation of powers among the branches of a government. Was it not reasonable to rely upon the Country as a whole, republican in and at its founding, to police what would happen here and there, intervening when a particular State moved clearly out of line? Such intervention on behalf of the Country could be through one branch or another of the General Government, as circumstances indicated.

The infrequency with which the Republican Form of Government Guarantee has been resorted to for two centuries now may mean that it has not been much needed. The people are in control in this Country, and they manage to assert themselves wherever they are threatened, in one State or another, with loss of power, especially if they can retain the freedom of speech. There has been little for the General Government to do in local situations. A major exception has been in response to the radical malapportionment into which State legislative arrangements have been permitted to deteriorate from time to time. The Supreme Court, relying primarily upon the Equal Protection Clause of the Fourteenth Amendment, has stimulated considerable reform here.[118] But it might have been even better, allowing more flexibility and hence less of a mechanical, numbers-based approach, if the Court had relied instead upon the Republican Form of Government Guarantee to shake up those State legislatures in which minorities had systematically, and permanently, come to rule majorities. It might have been still better if the Congress had intervened to do all at once and uniformly what the Court has been obliged to do on a case-by-case basis.

But, it is sometimes said, the Congress presumes that a State has a republican form of government if Congress permits members from that State to take their seats.[119] Still, may not the institutions of a State be republican for some purposes and not for others?

On the other hand, the Supreme Court said long ago that the Republican Form of Government Guarantee is not something that courts can do anything with. That guarantee must be left to the other branches of government to enforce.[120] It is not clear why this should be insisted upon, especially since the United States is addressed in Section 4 of Article IV. One consequence of the Court's abdication of its duty and power here is to require the Court to look to other provisions in the Constitution, as was done in the Reapportionment Cases, in order to deal with the problems presented to it. But to resort to other provisions is likely to produce distortions and further to conceal from view how well crafted the Constitution is.

In any event, the Republican Form of Government Guarantee for the States reflects the principles of our political way of life or regime.[121] We notice that no such explicit guarantee applies to the United States as a whole, just as there is no Equal Protection Clause or Contracts Clause applicable to the United States. Must not the American people as a whole be depended upon to keep the Government of the United States republican? There does not seem to be any other authority available for this purpose.

The linking, in Section 4, of the Republican Form of Government Guarantee with the protection against invasion and against domestic violence reminds us that the health of the soul—for the form of government is the soul of a regime—may presuppose the soundness of the body which is subject to physical attack. This is one more instance of the general awareness of the Founding Fathers that there is, in practical affairs, an intimate relation between the high and the low, between principled aspirations and material interests.

VI

The need to defer to material interests, even when principles might seem to suggest otherwise, may be seen in the accommodations to slavery in the Constitution of 1787.

These accommodations took several forms in the Constitution. We have noticed in Article I, Section 2, the counting of slaves in the allocation of seats in the House of Representatives. And we have noticed in Article I, Section 9, the immunity of the international slave trade from Congressional interference until 1808. In Article IV, we can see provision made for the return of fugitive slaves to their masters. Also, the "domestic Violence" protected against may have anticipated, among other disturbances, slave uprisings in various States.

The debates should never end among us as to whether those compromises should have been agreed upon in 1787. Powerful arguments can be made on both sides, arguments that we today may not be able to appreciate fully since we are not likely to grasp how intractable the problem of slavery seemed then, even as it could be hoped (not without reason) that slavery would be gradually eliminated. Whatever the merits of the various arguments, many among the Founders hated slavery as deeply as we all do now. But they had good reason to believe that unless accommodations were made to the slavery interests of the South, there would be no continuing Union of the thirteen States. This prospect seemed to them even more dangerous than the risks of a temporary compromise with slavery. Permanent disunion would not only have meant that two or more contending confederations would have existed in North America, but it would also have meant that at least one of those confederations would have been completely under the control of the slavery interests, able to import slaves as it pleased and able also to expand freely to the South, to the Southwest, and into the Caribbean, if not even into Central and South America. It must have been difficult for the Framers of the Constitution to see how either the cause of freedom or the fortunes of the slaves were likely to be served by such developments.

The only defensible alternative to compromise, then, may have been recourse to war, but the Free States were not strong enough in the late eighteenth century, compared with the Southern States, to be able to promote the abolition of slavery by the sword. On the other hand, if those Southerners ultimately moved by slavery interests had recognized in 1787 how much stronger the Free States would become, relative to the Southern States, they might well have wondered whether it made sense for them to accept the Constitution, even with its toleration of slavery.

VII

Time, I am suggesting, was on the side of freedom in this Country. The longer the Union prospered and grew under the Constitution of 1787, the weaker the Southern States became relative to the Free States. Had the Southern States waited still another generation before making the move they did make in 1860, they probably would have been put down much more easily than they were during the Civil War.

Some may argue, however, that it was a matter of chance that things turned out even as well as they did, because slavery was finally eliminated under a Constitution that was unconcerned about, if not even friendly to, slavery. Such an argument does not give due weight to the fundamental antipathy of the American constitutional system, from the beginning, to slavery. That antipathy goes back, as we all know, to the Declaration of Independence, which ratified a principle of equality that in turn inspired and shaped antislavery sentiments for generations to come.

In addition, the American dedication to a republican form of government implicitly called slavery into question. The Constitution takes the rule of law for granted, even as it guards against violence both from abroad and at home. Yet slavery is itself usually a denial of the rule of law, resting ultimately upon sustained violence that cannot justify itself.

The overall inclination of the regime under the Constitution of 1787 was toward freedom and equality. Even the protection of the international slave trade until 1808 recognized that Congress, left to itself, was likely to abolish the slave trade as soon as it could (as it did as of January 1, 1808). Furthermore, the controversial allocation to the Southern States of some seats in Congress based on their slave populations tacitly acknowledged that slaves were human, that they could not be considered as mere property. The even more controversial fugitive-slave provision recognized that, left to themselves, the Free States could not be relied upon to return slaves who escaped into them.

Various uses of language in the Constitution also testify to the dubious status of slavery in 1787, however marked the accommodation to it had to be. There is, first, the deliberate avoidance of the use of the words *slave* and *slavery* in the Constitution of 1787, reflecting both a general abhorrence of the institution and the universal hope that it would be eventually eliminated. There is also something revealing in the way the fugitive slave is referred to, compared with the fugitive who has been charged in another State "with Treason, Felony, or other Crime" and who can hence be referred to as "flee[ing] from Justice." Not the slave: he is referred to as "escaping" from "Service or Labour in one State, under the Laws thereof." We are thus reminded that slavery is keyed to State laws and that such laws simply may not be just.

It was no accident then that the decided majority of the people shaped by the Constitution of 1787 should have become, if they were not from the outset, so "dedicated to the proposition that all men are created equal" that they were eventually willing and able to make great sacrifices in behalf of strangers among them held in bondage by fellow citizens whose material interests had blinded them to their ancient republican faith.

VIII

The Secession to which the desperate slavery interests resorted in 1860–1861 reminds us not only of the distortions that material interests can induce, but also of the perversion to which salutary principles can be put. For the South did stand for the critical prerogatives of States and for the importance of liberty, including unfortunately the liberty of men who seemed to be beneficiaries of a system of slavery that they could see no way out of, a system that enslaved master and servant alike.

It is well to be reminded that the States did exist. They derived their principal powers not from any government of the United States but from the same people who, collectively, gave the General Government all of its powers. It is also well to be reminded that the powers originally recognized in the States were considerable, even with respect to many matters about which Congress can legislate. Congress is supreme, when it decides to act, but much is left for the States to do where Congress is not empowered to act or when Congress has chosen not to act.

How much Congress or the States should do may vary from time to time. The determination of who should use which powers and when is ultimately left in our constitutional system to the American people, the people who have ordained and established both the Constitution of the United States and the constitutions for all of the States in the Union. It is the people, after all, who choose, directly or indirectly, all the constitutional conventions, legislative assemblies, executive officers, and even judicial officers in the United States.

IX

The States, we have seen, are somewhat systematically dealt with in Article IV: their character is assured; their relations with one another are prescribed; and their augmentation is provided for.

The Constitution can then turn in Article V to how the document may be amended. The States provided for in Article IV are essential to the amendment process. I will discuss the subject of amendments in my next lecture, where we will return to the always challenging problem of slavery under the Constitution of 1787.

Thereafter, the Constitution can turn in Article VI to how this new constitution fits into the general scheme of things, a scheme that includes both the arrangements made before the advent of this Constitution and the demands to be made of all officers, National and State, subsequent to the ratification of this Constitution.

Finally, the Constitution can turn in Article VII to its ratification. With the lecture devoted to that subject, we will be prepared to end this Commentary, having begun to get a sense of the way the Constitution of 1787 is crafted.

14. Article V

I

The Constitution pursuant to which both the General and the State Governments are to conduct themselves in national affairs is arranged by the end of Article IV. Powers are distributed among the branches of the General Government; the relations of the States with one another and with the General Government are provided for.

The Framers of the Constitution anticipated that amendments would be needed from time to time. They agreed that the unanimous consent required in the Articles of Confederation for any constitutional alteration should definitely not be retained for the new constitution.

One of the modes of proposing amendments—and the only mode relied upon thus far in amending the Constitution of 1787— is that amendments be proposed by the Congress and ratified in one designated way or another by the States. There have been more than five thousand amendments introduced in Congress since 1789. Only thirty-three have been proposed by Congress to the States for ratification; twenty-six of these have been ratified by the States (ten at one time, in 1789–1791).[122]

State ratifications of amendments proposed by Congress have usually moved much faster than one might expect. It has been reported, "The Twenty-second Amendment required the longest time, forty-seven and one-half months; the Twenty-sixth Amendment required the shortest period, four months. The average time for ratification of a constitutional amendment has been eighteen months."[123] This reflects the fact that amendments are likely to be proposed by Congress only when there is widespread support for a change. Often an amendment does little more than formally confirm what has already been generally accepted, as in the case of the Bill of Rights.

The Congressional mode of proposing amendments, Article V specifies, requires decisions by "two thirds of both Houses" of Congress. It is understood that each House must vote separately. It has been suggested that "'two thirds of both Houses' means two-thirds of a quorum in both houses."[124] But the Constitutional provision here is immediately followed by a provision for amendments being initiated also by "the Application of the Legislatures of two thirds of the several States," and in that case, the two-thirds proportion is obviously keyed to the entire roster of States, as is also the three-fourths proportion required for ratification of amendments. Legislation may be enacted in ordinary circumstances, it seems, by the majority of a quorum in each House, which quorum, able "to do Business," is identified by the Constitution as "a Majority of each [House]" (Article I, Section 5). In other instances, also, the proportions referred to can be keyed only to "the Members present" (Article I, Section 3), or to "those Present" (Article I, Section 5), or to "the Senators present" (Article II, Section 2). Is it not likely, therefore, that all other voting requirements are keyed to the entire membership of each House of Congress, just as they are to the entire body of Presidential electors (Article II, Section 1) and to the entire roster of States when the House of Representatives has to choose the President (Article II, Section 1)? But whatever the Constitutional requirements, virtually all members are likely to be present for the more momentous occasions, especially if the rules of the body provide safeguards against surprise votes.

Nothing is said in Article V about any formal role for the President in the amendment process. But since a two-thirds vote is enough to override a Presidential veto in ordinary circumstances, there might not have seemed to be any need to give him a formal part to play here. Besides, the States are to provide in this matter the check upon Congress that the President supplies when legislation is being considered. From the beginning, then, Congress alone has handled amendment proposals, however much the President may do in making recommendations and marshaling Congressional and State support for his position.

II

The irrelevance of executives in the amendment process may also be seen in the alternative mode provided by the Constitution for proposing amendments. The Congress, "on the Application of the Legislatures of two thirds of the several States, shall call a Convention for proposing Amendments."

We again notice that it is assumed that the Legislative branch of government is supreme. The governors of the States do not seem to be depended upon here; whatever the State legislatures say seems decisive. An emphasis upon State legislatures, or upon conventions in each State presumably organized under the direction of their respective State legislatures, may be seen as well in the ratification process.

The Federal Convention mode of proposing amendments means that the State legislatures are empowered to initiate action if Congress should prove delinquent. Of course, Congress could ignore the State applications for a Federal Convention, and there would be no way within the General Government to make Congress act. That would be, however, a rather blatant dereliction of duty on the part of Congress, subjecting its members to reproof and sanctions at the hands of their constituents. All of this means, therefore, that the people can get at a problem in more than one way.

May the State legislatures themselves officially propose amendments rather than ask Congress to call a convention for proposing amendments? And, one might also wonder, may Congress itself call for a Federal Convention rather than depend upon the States to do so? I consider each of these questions in turn.

No provision is made for the States to propose amendments of their own, since they are the ones to decide whether to ratify proposed amendments. Two quite different sets of judgment have to be made in the course of the amendment process. For the same reason, Congress is not asked to decide whether to ratify proposed amendments but only to prepare and offer them up for ratification. Such division of labor would seem to argue against permitting

State legislatures to designate the specific amendment proposals that a Federal Convention should consider, since the same legislatures would thereafter have to consider ratifying such proposed amendments. We should also notice, as a reason for not allowing State legislatures to propose amendments, that a well-crafted amendment probably requires a deliberative body to develop it properly. Consultation between two houses of one legislature is feasible, and is done routinely, but hardly among dozens of legislatures. This too bears upon the question of whether State legislatures should be able to specify the precise language of amendments to be considered by a convention called to propose amendments, except perhaps as nonbinding suggestions to be considered by such a convention.

Nor does it seem that Congress itself may call for a Federal Convention. But Congress can in effect sit as a constitutional convention to consider one or many possible amendments. In fact, Congress does this all the time, and in doing so, it can no doubt establish panels or committees on a representative basis or otherwise to advise Congress about possible amendments for it to propose. But Congress in proposing amendments to the States must act by a two-third votes, not by the majority vote that a convention could use.

III

A Federal Convention called by Congress upon the application of the State legislatures is something that remains available at all times, even though it has not yet been resorted to for proposing amendments to the Constitution of 1787.

Many questions remain open as to how such a convention may be organized. The circumstances of the only plausible precedent, the Federal Convention of 1787, were so special that that convention does not readily lend itself as a guide to future conventions called by the State legislatures for proposing amendments.

Three sets of questions present themselves: the first set concerns how such a convention may be called and whether its subject matter can be limited; the second set concerns how such a convention should be organized and how it should conduct itself; and the third set concerns what might be done by Congress and by the States in response to whatever such a convention does.

Much depends, in dealing with all such questions, upon what Congress says. Several substantially different positions, each backed up by respectable arguments, confront us with respect to these questions. This means that Congress would have to answer such questions in the event a Federal Convention seems to have been called for. The first thing Congress might have to decide is what kind of call by the State legislatures truly binds Congress, and in what way. Many conservatives today are in favor of calling a convention for proposing a balanced-budget amendment, while many liberals are dubious about such an amendment. But most liberals and most conservatives emphatically agree that precautions should be taken to guard against a "runaway convention," one that does not limit itself to the single designated subject of a balanced-budget amendment.

It has been argued, with some force, that State legislatures can apply only for a general convention, that they cannot limit their applications. Does this mean that every application is to be treated as an application for a general convention, even if directed to one subject? But what of those applications from State legislatures that insist that their applications are to be treated as "null and void" if a convention cannot properly be limited to a single subject? This means, some argue, that many, if not all, of the thirty-two State applications sent to Congress thus far calling for a balanced-budget-amendment convention should be treated as defective.[125]

Even so, if two more balanced-budget-amendment applications from State legislatures should be added to this list, will it not be difficult for Congress to ignore the demand? Will not Congress then probably avoid the problem of Constitutional interpretation, as well as the risk of a "runaway convention," by sending out its own balanced-budget proposal for consideration by the States? (This is substantially what the First Congress did in preparing its Bill of Rights proposals, thereby heading off a call for a second Federal Convention to amend the just-ratified Constitution.)

Whatever happens in such circumstances, Congress would still have much to say about what any Federal Convention would be like, how the Convention would be organized, how the States would vote in the Convention, how the Convention would conduct itself, and what would become of the proposals it prepared.

Furthermore, whatever any Convention or, for that matter, any Congress produces is no more than a proposal. It still has to be ratified by three-fourths of the States, pursuant to the arrangements designated by Congress, including arrangements as to how much time would be available and perhaps even precisely what questions would be put to the States. It should be remembered that the Federal Convention of 1787 had to make its own proposed Constitution acceptable to the Confederation Congress before that body would transmit that Constitution to the States for their consideration.

In short, a prudent Congress, supported by a sensible people, is not likely to permit either a Federal Convention, even if "runaway," or the State legislatures to do anything that would wreck the Constitutional system we now have, a system that has long been regarded with favor by the people of this Country.

IV

Another useful way of talking about the amendment process is to look, however briefly, at a half-dozen suggestions that have been made much of in our own time but that have not yet been converted into Constitutional amendments.

An equal-rights amendment came within a few States of ratification before time ran out for it in 1982. One must wonder, however, whether such an amendment would have made much difference upon ratification. Have not judicial decisions, especially under the Fourteenth Amendment, made it seem unnecessary? Some efforts are now being made to revive it, even though it is coming to be regarded as moot, with Congressional legislation and the growing political power of women also accomplishing most of what was intended. Such an amendment has largely come to be regarded as primarily symbolic both by its proponents and by its opponents.

A reapportionment amendment aroused considerable interest in the 1960s. "Of the many attempts to get Congress to call a constitutional convention," it was pointed out a few years ago, "so far the closest to success came in the spring of 1967 when thirty-three state legislatures, only one short, petitioned Congress to call a convention to propose an amendment to reverse Supreme Court rulings requiring both chambers of state legislatures to be apportioned on the basis of population."[126] But, it has turned out, the court-ordered reapportionments of State legislative districts, which began in 1962, have so changed the composition of State legislatures that it is unlikely that a reapportionment amendment permitting a return to the old way of doing things (or, rather, of not doing things) would stand much chance of success.

Supreme Court rulings forbidding State-sponsored prayers in public schools have also prompted calls for amendments. Here, as elsewhere, there are condemnations by some of what are considered de facto judicial "amendments" of the Constitution.[127] Still, it has proved difficult to get agreement upon a school-prayer formula that would be acceptable even to those sects of believers interested in such prayers, with perhaps a recourse to silent meditation the only thing that can be generally agreed upon, and that could well pass judicial muster during the next decade without a Constitutional amendment.

Far more troublesome, and also in response to court decisions, is the call for an amendment permitting the States once again to regulate abortions even in the first trimester of pregnancies. Whether there was indeed either a Constitutional basis or a political need for what the National Courts have done here remains a serious question, especially since there had been, before the Supreme Court innovations in 1973,[128] a steady relaxation by State legislatures of abortion regulations. This seems to be the one issue of our time that simply will not go away in the fashion of the equal-rights amendment and the reapportionment amendment, both of which seem to be superseded by events. Still, it should be observed that it is hardly likely that many State legislatures, even if left free to do so, would return abortion law simply to what it was before 1973.

An effort has been made to invest the District of Columbia with representation in Congress like that of a State, and an amendment was proposed by Congress to that effect in 1978. But the seven-year time limit for its ratification has expired, leaving its proponents with the alternative of attempting to accomplish their purpose by simply having Congress convert most of the District of Columbia into a regular State.[129]

I addressed in Lecture No. 8 the proposals we hear from time to time about changing the mode of selecting the President of the United States. This is, I have argued, one Constitutional amendment that could have a considerable effect upon the way we do things. But, I have also argued, it is far from clear precisely what that effect would be.

I have also suggested that it is difficult to believe that any balanced-budget amendment, however it should be proposed and ratified, would have its intended effect. All of the proposals that have been taken seriously include prudent provisions allowing Congress, by three-fifths or some other supermajority, to override any balanced-budget restriction. Even more serious, this general approach assumes that there exists a thing readily identifiable as a budget and that it is reasonably evident when it is balanced, or when expenditures are matched by receipts.

Is not the balanced-budget-amendment approach naive, depending much more upon incantations than is politically sound? Such approaches can be little more than rhetorical exercises, which can have the bad effects not only of cluttering up the Constitution but also of misleading people as to what a constitution can and cannot do. The best popular critique I have seen of a balanced-budget amendment is by a conservative columnist who had this to say about the matter:

> The Senate last week fell just one vote short of approving a constitutional amendment intended to compel a balanced federal budget. It would be pleasant to say good riddance to bad rubbish, but we have not heard the last of this folly.
>
> This was the proposed amendment: "Outlays of the United States for any fiscal year shall not exceed receipts to the United States for that year, unless three-fifths of the whole number of both houses of Congress shall provide for a specific excess of outlays over receipts."
>
> A second section would permit Congress to waive these restrictions in wartime. A third section would make the amendment effective in the second fiscal year after its ratification.
>
> [T]he best speech in the Senate against the proposed amendment . . . made four points: (1) The resolution lacks constitutional feel. (2) From a parliamentary standpoint it is plainly grotesque. (3) Its terms could easily be evaded. (4) It is unenforceable by any acceptable means.

The amendment, [it was] said, "would wage war on the Constitution's majesty simplicity."

Indeed it would. Constitutional amendments ought to address either the rights of the people or the structure of government.[130]

The column ends with observations that apply to much more than the current controversy:

A balanced federal budget ought not to be constitutionally mandated, whether by an amendment that originates in Congress or by an amendment that originates in a constitutional convention. It is a bad idea in either event.

The way to get a balanced budget is to elect responsible men and women to Congress. It is a humiliating confession of irresponsibility that this amendment should ever have been considered.[131]

If a balanced-budget amendment should work, we might then resort to an amendment absolutely forbidding crime in the streets and still another insuring that only the most virtuous should serve in public office. We could adapt to this latter amendment the provision in the 1776 Maryland Constitution that "a person of wisdom, experience, and virtue, shall be chosen Governor, on the second Monday of November, seventeen hundred and seventy-seven, and on the second Monday in every year forever thereafter, by the joint ballot of both Houses [of the General Assembly]."

V

The balanced-budget-amendment proposals have the merit of stimulating us to think about just what a constitution is and is not. Similarly, the equal-rights-amendment proposal and the abortion controversy stimulate us to consider first principles and even the very nature of things.

The provision of a workable amendment process presupposes, as we have noted, both that the American people retain their ultimate authority and that standards exist by which they may judge and modify Constitutional arrangements as the need arises. Even the concern expressed from time to time by the Framers of the Constitution about guarding against the tyranny of the majority reflects both the people's authority and the existence of enduring standards. To speak of *tyranny* means that a distinction is recognized between good government and bad; there is not likely to be much concern about any tyranny of the majority except in a regime where the people are powerful.

It is evident throughout the Constitution of 1787, and especially in the Article V provisions for amendments, that efforts have been made to permit the considered opinion of the people to have its effect. It is the whole people, not just the majority of the moment, that is to have its way.

Throughout the Constitution it is taken for granted that standards exist in the light of which the General Government, the people, and the State Governments are to conduct themselves. Such standards are, of course, to be brought to bear in determining what amendments are to be proposed and what amendments are to be ratified. Since the very word *amendment* presupposes *the good*, Article V looks to changes for the better.

Article V of the Constitution of 1787 implies, just as does the provision in Article VII for the ratification of the Constitution, that there are standards by which the Constitution itself may be judged. This implication goes back at least to the Declaration of Independence, where it is recognized that peoples are entitled to choose constitutional arrangements to serve the enduring ends of government, several of which are reaffirmed in the Preamble to the Constitution.

And so Article V can anticipate that the Congress may sometimes "deem it necessary" to propose amendments. This, too, is consistent with the Declaration of Independence in that it recognizes that the people of the United States may, and should, examine their Constitution and its effects, testing them by some set of principles.

Where do such standards come from? Do they always exist? How are the people to be made and to be kept good, at least to the extent of permitting them to make proper use of their Constitution? One thing at least is certain: the standards to be employed by the people, however much they may be reflected in and reinforced by the Constitution and the way it is put together, are not themselves either created or established by the Constitution. They are the standards ultimately seen in the recourse a people always has to the right of revolution, a doctrine that can be offensive to the ears of the fearful, the thoughtless, and the tyrannical.

We might wonder whether certain kinds of amendments would be inappropriate in that they would go against the spirit of the Constitution as a whole. Is not freedom of speech implied by the amendment process itself, to say nothing of the way the entire Constitutional system is supposed to work? Would not amendments that deny the ultimate power of the people be improper and of no permanent authority?

The Constitution does recognize, again and again, that there are better and worse ways of arranging for the people's ultimate power to exert itself. The amending power, like any other political power, is hedged in, whether or not people are aware of it, by natural-right considerations of justice and the common good. We might wonder as well what effect such considerations can eventually be expected to have even in the long-established tyrannies around the world. Self-made tyrants are not apt to be moved, but what about their successors three or four generations later?

VI

Congress applies enduring standards and especially, it is to be hoped, the dictates of prudence, not only in considering what amendments are to be proposed to the States, but also in determining what the mode of ratification is to be in the States. In all but one instance since 1789, Congress has provided that proposed amendments were to be considered for ratification by the State legislatures, not by State conventions chosen for that purpose.[132]

It can make a difference, of course, which ratification mode is used, just as it can make a difference when an amendment is proposed or how long a time is allowed for its consideration by the States. The Federal Convention in 1787 made it clear that it believed that ratification of its proposed constitution should be done by State conventions called for that purpose, not by the State legislatures dominated by local politicians. And that Federal Convention had the prestige to get its way with the Confederation Congress, which in turn sent out the Constitution to the States for their consideration.

It is evident from the Constitution, as well as from our Constitutional practice, that it is completely up to Congress to determine, if it should choose to do so, how proposed amendments are to be handled in the States. The State power to ratify amendments is not inherent in the States, but rather is assigned to them by the Constitution.

Congress can determine how long an amendment proposal remains alive. It could probably even provide that all State legislative decisions on such matters should be by majority vote. Congress can also provide guides to States calling for a Federal Convention to propose amendments. Some, however, may consider it prudent for Congress to say as little as possible on this subject, leaving itself free to maneuver in various contingencies.

The formal amendment provisions of Article V have been criticized as undemocratic: "One-fourth of the states plus one, which could reflect the will of much less than one-fourth of the people, could block amendments desired by a large majority [of the Country]."[133] These arguments are very much like those we have considered in Lecture No. 8 with respect to the mode of selecting Presidents. Is it not likely, however, that the differences between States, on the question of a Constitutional amendment, will be dependent upon other differences than those of population?

Be all this as it may, we see in the amendment arrangements both the ultimate authority of the people and the restraints the people place upon themselves so as to be able to make the best use of that authority.

VII

It has been generally recognized that it is up to Congress to determine when an amendment has been ratified. Here, as elsewhere, someone must have the last word. The National Courts have generally stayed out of this, and properly so, because it is evident that constitution-writing and constitution-amending are more like what a legislature does than what a court or an executive can or should do.

It is sometimes said, however, that the Supreme Court is "a constitutional convention in continuous session."[134] And so it can be further said,

Chief Justice Marshall characterized the constitution-amending machinery as "unwieldly and cumbrous." Undoubtedly it is, and that fact has had an important influence upon our institutions. Especially has it favored the growth of judicial review, since it has forced us to rely on the Court to keep the Constitution adapted to changing conditions.[135]

Do not such observations expose judicial review, if used thus, as an unconstitutional assignment to the National Courts of the amendment power provided exclusively for the Congress, Federal Conventions, and the States to exercise? Have not such innovations, which did not take hold until late in the nineteenth century, been justified in large part because of a general failure to appreciate how well the original Constitution of 1787 *is* "adapted to changing conditions"?

Constitutional customs can gradually change, of course, without any explicit amendments, and that has to be expected. Such change has been seen in the emergence of political parties and in the way Presidential electors are expected to vote. Also to be expected are the rules and precedents developed over centuries by Congress and the States with respect to various aspects of the amendment process, such as the effect of any State's attempt to rescind its ratification before three-fourths of the States have ratified a proposed amendment. Is not the important thing here that there be a fairly clear understanding, preferably well ahead of time, as to what the rules are? Much may depend upon how Congress writes the rules or what customs have developed.

All this is related to the rule of law. Certainly, it is important, if the spirit of fair play is to prevail, that the people be assured that there is a plausible, *and known*, way for everyone to follow. Congress, subject to checking by an alert people, is the only branch of government able to provide "traffic control" here, just as the Confederation Congress had been in 1786–1789 with respect to the development of a new constitution. Things don't just happen: there is a route to be followed if the proposing and the ratifying of amendments are to proceed in a manner apparent to all.

Justice Hugo L. Black, himself a legislative veteran, summed up the authority of Congress in this fashion:

The Constitution grants Congress exclusive power to control submission of constitutional amendments. Final determination by Congress that ratification by three-fourths of the States has taken place "is conclusive upon the courts." In the exercise of that power, Congress, of course, is governed by the Constitution. However, whether submission, intervening procedure or Congressional determination of ratification conforms to the commands of the Constitution, calls for decisions by a "political department" of questions of a type which this Court has frequently designated "political." And decision of a "political question" by the "political department" to which the Constitution has committed it "conclusively binds the judges, as well as all other officers, citizens and subjects of . . . government." Proclamation under authority of Congress that an amendment has been ratified *will carry with it a solemn assurance by the Congress that ratification has taken place as the Constitution commands.* Upon this assurance a proclaimed amendment must be accepted as a part of the Constitution, leaving to the judiciary its traditional authority of interpretation.[136]

Is not this radically different in spirit from *Marbury* v. *Madison,* and properly so?

VIII

We have considered the limitations placed upon the amending power by the very nature of the Constitution, if not by nature herself. There remains only to consider the restrictions placed in Article V upon the amending power, the restrictions that "no Amendment which may be made prior to the Year One thousand eight hundred and eight shall in any Manner affect the first and fourth Clauses in the Ninth Section of the first Article; and that no State, without its Consent, shall be deprived of it's equal Suffrage in the Senate."

Some have wondered whether a two-stage amendment process might not be resorted to, first to eliminate this proviso in Article V, which protects certain arrangements from ordinary amendment, and thereafter to amend those arrangements. But would not such a devious way of proceeding be against the spirit of the Constitution? If Congress and the States are willing to do this, then they admit that they consider themselves bound only by the letter of the Constitution.

No matter how many "back-ups" there may be in the Constitution to protect any arrangement from ordinary amendment, they can be circumvented by those who do not recognize that the Constitution relies on both good sense and good faith, which may be intimately related to each other.

The references in the Article V proviso to "the first and fourth Clauses in the Ninth Section of the first Article" are to these two provisions:

> The Migration or Importation of such Persons as any of the States now existing shall think proper to admit, shall not be prohibited by the Congress prior to the Year one thousand eight hundred and eight, but a Tax or duty may be imposed on such Importation, not exceeding ten dollars for each Person.

> No Capitation, or other direct, Tax shall be laid, unless in Proportion to the Census or Enumeration herein before directed to be taken.

These two clauses are connected in the Article V proviso as being beyond any amendment whatsoever before 1808. The first of these clauses protects the power of any original State, and particularly North Carolina, South Carolina and Georgia, to continue to import slaves from abroad until 1808. The inclusion here of the second clause, with respect to capitation or other direct taxes, fits in with the provision in the first clause protected here, "but a Tax or duty may be imposed on such Importation, not exceeding ten dollars for each Person." The Framers recognized that taxes might be used, properly or otherwise, to accomplish social-political purposes, and these provisions are intended to guard against the use of the tax power to discourage, if not even to abolish, the international slave trade before 1808.

We can thus see how the Framers anticipated possible evasions of the restrictions that had been laid down. The fact that such evasions had to be anticipated reflects an awareness at that time of the peculiar vulnerability both of the slave-trade provision and of the Senate-equality provision. But, it might be wondered, if the slave trade is vulnerable, why not the institution of slavery itself? Why is not the Fugitive Slave Clause in Article IV also protected against amendment, as well as the provision in Article I whereby slaves are counted toward representation?

193

The domestic institutions of slavery were evidently believed to be already secure enough from interference through Constitutional amendments because there were enough Southern States to prevent unfriendly amendments. South Carolina, Georgia, and North Carolina must have recognized in 1787 that they were alone in the demand for international slave-trade protection and that the other States, Southern and Northern alike, might try to stop the slave trade by amendments as soon as the Constitution was ratified and everyone was "in." This provision exposes, therefore, the unpopularity of the international slave trade. This is unlikely to be recognized by those who fail to appreciate how troubled the Framers were by the compromises they were compelled to make with slavery in 1787.

We see, once again, that we have to think about the parts of the Constitution and fit them together with care if either the meaning of any particular part or the overall sense of the document is to be grasped.

IX

The Constitutional compromise that permitted even the smallest States the same representation in the Senate as the largest was also vulnerable from the outset. The disparity among the States in 1787 was such that each of the three largest States—Virginia, Pennsylvania, and Massachusetts—had as much representation allocated to it in the House of Representatives, where population determines numbers, as the four smallest States combined—New Hampshire, Rhode Island, Delaware, and Georgia. It did not seem to the larger States either fair or workable, therefore, that the small States should be treated equally in the Senate. The smallest States were aware of this opinion, and so insisted upon appropriate protection in Article V against any use of the amendment power to change their standing in the Senate. We are reminded, once again, that if something is not obviously fair, it is vulnerable.

Fortunately, the Senate equality irrevocably assured by the Constitution is far less of a concern today than it once was. Now that we have national political parties that cut across State lines, the two Senators from a State may be divided in party loyalties. In fact, we now see perhaps unanticipated merits of the original Senatorial arrangement, not least of which is that it produces two Houses in the Congress that are apt to be significantly different in composition and experience, thereby making it more likely that legislative proposals will receive thorough consideration.

The two sets of guarantees against amendments in Article V suggest that the States ratifying the Constitution in 1787–1788 recognized the likelihood that once they ratified it they would not be able to leave the Union on their own. Is not this recognition reflected in the fact that Georgia, South Carolina, and North Carolina required the slave-trade assurance against amendments and that the smallest States required the Senate-equality assurance against amendments?

Does not the amendment process laid down in Article V itself imply, as we have noticed, that there may be no way to secede unilaterally, short of an exercise of the natural right of revolution? If three-fourths of the States have to agree to effect any explicit change in the Constitutional arrangement, however minor, should a smaller proportion of the States be able to make a major change, such as withdrawal from the Union, on their own? The requirement, in effect, of unanimous consent before there can be a change in the Senatorial arrangement in the Constitution also contributes to the expectation that those who are "in" are fully and irrevocably in.

Senate equality goes back, we have noticed, to the equality of the States in the one-house legislature under the Articles of Confederation. These and other elements in the Constitution of 1787 remind us that a people cannot easily, if ever, get altogether away from their origins, even when those origins are somewhat accidental in character. They remind us as well of the practical limits placed upon Constitutional amendments because of what is deeply ingrained in a way of life, a way of life that is better or worse depending upon the deference paid to standards grounded in justice and the common good. Should not our considerable reluctance to exercise the amendment power to which we have continual access be taken to reflect a general satisfaction with, and a constant reaffirmation of, the Constitution we have inherited?

15. Article VI

I

The Constitution of 1787 is, in a manner of speaking, completed by the end of Article V. The Legislative, Executive, and Judicial branches of the General Government are provided for in Articles I, II, and III, respectively; the States, which are dealt with and relied upon throughout the Constitution, are systematically addressed in Article IV; and amendments to the Constitution are provided for in Article V.

Now, in Article VI, the Constitution must be put in context. This article explains how the new constitution fits into the general scheme of things, a scheme that includes both a recognition of the undertakings entered into before this Constitution was drafted and a specification of the demands to be made of all officers, National and State, after it was ratified.

Central to Article VI is the celebrated Supremacy Clause, the designation of the Constitution and certain laws and treaties as "the supreme Law of the Land." Let us consider in turn the three paragraphs in this article.

II

The first paragraph of Article VI provides: "All Debts contracted and Engagements entered into, before the Adoption of this Constitution, shall be as valid against the United States under this Constitution, as under the Confederation." It is taken for granted here that the United States existed before the Constitution of 1787.

When did the United States come into being? The language, "under the Confederation," refers to the United States under the Articles of Confederation. We know that Congress acted pursuant to the Articles long before they were ratified in 1781, perhaps before they were proposed to the States by Congress in 1777 and, in effect, ever since July 4, 1776, when the United States was first announced as such to the world, if not earlier. It may even be said that the Constitution of 1787 merely reconstituted the political order of the United States, something that the Declaration of Independence recognized that a people is always entitled to do in attempting to better its lot.

There have been those, such as many in the antebellum South, who have argued that the present United States came into being only in 1788 upon the ratification of the Constitution or in 1789 upon the inauguration of the first government under the Constitution. They have further argued that this Constitution was made by the States, not by the people of the United States, notwithstanding the "We the People" language of its Preamble. This approach has been taken to mean that the States that made the Constitution could, without majority consent, unmake it and go their separate ways.

Abraham Lincoln presented the argument in opposition to this in its most poetic form when he said, "Four score and seven years ago our fathers brought forth on this continent a new nation, conceived in Liberty, and dedicated to the proposition that all men are created equal." His mode of dating goes back to 1776 and the Declaration of Independence. Does not his use of *fathers* point to ancestors and hence to the people and not to the States as the makers of the Country, something that is further emphasized by the uses of *brought forth*, of *nation*, and of *conceived*, terms that imply birth or, again, a people?

The Civil War was fought, in part, over how the origins of the Country were to be understood, from which understanding follow various powers both of the States and of the General Government of the United States.

III

The first paragraph of Article VI of the Constitution gives assurance that the United States will consider itself bound under the

Constitution by those debts and engagements of the United States that were valid under the Confederation. The claimants thus assured included Americans as well as foreigners. The distinction between "Debts contracted" and "Engagements entered into" may be a distinction between commercial and financial obligations on the one hand and treaty and other such obligations on the other hand.

It is taken for granted that the Country's word is to be kept, something that constitutional government itself very much depends upon. It was several times indicated in the Federal Convention of 1787 that any prospective general government under a new constitution should honor the undertakings of its predecessor governments under the Articles of Confederation. One such undertaking, several times referred to in the Federal Convention, was with respect to the Northwest Territory. The Northwest Ordinance had promised that the people of that Territory could eventually form States that would be accepted in the Union as full partners of the original thirteen.

No doubt, it was considered both expedient and just to honor the debts and engagements of the United States. Questions may remain as to precisely what debts and engagements had been "valid . . . under the Confederation." Would not that depend upon the law at the time of the transactions being referred to as well as upon a general sense of right and wrong?

Property and promises are to be respected. We can thus see that the common law, which is itself critical to the constitutional context that the Federal Convention took for granted, would probably be looked to for some guidance as to what the valid debts might be that the United States owed. Here and elsewhere, in any event, enduring standards outside the Constitution must be drawn upon if the General Government established by the Constitution of 1787 is properly to serve justice and the common good.

IV

The second paragraph of Article VI provides: "This Constitution, and the Laws of the United States which shall be made in Pursuance thereof; and all Treaties made, or which shall be made, under the Authority of the United States, shall be the supreme Law of the Land; and the Judges in every State shall be bound thereby, any Thing in the Constitution or Laws of any State to the Contrary notwithstanding."

Only the laws made pursuant to this Constitution are to be part of "the Supreme Law of the Land," which seems to exclude the laws made by the Congress under the Articles of Confederation. But, of course, the new Congress can reenact, or otherwise ratify, whatever laws made by its predecessors that it wishes to retain.

Treaties, however, are a different matter. Other countries are entitled to treat the United States as continuous, since from the "outside" they must deal with this country as it presents itself, whatever may be happening to its constitutional organization at home. An agreement made "under the Authority of the United States" can bind the Country indefinitely, unless perhaps there is something so obviously questionable about any treaty arrangement entered into that the other contracting parties should have recognized that that treaty might well be repudiated by a successor government.

But, assuming a proper treaty has been duly ratified, there is not likely to be the kind of validity concern about a treaty that there may be about supposed debts and other engagements. It is unusual to bring to bear upon an assessment of treaties and their effects the kinds of considerations of right and wrong that common-law issues raise.

We again see in this paragraph an acceptance of the past even as the future is being prepared for. However, the treaties referred to here do not take precedence over the laws of the United States but only over the constitutions and laws of the States. The General Government of the United States should be able to determine what, if any, effect a treaty is to have in the domestic life of the Country. Here, as elsewhere, the Congress as lawmaker must have the authoritative voice, subject always to the superior authority of the people.

V

The Supremacy Clause—the second paragraph of Article VI—seems to be primarily concerned with directing the States, and particularly "the Judges in every State," in the way they are to conduct themselves. State judges have particularly to be addressed thus since they may be moved primarily by local loyalties, that is, by "the Constitution or Laws of [their] State." The important requirement here seems to be that the judges as well as the other officers of a State *not* presume to sit in judgment upon the Constitution, laws, and treaties of the United States. The Framers were prudent to insist upon this because it then seemed that much of the judicial business of the United States might be conducted in State courts for some years to come. It remained to be seen, that is, how soon Congress would institute National Courts and how extensive they and their jurisdictions would be.

The National Courts do not have to be addressed by the Supremacy Clause, if only because they are much more immediately under the control of Congress, and not only through its impeachment power. Besides, it was evidently expected that judges in the National Courts would routinely defer to the Constitution, laws, and treaties of the United States.

The Constitution, laws, and treaties of the United States are all to be regarded as authoritative by State judges. If these instruments should seem to contradict one another, then State judges must look to the General Government for guidance, with presumably the most recent action of Congress or of the National Courts serving as their most reliable guide. The critical power of passing judgment upon laws and treaties of the United States is left to the General Government, not to the States.

The language, "the Laws of the United States which shall be made in Pursuance [of the Constitution]," seems to refer to the laws that are made by the Congress established by the Constitution, as distinguished from the Continental or Confederation Congresses. This language looks to the laws which shall be made, in contradistinction to the treaties "made, or which shall be made." It is hardly likely that State judges are hereby being empowered to do something that the National Courts are never empowered to do. That is, State judges are not being licensed by the "in Pursuance" language to examine acts of Congress for their Constitutionality. The judges are only required to determine whether something that is submitted to them as a relevant law of the United States has been made, and is still in force, pursuant to the legislative mode prescribed in Article I of the Constitution.

Thus, the Supremacy Clause, which many look to as providing

some basis for the power of judicial review of acts of Congress, says little, if anything, about the prerogatives of the National Courts. Rather, it assumes much about the powers of the Congress of the United States when it makes laws and of the powers of the President when he acts in cooperation with the Senate in the making of treaties.

VI

The "in Pursuance" language, therefore, looks more to the source and formal adequacy of a purported law of the United States than to its "constitutionality." This language is more likely to mean "following upon" or "made after this Constitution is adopted" than it is to mean "in conformity to the Constitution" in the sense used today to denote "constitutionality."

And so, once again, I have touched upon that question of judicial review already examined at some length in this Commentary, a question that can challenge in various ways one's understanding of the principles of the Constitution. It should be noticed here, since the status of State constitutions and laws has been referred to, that the Judiciary Act of 1789 anticipated that State laws may routinely be challenged as "being repugnant to the Constitution . . . of the United States," but not, it seems, any laws duly enacted by Congress. This is consistent with the arrangement laid out in the Supremacy Clause.

It is sometimes said, however, that judicial review of acts of Congress is to be expected under a written constitution. But, as I have already noted, parts of the British Constitution, such as Magna Carta and the Habeas Corpus Act, are written. Yet, I dare say, no British judge would presume to use a written part of the British Constitution to set aside an act of Parliament. On the other hand, he may well try to interpret such an act to make it consistent with the constitution as it is generally understood.

This is not to suggest that a State government may never encounter an act of Congress that it regards as unconstitutional. If it does, it should certainly say so and should at least urge the members of Congress from that State to try to do something about it. It was in the Congress, with echoes in the State legislatures, that the great public debates about Constitutionality were to be heard in the early decades of the Republic. This could be seen, for example, in the Alien and Sedition Acts controversy, in the Embargo Acts controversy, and in the Tariff Acts controversy.[137]

In the United States Supreme Court, on the other hand, only two acts of Congress were generally recognized to have been declared unconstitutional before the Civil War—one in 1803, the other in 1857—and of these, I have suggested, the second (*Dred Scott*) was clearly wrongly decided and the first (*Marbury* v. *Madison*) was probably wrongly decided. Both cases presumed to call into question exercises of power that went back to the First Congress made up of several members fresh from the Federal Convention.

Nor is all this to suggest that the courts, National and State, should not use the Constitution in interpreting acts of Congress. The courts are entitled, perhaps even obliged, to assume that Congress intended to proceed in accordance with the obvious meaning of the Constitution, at least until Congress emphatically indicates otherwise. In addition, the courts have to look to the Constitution for guidance in those circumstances where Congress has not yet spoken, especially in those controversies between the States that the United States Supreme Court is expected to decide.

Would it not be salutary as well to consider looking to the National Courts to obtain compliance with the various restraints upon the States found in Section 2 of Article IV, at least in those instances in which Congress has not yet acted? In some instances, a sensible Congress would recognize that such a controversy is more judicial than legislative in character and hence best left to the United States Supreme Court to deal with.

VII

The third paragraph of Article VI provides: "The Senators and Representatives before mentioned, and the Members of the several State Legislatures, and all executive and judicial Officers, both of the United States and of the several States, shall be bound by Oath or Affirmation, to support this Constitution; but no religious Test shall ever be required as a Qualification to any Office or public Trust under the United States."

It is consistent with the precedence recognized throughout the

Constitution that here, too, legislators, both National and State, should be mentioned first. The order seen here—the Legislative, the Executive, and the Judicial—is that found in the order of the first three articles of the Constitution, as well as, later, in the order of the elements in the Bill of Rights. The history of the General Government under the Constitution is also relevant here: Congress was the first branch to come into being, in March 1789; it determined who had been chosen President and arranged for his inauguration; later, the President nominated Supreme Court Justices for the Senate to confirm.[138]

The references here to the legislators and executives of the States remind us that in the preceding paragraph, the Supremacy Clause, only the judges of the States are referred to. It seems to have been expected that maintaining general respect in the States for the Constitution, laws, and treaties of the United States would depend in large part upon State judges, for it is they who would routinely sort out the contending official directives that impinge upon the lives of people. State judges are implicitly empowered by the Constitution to decide whether State enactments have been superseded by the Constitution, laws, and treaties of the United States.

In effect, State judges are told that the legislature they must consider ultimately authoritative is Congress, not the State legislature they would ordinarily defer to. When State legislators and executives step out of line in circumstances where judicial proceedings are not implicated, the General Government may have to resort to political measures to protect the interests of the United States.[139]

VIII

It is evident throughout the Constitution that officers of government are to be kept in line partly because of their competing interests, partly because of their rectitude, and partly because of the people's as well as official supervision. The rectitude of officers of government, both National and State, is looked to in the requirement for the oaths prescribed by the Constitution.

Presumably, Congress can supply the text of the required oaths for General Government officers and, if the State legislatures do not do so adequately, for State officers as well. Presumably, also, the oath required need not be as elaborate as, even though it may be modeled upon, the oath laid down for the President in Article II.

We can once again see, in this provision for oaths, that there are standards drawn upon that are independent of the law. Certainly, belief in the efficacy of an oath depends upon the habits, opinions, and character of the people from whom the officers of government are taken. Thus, as we have seen, both the Country and a body of standards exist independently of the Constitution, however important the Constitution may become for both the Country and its standards.

The oath required need include only the promise to support the Constitution. It is hardly likely that such an oath, required as it is of every National and State officer in the Country, presupposes that each such officer understands the Constitution, but rather only that he concedes it takes precedence over all other political arrangements and allegiances in the Country. This means a recognition of the superior authority of the General Government, at least in its proper sphere. Among the implications of such an oath would certainly be the disavowal of any continued allegiance to the British government. (We shall see that explicit disavowals were often required during the Revolutionary War.)

A sampling of oaths drawn from State constitutions in force at the time the Constitution of 1787 was drafted should suggest what an oath to support the Constitution was intended to deal with. We are reminded as well of the important, if not even the dominant, political opinions of the day.

The Maryland Constitution, completed in November 1776, provided:

> That every person, appointed to any office of profit or trust, shall, before he enters on the execution thereof, take the following oath; to wit: "I, A. B., do swear, that I do not hold myself bound in allegiance to the King of Great Britain, and that I will be faithful, and bear true allegiance to the State of Maryland;" and shall also subscribe a declaration of his belief in the Christian religion.

Eighteen months later into the war, such an oath could become more elaborate, as may be seen in the March 1778 South Carolina Constitution:

> That all persons who shall be chosen and appointed to any office or

to any place of trust, civil or military, before entering upon the execution of office, shall take the following oath: "I, A. B., do acknowledge the State of South Carolina to be a free, sovereign, and independent State, and that the people thereof owe no allegiance or obedience to George the Third, King of Great Britain, and I do renounce, refuse, and abjure any allegiance or obedience to him. And I do swear (or affirm, as the case may be) that I will, to the utmost of my power, support, maintain, and defend the said State against the said King George the Third, and his heirs and successors, and his or their abettors, assistants, and adherents, and will serve the said State, in the office of ———, with fidelity and honor, and according to the best of my skill and understanding: So help me God."

Two years further into the war, the oath of allegiance could become still more elaborate, as may be seen in the March 1780 Massachusetts Constitution:

And every person chosen to either of the places or offices aforesaid, as also any person appointed or commissioned to any judicial, executive, military, or other office under the government, shall, before he enters on the discharge of the business of his place or office, take and subscribe the following declaration and oaths or affirmations, viz:

"I, A. B., do truly and sincerely acknowledge, profess, testify, and declare that the commonwealth of Massachusetts is, and of right ought to be, a free, sovereign, and independent State, and I do swear that I will bear true faith and allegiance to the said commonwealth, and I will defend the same against traitorous conspiracies and all hostile attempts whatsoever; and that I do renounce and abjure all allegiance, subjection, and obedience to the King, Queen, or government of Great Britain, (as the case may be,) and every other foreign power whatsoever; and that no foreign prince, person, prelate, state, or potentate hath, or ought to have, any jurisdiction, superiority, preeminence, authority, dispensing or other power, in any matter, civil, ecclesiastical, or spiritual, within this commonwealth; except the authority and power which is or may be vested by their constituents in the Congress of the United States; and I do further testify and declare that no man, or body of men, hath, or can have, any right to absolve or discharge me from the obligation of this oath, declaration, or affirmation; and that I do make this acknowledgment, profession, testimony, declaration, denial, renunciation, and abjuration heartily and truly, according to the common meaning and acceptation of the foregoing words, without any equivocation, mental evasion, or secret reservation whatsoever: So help me, God."

"I, A. B., do solemnly swear and affirm that I will faithfully and impartially discharge and perform all the duties incumbent on me as ———, according to the best of my abilities and understanding, agreeably to the rules and regulations of the constitution and the laws of the commonwealth: So help me God."

One can imagine from the tenor of such oaths the plight of Empire Loyalists, or Tories, among the Americans. A move into somewhat calmer times is evident in the June 1784 New Hampshire Constitution, which had been prepared during the last year of the Revolutionary War, where it is said:

Any person chosen president, counsellor, senator, or representative, military or civil officer, (town officers excepted,) accepting the trust, shall, before he proceeds to execute the duties of his office, make and subscribe the following declaration, viz.

"I, A. B. do truly and sincerely acknowledge, profess, testify and declare, that the state of New-Hampshire is, and of right ought to be, a free, sovereign and independent state; and do swear that I will bear faith and true allegiance to the same, and that I will endeavor to defend it against all treacherous conspiracies and hostile attempts whatever: and I do further testify and declare, that no man or body of men, hath or can have, a right to absolve me from the obligation of this oath, declaration or affirmation; and that I do make this acknowledgement, profession, testimony, and declaration, honestly and truly, according to the common acceptation of the foregoing words, without any equivocation, mental evasion or secret reservation whatever. So help me GOD.

"I, A. B. do solemnly and sincerely swear and affirm, that I will faithfully and impartially discharge and perform all the duties incumbent on me as ——— according to the best of my abilities, agreeably to the rules and regulations of this constitution, and the laws of the state of New-Hampshire. So help me GOD."

It should be evident from this sampling of oaths that such solemn undertakings were regarded as significant acts, perhaps even as a summary, especially in trying times, of one's constitutional principles.

IX

The United States Constitution of 1787 provides that "no religious Test shall ever be required as a Qualification to any Office or public Trust under the United States." It is important, if we are to understand the Constitutional thought of the Framers, to be clear about what this provision does *not* mean. Certainly, it does not mean what it is often taken to mean: that the Framers expressed their disapproval here of religious tests, thereby teaching us that religion and politics (or, as we would say, church and state) should be rigorously separated.

Their deference to religious sensibilities is reflected in their allowance of an affirmation in place of an oath, a substitution routinely permitted as well by various State constitutions of the day. This substitution defers, as we shall see, to the religious scruples of people such as the Quakers. On the other hand, the Framers' reliance upon religious sensibilities may be seen in their very recourse to oaths.

The prohibition in Article VI of a religious test seems to have been shaped not by abhorrence of these tests, although, no doubt, some members of the Federal Convention might have had their doubts about such things, but rather by an awareness of the problem, and hence the danger, of any effort by the General Government to order a religious test for the Country at large, especially considering the diversity in religious sentiments from State to State. (There is a parallel here, we have seen, to the provision in Section 2 of Article I that "the [House of Representatives] Electors in each State shall have the Qualifications requisite for Electors of the most numerous Branch of the State Legislature.")

How the religious-test prohibition in Article VI and the no-establishment provision in the First Amendment should be interpreted will be affected, then, by what is known about the Constitutional context in which these provisions were prepared. Again, one sees the need to have a reliable notion about British constitutional history and the common law if one is to appreciate fully the craftsmanship, and hence the sensibleness, of the Constitution of 1787.

Let us consider once again the thirteen State constitutions in force at the time the Constitution of 1787 was drafted. It is evident from these constitutions, eleven of which were drafted during the decade preceding the Federal Convention, that the general opinion of the community with respect to "the separation of church and state" was not what it has lately been taken to have been. A reliance upon religious tests was often believed to be consistent with religious toleration, which *was* generally approved of, and even with a prohibition of the establishment of a religion, which can be found in various of the earliest State constitutions.

I review the eleven State constitutions prepared shortly before the Federal Convention met. (It will be recalled that two of the State constitutions in force in 1787 were merely adaptations of ancient Colonial Charters.) It may be seen here how religion was made use of politically even as a considerable, perhaps unprecedented, degree of religious liberty was insisted upon.[140]

The 1776 New Jersey Constitution provides for religious toleration, even as it requires one to be a Protestant in order to hold public office:

> That no person shall ever, within this Colony, be deprived of the inestimable privilege of worshipping Almighty God in a manner agreeable to the dictates of his own conscience; nor, under any pretence whatever, be compelled to attend any place of worship, contrary to his own faith and judgment; nor shall any person, within this Colony, ever be obliged to pay tithes, taxes, or any other rates, for the purpose of building or repairing any other church or churches, place or places of worship, or for the maintenance of any minister or ministry, contrary to what he believes to be right, or has deliberately or voluntarily engaged himself to perform.

> That there shall be no establishment of any one religious sect in this Province, in preference to another; and that no Protestant inhabitant of this Colony shall be denied the enjoyment of any civil right, merely on account of his religious principles; but that all persons, professing a belief in the faith of any Protestant sect, who shall demean themselves peaceably under the government, as hereby established, shall be capable of being elected into any office of profit or trust, or being a member of either branch of the Legislature, and shall fully and freely enjoy every privilege and immunity, enjoyed by others their fellow subjects.

The Georgia Constitution, drafted in 1776 and agreed to in 1777, also requires that members of the State legislature "be of the Protestant religion."

The 1776 Delaware Constitution provides that every person who serves in the State legislature or who is appointed to any office or place of trust must "subscribe the following declaration":

> I, A. B., do profess faith in God the Father, and in Jesus Christ His only Son, and in the Holy Ghost, one God, blessed for evermore; and I do acknowledge the holy scriptures of the Old and New Testament to be given by divine inspiration.

And yet this Delaware Constitution can also provide this assurance:

> There shall be no establishment of any one religious sect in this State in preference to another . . .

The 1776 Pennsylvania Constitution acknowledges in its preamble "the goodness of the great Governor of the universe." It then provides, in its Declaration of Rights:

> That all men have a natural and unalienable right to worship Almighty God according to the dictates of their own consciences and understanding: And that no man ought or of right can be compelled to attend any religious worship, or erect or support any place of worship, or maintain any ministry, contrary to, or against, his own free will and consent: Nor can any man, who acknowledges the being of a God, be justly deprived or abridged of any civil right as a citizen, on account of his religious sentiments or peculiar mode of religious worship: And that no authority can or ought to be vested in, or assumed by any power whatever, that shall in any case interfere with, or in any manner controul, the right of conscience in the free exercise of religious worship.

Yet this Pennsylvania Constitution can go on to lay down this requirement:

> And each member [of the legislature], before he takes his seat, shall make and subscribe the following declaration, viz: "I do believe in one God, the creator and governor of the universe, the rewarder of the good and the punisher of the wicked. And I do acknowledge the Scriptures of the Old and New Testament to be given by Divine inspiration."

> And no further or other religious test shall ever hereafter be required of any civil officer or magistrate in this State.

Thus, it is made explicit here that the required declaration is indeed a "religious test."

The 1776 Maryland Constitution combines, in one article, a concern for "religious liberty" and a power in the legislature to secure revenues "for the support of the Christian religion."[141] It can then add:

> That no other test or qualification ought to be required, on admission to any office of trust or profit, than such oath of support and fidelity to this State, and such oath of office, as shall be directed by this Convention, or the Legislature of this State, and a declaration of a belief in the Christian religion.

Immediately thereafter provision is made in the Maryland Constitution for those who find themselves unable to *swear* an oath:

> That the manner of administering an oath to any person, ought to be such, as those of the religious persuasion, profession, or denomination, of which such person is one, generally esteem the most effectual confirmation, by the attestation of the Divine Being. And that the people called Quakers, those called Dunkers, and those called Menonists, holding it unlawful to take an oath on any occasion, ought to be allowed to make their solemn affirmation, in the manner that Quakers have been heretofore allowed to affirm; and to be of the same avail as an oath, in all such cases, as the affirmation of Quakers hath been allowed and accepted within this State, instead of an oath.

The 1776 North Carolina Constitution deals much more tersely with these matters in two separate articles:

> That all men have a natural and unalienable right to worship Almighty God according to the dictates of their own consciences.

> That no person, who shall deny the being of God or the truth of the Protestant religion, or the divine authority either of the Old or New Testaments, or who shall hold religious principles incompatible with the freedom and safety of the State, shall be capable of holding any office or place of trust or profit in the civil department within this State.

Perhaps the most elaborate treatment of these matters is in the 1778 South Carolina Constitution. It provides that "the Christian Protestant religion shall be deemed . . . the established religion of

[the] State." It is further provided that every religious society "of fifteen or more male persons" "to be incorporated and esteemed as a church of the established religion" must subscribe to five articles:

1st. That there is one eternal God, and a future state of rewards and punishments.

2d. That God is publicly to be worshipped.

3d. That the Christian religion is the true religion.

4th. That the holy scriptures of the Old and New Testaments are of divine inspiration, and are the rule of faith and practice.

5th. That it is lawful and the duty of every man being thereunto called by those who govern, to bear witness to the truth.

The 1780 Massachusetts Constitution is much more modest in its requirements:

Any person chosen governor, lieutenant-governor, councillor, senator, or representative, and accepting the trust, shall, before he proceed to execute the duties of his place or office, make and subscribe the following declaration, viz:

"I, A. B., do declare that I believe the Christian religion, and have a firm persuasion of its truth; and that I am seized and possessed, in my own right, of the property required by the constitution, as one qualification for the office or place to which I am elected."

We then have an extended indication of the dependence of public morality upon institutional piety in the 1784 New Hampshire Constitution, the last State constitution prepared before the Federal Convention met in 1787:

As morality and piety, rightly grounded on evangelical principles, will give the best and greatest security to government, and will lay in the hearts of men the strongest obligations to due subjection; and as the knowledge of these, is most likely to be propagated through a society by the institution of the public worship of the DEITY, and of public instruction in morality and religion; therefore, to promote those important purposes, the people of this state have a right to impower, and do hereby fully impower the legislature to authorize from time to time, the several towns, parishes, bodies-corporate, or religious societies within this state, to make adequate provision at their own expence, for the support and maintenance of public protestant teachers of piety, religion and morality:

Provided notwithstanding, That the several towns, parishes, bodies-corporate, or religious societies, shall at all times have the exclusive right of electing their own public teachers, and of contracting with them for their support and maintenance. And no person of any one particular religious sect or denomination, shall ever be compelled to pay towards the support of the teacher or teachers of another persuasion, sect or denomination.

And every denomination of Christians demeaning themselves quietly, and as good subjects of the state, shall be equally under the protection of the law: and no subordination of any one sect or denomination to another, shall ever be established by law.

This New Hampshire Constitution goes on to provide that the legislative and executive officers of the State must be of the Protestant religion.

I return now to two State constitutions that seem closer in spirit to our contemporary approach than the nine constitutions I have just reviewed. The 1776 Virginia Declaration of Rights provides:

That religion, or the duty which we owe to our Creator, and the manner of discharging it, can be directed only by reason and conviction, not by force or violence; and therefore all men are equally entitled to the free exercise of religion, according to the dictates of conscience; and that it is the mutual duty of all to practise Christian forebearance, love, and charity towards each other.

This provision can be said to have inspired in 1785–1786 the celebrated Virginia Act for Establishing Religious Freedom.

The 1777 New York Constitution nullifies all parts of the common law and statutes inherited from Great Britain "as may be construed to establish or maintain any particular denomination of Christians or their ministers." It further provides:

And whereas we are required, by the benevolent principles of rational liberty, not only to expel civil tyranny, but also to guard against that spiritual oppression and intolerance wherewith the bigotry and ambition of weak and wicked priests and princes have scourged mankind, this convention doth further, in the name and by the authority of the good people of this State, ordain, determine, and declare, that the free exercise of religious profession and worship, without discrimination or preference, shall forever hereafter be allowed, within this State, to all mankind:

Provided, that the liberty of conscience, hereby granted, shall not be so construed as to excuse acts of licentiousness, or justify practices inconsistent with the peace or safety of this State.

(We are reminded of Shakespeare's English History Plays and of the Declaration of Independence by this reference to "the bigotry and ambition of weak and wicked priests and princes [that] have scourged mankind.")

It is well to recognize, if one is to think properly about these eleven State constitutions, that the Framers of the Constitution of 1787, and their counterparts in the States, were politically sophisticated men, some of them no doubt of a relaxed attitude personally about revealed religion. They seem, however, to have appreciated the political usefulness of religion, if only in the form of deference to local orthodoxy. The most exalted manifestations of such usefulness may be seen in what President Lincoln was able to do in his Gettysburg Address and Second Inaugural Address. (The texts of these talks are set forth in Appendix M.)

Is it likely, therefore, considering the various religious tests that had been so recently provided for in State constitutions, that the Framers of the Constitution of 1787 considered religious tests simply bad or improper? The samples I have collected here, except perhaps those from the New York and Virginia Constitutions, suggest otherwise. Even so, the "no religious Test" provision in the Constitution of 1787 eventually had the effect, once the circumstances of its original development had been forgotten, of contributing to the now general opinion among Americans that government should never make use of such tests. And so nineteenth-century State constitutions, began to imitate the Constitution of 1787 here as in many other ways.

No doubt there are sound arguments in support of this liberalizing development, but surely not the argument that this is what the Framers intended, however salutary the restraint they exhibited. This is not to deny that there is in the Constitution of 1787 far less of that indulgence in passion evident in various of the early State constitutions, which passion may be seen in the passages I have quoted. All this is well to keep in mind as a reminder of how the Constitution may be misunderstood, especially if either the political astuteness or the legal craftsmanship devoted to it should be underestimated.

We have seen in Article VI a determination that the past be respected and that the future be provided for. This article opens, in its acceptance of old debts, with a confirmation of agreements previously relied upon, and it closes, in its recourse to oaths, with a guarantee of still more agreements to be relied upon hereafter.

The Constitution of 1787 is now ready for ratification. Critical to the Ratification Campaign was the justified expectation that a well-wrought constitution so combines the past and the future as to make a vital present likely for centuries to come.

16. Article VII

I

I have, in this Commentary, examined the Constitution of 1787 article by article. Now that the first six articles are finished, our constitution is ready for adoption. The seventh and final article provides for ratification.

Each of the first four articles deals with one of the four branches or departments of government in the United States. Article I deals with the Legislative department of the General Government; Article II deals with the Executive department of the General Government; and Article III deals with the Judicial department of the General Government. Article IV then deals with State government, which constitutes the fourth "branch" of government in this Country.

From the perspective of the Constitution of 1787, State government is unitary: that is, the primary concern of the Constitution is not with which department of State government does what, but rather with what State governments generally do, especially as that bears upon the effective use by the General Government of its powers. We have seen that those State government doings, which are touched upon in the first three articles of the Constitution, are addressed somewhat systematically in Article IV, as are the very existence of new States and the character of, and relations among, all States.

Once the four branches of government are accounted for—that is, once constitutional guidelines are laid down for the three departments of the General Government and for the States—provision can then be made in Article V for amendments that permit changes in Constitutional relations and in what government may do for or with the people of the Country. The importance of the States in the national constitutional scheme is again evident here.

Article VI, we have seen, recognizes the past and looks to the future as both old and new agreements are provided for. In Article VII, the next step in the constitutional career of the Americans is anticipated with the provision, "The Ratification of the Conventions of nine States, shall be sufficient for the Establishment of this Constitution between the States so ratifying the Same." Here, too, we may see the prudence of the Framers of the Constitution at work.

II

This ratification arrangement exhibits considerable astuteness. The proposed Constitution, it is assumed, will not be vetoed by the already-existing Congress of the United States. The Confederation Congress is relied upon to transmit to the States the Constitution that had been drafted by the Federal Convention of 1787. It is also relied upon to accept, in doing so, the significance of the nine State ratifications provided for in Article VII.

The Federal Convention knew, from the outset, that it had to produce something that the Confederation Congress could indeed accept, if only for purposes of transmittal to the States. Although Congress had the advantage of a constitutional status under the Articles of Confederation, it in turn recognized that the proposals made by the extraordinary, if not extra-constitutional, Federal Convention had to be treated with the utmost respect, partly because of the reputations of many of the Convention delegates and partly because of what the Country had come to expect from that Convention.

The respect accorded the proposal made by the Convention invested that body with the constitutional significance now associated in Article V of the Constitution of 1787 with any convention called "on the Application of the Legislatures of two thirds of the several States . . . for proposing Amendments." It is salutary to be reminded that whatever comes out of any Article V convention must in effect pass muster with Congress before it is transmitted to the States for their consideration, just as was true in 1787 with the proposal that came out of the Federal Convention. Although a national convention speaks with some authority, as the voice of the people of the Country, it does not have the last word. The voice of the people must be expressed in more than one mode for that voice to be fully authoritative. The people, this time as organized in the several States, must again be heard from, once a federal convention has done its work.

The Convention proposed, and the Congress agreed, that the best way to determine, in the circumstances, the response of the people to the Constitution prepared for them at Philadelphia was through conventions convened in the various States for this purpose. Once Congress designated this mode of proceeding, it was left to the State legislatures to arrange for the organization of appropriate conventions in their respective States.

The State governments were recruited to assist in the establishment of an arrangement designed, at least in part, to permit the people of the Country to register with a certain immediacy their opinion about the proposed Constitution. No doubt, local politicians knew they were being circumvented, but they must have recognized as well that they had no practical choice but to arrange for the conventions generally anticipated in the States. No doubt, also, attempts were made so to provide for the composition and the procedures of those conventions as to favor one result over another.

We should again be reminded by this sequence of events that the effects of Constitutional provisions can very much depend upon the circumstances in which they happen to be applied.

III

A federal constitutional convention was not provided for by the Articles of Confederation, but that was not considered an insuperable obstacle to overcome in 1786–1787. The Convention that did meet can be considered, in effect, to have acted as a special committee of the Congress, providing it a proposal that it could then share, if it wished, with the States. Such a mode of preparing a proposal for Congress to send out to the States was evidently considered consistent with the prevailing constitutional arrangements.

What was clearly inconsistent with prevailing norms was the

proposal made by the Federal Convention, which was accepted by Congress, that ratification by nine States would suffice for the establishment of the Constitution between the States so ratifying. This proposal had the character of a revolutionary act, since any alteration of the then-authoritative Articles of Confederation required the unanimous consent of the thirteen States.

Still, the Convention did not propose coercion of any reluctant States. The principle of unanimous consent was observed in this way at least. If all thirteen States agreed, there would be no constitutional problem and therefore little was said about what would happen if there should be less than unanimous agreement by the States. Besides, irregularity in such matters was something the Americans of that day had learned to accommodate themselves to, as we have seen in their willingness to have Congress exercise its powers under the Articles of Confederation for several years before the Articles themselves were ratified. Eighteenth-century Americans can be seen to have acted, on more than one occasion, pursuant to what the Constitution could reasonably be expected to become.

Reliance upon nine States for a comprehensive amendment of the existing constitution anticipated, in effect, the reliance in Article V of the Constitution of 1787 upon three-fourths of the States for the ratification of amendments. (Because Rhode Island had refused to participate at all in the Federal Convention, *nine* did amount to three-fourths of the active States there.) The eventual ratification of the Constitution of 1787 by all thirteen of the original States meant, in effect, that the radical changes proposed by the Federal Convention were authorized in substantial compliance with the mode of alteration laid down in the Articles of Confederation.

IV

Another way of putting all this is to say that the delegates to the Federal Convention knew, and knew that it was generally believed, that they were expressing the considered sentiments of the Country at large. They were both bold and cautious in the way they proceeded—bold in the scope of the changes they wrote into the Constitution, cautious in the way in which they presented what they had done.

An intriguing manifestation of caution may be seen in how the Convention delegates signed the final draft of the Constitution on September 17, 1787. The thirty-nine signers are collected according to States, with the arrangement of the States being that used theretofore in similar listings (as in Section 2 of Article I of the Constitution and earlier in the Declaration of Independence): the States are set forth in accordance with their geographical relations on the Atlantic Coast, starting from the North and East with New Hampshire and moving South to Georgia. This particular arrangement may have to it more the feel of something natural than one relying only upon an alphabetical sequence or upon some chronological sequence.

The delegates are not listed as endorsing the proposed Constitution. Rather, they are listed as *witnessing* the fact that the Constitution had been "done," that is, made, "by the Unanimous Consent of the States present." We are told by James Madison that this "ambiguous form" had been drawn up by Gouverneur Morris "in order to gain the dissenting members."[142]

One could thereby sign as a "witness" even if one did not endorse the Constitution in its entirety. Elbridge Gerry of Massachusetts and Edmund Randolph and George Mason of Virginia held out against signing even on these terms.[143] Still, this mode of signing may have helped permit the Federal Convention to close on a harmonious note, in that those who refused to sign were shown that it mattered to the others whether they did sign or not.

An appearance of unanimity was given although, strictly speaking, it was the unanimity of "the States present," not the unanimity of all delegates present. Nor was it the unanimity of all the States that had been present at one time or another that summer. Although New York's delegation had not been voting for some weeks, because only Alexander Hamilton was present, the arrangement resorted to did permit Hamilton to sign as a witness under the name of New York. The general impression might even have been left, perhaps inadvertently, that the New York delegation too had agreed to the Constitution.

It seems to have been recognized in 1787 that it mattered immediately, for the fate of the Constitution, whose names were attached to it in whatever capacity. Once the Constitution had been ratified and had proved successful, however, the name of the Constitution itself came to be more esteemed than the names of most of the delegates who had signed it, names that have since become fairly obscure for the most part.

Or, as James Madison put it in the Federal Convention on July 5, 1787:

> It should be considered that altho' at first many may judge of the system recommended by their opinion of the Convention, yet finally all will judge of the Convention by the System.[144]

V

The delegates hoped that the apparent unanimity of the Federal Convention in proposing the Constitution would become the genuine unanimity of the States in ratifying it. The delegates knew that they would be likely to get all of the States to ratify only if it was understood that not all of the States were necessary to the validity of the Constitution. Holdouts could not expect to thwart implementation.

Whether nine States could suffice for an effective establishment of the Constitution depended, in part, upon which nine States these were. There would have remained the ticklish problem of what the relations should be between the States that had ratified and the States that had not.

Conceivably, accommodations might have been reached whereby all thirteen States remained associated with one another pursuant to the Articles of Confederation, while, at the same time, that association had a special relation with the General Government for nine or more States under the Constitution of 1787. No doubt, this would have been irregular, but then, as we have seen, the Continental and Confederation Congresses had themselves been somewhat irregular for almost a decade.

Furthermore, Americans have long been accustomed to living under more than one "sovereign" constitution at a time. This may be seen down to our day in the way that the United States and the State Constitutions are concurrently relied upon by us.

It was evidently believed by the Framers of the Constitution of 1787 that the less said in advance about the problem of the nonratifying States, the better. Another problem that was too sensitive to deal with explicitly in the Federal Convention was whether a State could ever leave the Union on its own once the Constitution of 1787 had been ratified.

An often practical approach to complex affairs is suggested by the reminder, "Sufficient unto the day is the evil thereof."[145] This is something the Framers were no doubt aware of, even though they themselves were not likely to make explicit use of the Bible in their deliberations.

VI

Only here and there in the Constitution of 1787 do we get glimpses of the religious sentiments of the American people in 1787. I discussed in my last lecture the prevailing reliance upon oaths and the concern about religious tests.

Consider the exception of Sundays from the computation of the ten days that the President has to review a bill passed by Congress. Also, recall again how the mode of dating the Constitution draws upon both the "universal," that is, Christian, calendar and the particular American calendar, keyed to the Declaration of Independence: "the Seventeenth Day of September in the Year of our Lord one thousand seven hundred and Eighty seven and of the Independence of the United States the Twelfth." Both the spiritual order and the temporal order are looked to for placing properly the doings of the Federal Convention, however ambiguous might have been the response in that Convention, at a critical moment, to Benjamin Franklin's suggestion that each meeting thenceforth be opened with a prayer.[146]

I suggested in Lectures No. 1 and No. 2 that there is recourse in the Declaration of Independence to a natural constitutionalism. Such recourse would take due account, for an enduring political order, of both the sacred and the profane in ministering to human affairs.

Something of a reliance upon the sacred may even be seen in the status assigned among us, for two centuries now, to the Framers at Philadelphia. Consider, for example, the prophetic note upon which the Federal Convention is reported by Madison to have ended:

> Whilst the last members were signing [the Constitution], Doctor Franklin looking towards the Presidents Chair, at the back of which a rising sun happened to be painted, observed to a few members near him, that Painters had found it difficult to distinguish in their art a rising from a setting sun. I have, said he, often and often in the course of the Session [of the Convention], and the vicissitudes of my hopes and fears as to its issue, looked at [the sun] behind the President without being able to tell whether it was rising or setting. But now at length I have the happiness to know that it is a rising and not a setting Sun.[147]

VII

We make much more, in our celebrations of the Constitution, of the year it was made by its Framers than we do of the date it was ratified by the States. Are we not right to do so? The decisive step seems to have been the work done at Philadelphia in 1787, not what happened to have been done later in the various State Ratification Conventions.

One can see the mind of the American people superbly at work in the Federal Convention. Statesmen as diverse as John C. Calhoun and Abraham Lincoln could agree that the Framers of the Constitution were exceptionally wise and good.[148]

It must be a rare student of the Constitution of 1787 who does not come away from it impressed by its efficiency. Consider how Calhoun could, in 1831, sum up, albeit with a States' Rights emphasis, the majestic symmetry of the document:

> The majority of the States elect the majority of the Senate; [the majority] of the people of the States [elect the majority] of the House of Representatives; the two united [elect] the President; and the President and a majority of the Senate appoint the judges: a majority of whom, and a majority of the Senate and the House, with the President, really exercise all the powers of the Government, with the exception of the cases where the Constitution requires a greater number than a majority.[149]

Another student a century and a quarter later could say of the "coordinated electorates" upon which our form of government relies,

> The advantages of both Union and popular control are assured, or at least made more likely to be enjoyed, by an arrangement whereby those best equipped to select the men to fill each post under the Constitution are given the power to make such selections. Those best equipped are presumed to be those who are most likely to know the candidates best: the original Constitution provides, that is, for the coordination of the decisions of relatively small "electorates." Thus, the State legislatures (made up of members chosen in small legislative districts in each State) select the Senators; the members of the House of Representatives are chosen, in effect, by electoral districts within the States (even when the voting is at large rather than, as is now common, by Congressional districts); the President is chosen by a body of electors (whom we call the Electoral College: they are chosen as the State legislatures prescribe); the other officers of the General Government, including the judges, are nominated by the President and consented to by the Senate or are selected by the President alone or by one of his lieutenants [or by the courts].

> The largest "electorate" under the Constitution of 1787—the largest body of men who have to pass on the qualifications of "candidates" for any office in the General Government—is likely to be that of the Congressional district. The "candidate" can be known, and known well, by those who must select him: one is never obliged to choose among complete strangers. The people retain ultimate control—but they are a people so organized as to bring out the best in them.[150]

I have suggested that it is in the Declaration of Independence and the Constitution of 1787 that we can see the mind of the American people truly at work. I further suggest that it is in the Constitution itself that we can see master draftsmanship at work, just as statesmanship of the highest order can be seen in the Declaration.

We have already observed that the sequence of and within the seven articles in the Constitution makes considerable sense. It is *not* the order in which Constitutional provisions were worked on or adopted in the Federal Convention. That is, these provisions had to be arranged by someone with a comprehensive view of the implications of the things that had been said and done by the Convention. This means that one does not fully understand the Constitution unless one understands why the parts are what and where they are.

I have attempted to explain how the Constitution is put together and why it is made the way it is. We should be reminded of the Gladstonian observation to the effect that the British Constitution excelled all those that have emerged from the womb of time, whereas the American Constitution is the most outstanding of those constitutions brought forth at a given moment out of the mind of man.[151]

17. The Americans of the Constitution

I

The Federal Convention of 1787 sent to the Confederation Congress, over the name of George Washington, its presiding officer, a September 17th letter of transmittal accompanying the proposed Constitution. The letter includes this instructive summary of the powers provided for by the Constitution:

> The friends of our country have long seen and desired, that the power of making war, peace and treaties, that of levying money and regulating commerce, and the correspondent executive and judicial authorities should be fully and effectually vested in the general government of the Union: but the impropriety of delegating such extensive trust to one body of men is evident—Hence results the necessity of a different organization.[152]

The next stage in the development of this Constitution was its transmittal by Congress to the States for them to ratify. It was then that Congress adopted the recommendation of the Federal Convention that each State call a convention to pass upon the proposed Constitution. Almost all of the States proceeded to do this.

The extended debates in various of the State Ratification Conventions remain a useful source for any investigation into the meaning of the Constitution, however partisan and hence distorted those debates often might have been. Much the same can be said about the public debates of the day, especially as recorded in the highly polemical press. (Among such public debates are the contributions made by the *Federalist Papers* issued in the New York State ratification contest.) In the final analysis, however, a sound interpretation of the Constitution depends primarily upon a

225

careful reading of the document itself, to which this Commentary has been devoted.

Nine States had been designated in Article VII as required "for the Establishment of this Constitution between the States so ratifying the Same." The first State to ratify was Delaware, on December 7, 1787, less than three months after the drafting of the Constitution was completed; the ninth State to ratify was New Hampshire, on June 21, 1788, less than a year after the Constitution was drafted. Technically, the Constitution was then "established" or "adopted." Congress could properly begin providing for a transition once it learned that the ninth State had signed on. It was always recognized, however, that New York and Virginia would have to agree to the Constitution for it to stand a good chance of success, and these two States were not among the first nine.

It was only when Virginia and New York ratified, in the summer of 1788, that the Constitution could truly be considered a going concern. North Carolina and Rhode Island were to hold out until November 1789 and May 1790, respectively—the former until a Bill of Rights was proposed by the First Congress for the Constitution of 1787, the latter until it became all too evident that things were going to go on without her.[153]

II

The Confederation Congress, once it found that the Constitution had been sufficiently ratified, guided the State governments in what had to be done to select Members of Congress and Presidential electors. The new Congress assembled in March 1789 pursuant to the directions of the new Constitution and of the old Congress. The First Congress then determined who had been chosen President by electors in the States. George Washington was inaugurated on April 30, 1789.

The First Congress had to sketch out the new General Government. It provided for several Executive departments and for the National Courts. Appropriate nominations to these offices were made by the President and confirmed by the Senate. The Judiciary Act of 1789 has been vital to the operations of the Courts down to our time. (The first term of the Supreme Court began on February 2, 1790.)

Congress was also obliged to begin reviewing the laws enacted by its predecessor under the Articles of Confederation to determine which of those laws should be retained. Among them, as we have seen, was the Northwest Ordinance, which had been enacted in 1787 and which the First Congress reaffirmed in its First Session, thereby confirming the pattern for developing new States from the Territories. (That reaffirmation is found in Appendix D.)

And, of course, the First Congress had to finance the activities of the General Government. Particularly important in those early years were import taxes, some of which were provided for in the First Session of Congress in 1789.

III

It was in the First Session of the First Congress as well that the Bill of Rights was prepared. Twelve amendments were proposed by Congress in 1789; ten of these were ratified by the States, with Virginia's ratifications on December 15, 1791, completing the three-fourths of the States required for amendments. (Here the ratification date seems more significant than the date of composition.)

Amendments Two through Eight set forth, for the most part, guarantees that had long been considered parts of the great common-law heritage of the American people. And, as I have suggested from time to time, the First Amendment, especially with its assurances about freedom of speech and of the press, confirmed the understanding of Americans as to what was required for effective self-governance by a people. The Ninth Amendment was added out of caution, to make certain that the enumeration of certain rights did not implicitly relinquish others that had been claimed previously.

The prompt addition of the Bill of Rights is considered by many to have been a condition for ratification of the Constitution in several States. It can properly be regarded as virtually a part of the original Constitution, and hence as perfectly consistent with what had been done in the Federal Convention of 1787. The Eleventh and Twelfth Amendments, we have seen, can also be considered part of the original arrangement, in that they clarified what had been attempted in the judicial-power and Presidential-selection provisions of the Confederation.

It is well to be reminded once again, especially in a skeptical age, that recourse to amendments—indeed, the very recognition that amendments would be necessary from time to time—reflects an awareness that there are enduring standards in the light of which the Constitution, as well as the laws, of the day should be judged. The Constitution assumes and reinforces established moral and political principles, thereby shaping generations of Americans under the new dispensation.

IV

The Framers of the Constitution, I have suggested, were both principled and practical. This means, among other things, that they were not doctrinaire, and hence they could be truly virtuous.

Perhaps the most talented man in the history of the Country to devote himself to a political doctrine, at the expense of that combination of principle and practicality that we recognize as prudence, was John C. Calhoun of South Carolina. He died in 1850 on the eve of the Civil War that his doctrinaire approach to politics and to the Constitution helped bring on.

Calhoun sought a political proposition that would be "universally true,—one which springs directly from the nature of man, and is independent of circumstances."[154] He could never properly appreciate, for example, the significance of the fact that African slavery in this Country was due to unfortunate circumstances in which there was unleashed an indefensible self-interest. Rather, he was driven to insist that that institution, due to permanent significant varieties in the nature of men, represented a positive good for both slave and master. It was the slavery issue, and what the South could do to protect its "peculiar institution" from dangerous Northern interference, that guided Calhoun's reading of the Constitution, going back to the great tariff debates in the late 1820s and the 1830s.

Calhoun's reading of the Tenth Amendment was essential to his approach.[155] He repeatedly reads it as though it provides that Congress has only those powers expressly delegated to it. We again recall that the House of Representatives, when the First Congress drafted in 1789 what later became the Tenth Amendment, resolutely refused to add *expressly* to the proposed amendment, and in doing so, it refused to continue to use that limiting adverb as it had been used in the Articles of Confederation.[156]

The Federalists, as we have noted, controlled the First Congress and had, for the most part, written the Constitution in the Federal Convention only two years before. Their answer to those who wanted *expressly* added to the Tenth Amendment was, in effect, "No, the Ratification Campaign is over. The American people have established the Constitution drafted by the Federal Convention. And we intend to keep, and to put to good use, the Constitution with which Providence has blessed us." The repeated Calhounian efforts, down to our day, to read *expressly* into the Tenth Amendment dramatize the significance of the original determination of the Federalists to keep it out.

V

I am not the first to have noticed that the Tenth Amendment in effect says, at least with respect to the powers of the General Government, that the Constitution provides what it provides. It makes no change, therefore, in the distribution of powers recognized in the Constitution of 1787. Thus, it can be said, the Tenth Amendment really makes no difference in this respect.

I now venture to add that what the Tenth Amendment did do was to permit the State Legislatures, as distinguished from the State Conventions relied upon during the Ratification Campaign, to make explicit their assent to the Constitution of 1787. All of the original thirteen States have ratified this amendment, albeit three of them, ceremonially, in 1939, which can be taken to mean that the Constitution of 1787 may be seen as a comprehensive alteration of the Articles of Confederation even pursuant to the precise provision in the Articles themselves for their alteration by State Legislatures.

In any event, the Tenth Amendment confirms the original Constitutional arrangement, an arrangement in which the prominent place of the States must be forever recognized.

VI

"The question of the relation which the States and General Government bear to each other," Calhoun said in 1831, "is not one of recent origin. From the commencement of our system, it has divided public sentiment. Even in the Convention, while the Constitution was struggling into existence, there were two parties as to what this relation should be, whose different sentiments constituted no small impediment in forming that instrument."[157]

Calhoun's mode of answering his question about the relation of the States and the General Government included this suggestion:

> The great and leading principle is, that the General Government emanated from the people of the several States, forming distinct political communities, and acting in their separate and sovereign capacity, and not from all of the people forming one aggregate political community; that the Constitution of the United States is, in fact, a compact, to which each State is a party, in the character already described; and that the several States, or parties, have a right to judge of its infractions.[158]

Three years before, Calhoun had insisted that our system "consists of two distinct and independent Governments."[159] And so he could rely upon James Madison (the Madison of 1798, not the Madison of 1787–1789): "The Constitution of the United States was formed by the sanction of the States, given by each in its sovereign capacity."[160] Calhoun saw the General Government as nothing but the creature of the compact that the States had formed in 1787–1789.[161]

Abraham Lincoln was to insist, as we have seen, that the Union was older than the States.[162] Of course, a proper place was recognized by him for the States, just as Calhoun had recognized a proper place for the General Government. Lincoln made much more than Calhoun did, however, of the fact that the Preamble to the Constitution had announced that "We the People" were ordaining and establishing the Constitution.[163]

So Lincoln could speak, as at Gettysburg, of the fathers who had brought forth a new nation, not a mere compact, in 1776. I have noted that to speak thus of *fathers* is to look to a people who form a natural whole, not to those somewhat arbitrary subdivisions of a people known as States. The Civil War and its aftermath provided a decisive affirmation of the fundamental unity of the Americans as one people.

Lincoln knew that the States retained considerable authority under the Constitution, including the exclusive power of ratifying amendments to the Constitution. In fact, as we have also seen, the States can always insist upon an Article V Convention for proposing Constitutional amendments, thereby circumventing any Congressional reluctance to do so.

VII

Calhoun's fundamental problem was such, however, that the ultimate power of amending the Constitution available to any combination of three-fourths of the States could neither quiet his fears nor satisfy his desires. He knew that his cause could not enlist the support of even a majority of the States, or of the Congress, to say nothing of the supermajorities required for Constitutional amendments. A steady shift away from the South in population ratios, and hence in political power in the General Government, had become all too apparent by his time.

This development probably led Calhoun to insist that a State should be able to "interpose" itself between the General Government and the people of a State when vital interests of that people were threatened. The venerable Madison could be looked to as an authority here, since he had said in the Virginia Resolutions of 1798 that "in case of a deliberate, palpable, and dangerous exercise [by the General Government] of power not delegated [to it], [the States affected] have the right . . . 'to interpose [themselves] for arresting the progress of the evil, and for maintaining, within their respective limits, the authorities, rights, and liberties appertaining to them.'"[164] Only thus, it was argued, may the consolidating tendencies of the General Government be arrested in extreme circumstances.[165]

Calhoun recognized, of course, that no State power of interposition is explicitly provided for in the Constitution of 1787. In response to any objection that such a power of interposition "rests on mere inference," Calhoun would ask "whether the power of the Supreme Court to declare a law unconstitutional is not among the very highest and most important that can be exercised by any department of the Government,—and [yet can] any express provision . . . be found to justify its exercise?"[166]

Calhoun argued that the Supreme Court's power of judicial review and the States' power of interposition both rest upon inferences so clear "that no express provision could render [them] more certain."[167] We need not reconsider here the basis, if any, for the power of judicial review in the Constitution of 1787. We need only notice that it, like Calhoun's power of State interposition, can appeal to minorities as a check upon effective self-government by the people of the United States, especially when the people at large act through their Congress.

Calhoun's approach meant that any States that felt strongly about any issue could always exercise an effective veto against the judgment of a majority of the people of the Country. However tyrannical any majority rule may be at times, is there any justification for what would be, in effect, permanent minority rule? We are reminded of the perils of minority rule when we notice that Calhoun's demands are made ultimately in behalf of individual slaveholders who insisted upon their right to continue undisturbed in their enslavement of multitudes of their fellow humans. Calhoun himself repudiates, by implication, the very institutions he so desperately attempts to defend when he repeatedly condemns as *slavery* the effects upon certain States of the powers claimed and exercised by the General Government.

VIII

The immediate causes of Calhoun's agitation in 1828–1831 were the tariff laws enacted by Congress, laws that were no longer designed primarily for the collection of revenues but rather for the protection of American manufactures. The South, not without reason, criticized such an arrangement as benefiting the manufacturing interests, mostly in the North, at the expense of the staples-producing States, mostly in the South. The question whether the powers granted Congress may ever be used primarily for any purposes other than those naturally associated with such powers still divides students of the Constitution.[168]

We should be reminded by such debates that the Constitution simply cannot guarantee that its powers will always be exercised justly. Considerable discretion must be left with the public servants who, subject to our discipline, exercise these powers for us, and it is to misconceive the nature of a constitution to expect all troublesome questions about justice to be answered there. Such an expectation is likely to distort the provisions of the Constitution, thereby making it less useful, and ultimately less productive of justice, than it might otherwise be. This is not to deny that an informed and disciplined respect for the Constitution should generally serve the ends of government set forth in the Preamble, including the establishment of justice.

There did remain one remedy for Calhoun to consider once arguments from justice and common sense had been rejected—and that was recourse to that right of revolution recognized in, and acted upon by, the Declaration of Independence. Was that right tacitly invoked when extraordinary means were used, however discreetly, to replace the Articles of Confederation by the Constitution of 1787?[169]

IX

The Union efforts in the Civil War were a response to a purported exercise by the South of the natural right of revolution. The ultimate result of this attempt was even more revolutionary than the South anticipated, for not only was the right of secession by any State forcibly repudiated, but also the existence of slavery in the United States was permanently forbidden. And as further results, the prerogatives of the States in the Union have had to be reconsidered, not only as the Civil War amendments have come to be applied but also as still more amendments (guaranteeing the rights of women, of the young, and of others) have been added to the Constitution. (These developments are in marked contrast to the 1861 "States' Rights" offer, recorded in Appendix L, that was made to the South as part of a desperate Unionist effort to head off secession.)

Precisely what the effects have been of the dozen most recent amendments to the Constitution must be left by us to consider at length on another occasion. It suffices to notice here that the American respect for both liberty and equality, as well as for a sensible and known rule of law, is reflected in the Constitutional amendments we now have.

We are reminded by these amendments that everything the Framers did is truly open to reconsideration. We the People are always in principle their equals, and hence we are always left free to change what was ordained and established two centuries ago.

But we, like the Framers, should be sensible enough to treasure and to use properly what has gone before, respecting the tested wisdom of predecessors who are our peers, not least in the prudent manner in which they, sometimes in the name of equality, exercised their and our liberty.

APPENDIXES AND SOURCES

The documents reproduced in these appendixes are taken immediately from the sources indicated. The ultimate sources of the major documents are also indicated. There are a few departures here, from the sources drawn upon, in the use of headings, indentations, line placements, capitalizations of entire words, and italics. Notes are added to the documents in Appendixes A, C, D, E, I, J, and M. Punctuation, spelling, and other details can vary from one source of a document to another.

A. The Declaration of Independence (1776)

This is based upon the copy in *The Declaration of Independence and the Constitution of the United States*, 96th Congress, 1st Session, House Document No. 96–143 (Washington, D.C.: Government Printing Office, 1979). That version of the Declaration of Independence was reprinted in accord with the text and typographical style of the original printed by John Dunlap at Philadelphia for the Continental Congress. A note is added that sets forth, from the same source, a resolution in the Continental Congress proposing a declaration of independence, June 7, 1776.

B. The Articles of Confederation and Perpetual Union (1776–1781)

This is based upon the copy in *Documents Illustrative of the Formation of the Union of the American States*, 69th Congress, 1st Session, House Document No. 398 (Washington, D.C.: Government Printing Office, 1927). That version of the Articles of Confederation was taken from the original roll in the Bureau of Rolls and Library, Department of State. The Articles of Confederation were written by a committee of the Continental Congress in 1776 and agreed to by the Congress on November 15, 1777. They were, as appears from the list of signatures affixed to these Articles, signed at different times by the delegates of the various States, with ratification completed in 1781.

C. Congressional Resolution Calling the Federal Convention (1787)

This is based upon the copy in *Documents Illustrative of the Formation of the Union of the American States* (see Item B, above). A note is added that includes a passage from the Report of the Annapolis Convention, September 14, 1786. This passage is taken from the same source as the Congressional resolution.

D. The Northwest Ordinance (1787)

This is based upon the copy in *The Northwest Ordinance 1787: A Bicentennial Handbook* (Indianapolis: Indiana Historical Society, 1787) (insert). That version of the Northwest Ordinance is a facsimile of a document in the National Archives. The bracketed section headings are added here from another version of the Northwest Ordinance. A note is added that sets forth the 1789 Act of Congress reenacting the Northwest Ordinance. This act is taken from the *Public Acts of Congress* (as published in the *Annals of Congress* [Washington: Gales and Seaton, 1834]).

E. The United States Constitution (1787)

This is based upon the copy in *Documents Illustrative of the Formation of the Union of the American States* (see Item B, above). That version was taken from the engrossed Constitution, in four sheets, as signed by the delegates to the Federal Convention. A few minor changes have been made in light of the version of the Constitution reprinted in William W. Crosskey, *Politics and the Constitution in the History of the United States* (Chicago: University of Chicago Press, 1953).

F. Chart for Article I, Section 8 (Lecture No. 5)

This is based upon the version of the United States Constitution reprinted in Appendix E, above.

G. Resolutions of the Federal Convention Providing for Transmittal of the Proposed Constitution to the Confederation Congress (1787)

These are based upon the copy in *The Declaration of Independence and the Constitution of the United States* (see Item A, above).

H. Letter Transmitting the Proposed Constitution from the Federal Convention to the Confederation Congress (1787)

This is based upon the copy in *The Declaration of Independence and the Constitution of the United States* (see Item A, above).

I. Congressional Resolution Transmitting the Proposed Constitution to the States (1787)

This is based upon the copy in *Documents Illustrative of the Formation of the Union of the American States* (see Item B, above). A note is added that sets forth from the same source the circular letter, of September 28, 1787, sent by the Secretary of the Congress to the Governors of the States.

J. Congressional Act for Putting the Constitution into Operation (1788)

This is based upon the copy in *The Declaration of Independence and the Constitution of the United States* (see Item A, above). Included here is an editorial note from the same source recording the State ratifications of the proposed United States Constitution.

K. Amendments to the Constitution of the United States (1791–1971)

These are based upon the copies in *The Declaration of Independence and the Constitution of the United States* (see Item A, above).

L. Proposed Amendments to the Constitution Not Ratified by the States (1789–1978)

These are based upon the copies in *The Declaration of Independence and the Constitution of the United States* (see Item A, above).

M. The Gettysburg Address (1863)

This is based upon the copy in *The Collected Works of Abraham Lincoln* (New Brunswick, N. J.: Rutgers University Press, 1953). That version of the Gettysburg Address was taken from an Autograph Copy signed by Abraham Lincoln, a copy known as the "Bliss Copy." Included here, in a note, is President Lincoln's Second Inaugural Address as set forth in *The Collected Works of Abraham Lincoln.*

A. The Declaration of Independence (1776)

In Congress, July 4, 1776.
A DECLARATION
By the REPRESENTATIVES of the
UNITED STATES OF AMERICA,
In GENERAL CONGRESS assembled.

When in the Course of human Events, it becomes necessary for one People to dissolve the Political Bands which have connected them with another, and to assume among the Powers of the Earth, the separate and equal Station to which the Laws of Nature and of Nature's God entitle them, a decent Respect to the Opinions of Mankind requires that they should declare the causes which impel them to the Separation.

We hold these Truths to be self-evident, that all Men are created equal, that they are endowed by their Creator with certain unalienable Rights, that among these are Life, Liberty, and the Pursuit of Happiness—That to secure these Rights, Governments are instituted among Men, deriving their just Powers from the Consent of the Governed, that whenever any Form of Government becomes destructive of these Ends, it is the Right of the People to alter or to abolish it, and to institute new Government, laying its Foundation on such Principles, and organizing its Powers in such Form, as to them shall seem most likely to effect their Safety and Happiness. Prudence, indeed, will dictate that Governments long established should not be changed for light and transient Causes; and accordingly all Experience hath shewn, that Mankind are more disposed to suffer, while Evils are sufferable, than to right themselves by abolishing the Forms to which they are accustomed. But when a long Train of Abuses and Usurpations, pursuing invariably the same Object, evinces a Design to reduce them under absolute Despotism, it is their Right, it is their Duty, to throw off such Government, and to provide new Guards for their future Security. Such has been the patient Sufferance of these Colonies; and such is now the Necessity which constrains them to alter their former Systems of Government. The History of the present King of Great-Britain is a History of repeated Injuries and Usurpations, all having in direct Object the Establishment of an absolute Tyranny over these States. To prove this, let Facts be submitted to a candid World:

He has refused his Assent to Laws, the most wholesome and necessary for the public Good.

He has forbidden his Governors to pass Laws of immediate and pressing Importance, unless suspended in their Operation till his Assent should be obtained; and when so suspended, he has utterly neglected to attend to them.

He has refused to pass other Laws for the Accommodation of large Districts of People, unless those People would relinquish the Right of Representation in the Legislature, a Right inestimable to them, and formidable to Tyrants only.

He has called together Legislative Bodies at Places unusual, uncomfortable, and distant from the Depository of their public Records, for the sole Purpose of fatiguing them into Compliance with his Measures.

He has dissolved Representative Houses repeatedly, for opposing with manly Firmness his Invasions on the Rights of the People.

He has refused for a long Time, after such Dissolutions, to cause others to be elected; whereby the Legislative Powers, incapable of Annihilation, have returned to the People at large for their exercise; the State remaining in the mean time exposed to all the Dangers of Invasion from without, and Convulsions within.

He has endeavoured to prevent the Population of these States; for that Purpose obstructing the Laws for Naturalization of Foreigners; refusing to pass others to encourage their Migrations hither, and raising the Conditions of new Appropriations of Lands.

He has obstructed the Administration of Justice, by refusing his Assent to Laws for establishing Judiciary Powers.

He has made Judges dependent on his Will alone, for the Tenure of their Offices, and the Amount and Payment of their Salaries.

He has erected a Multitude of new Offices, and sent hither Swarms of Officers to harass our People, and eat out their Substance.

He has kept among us, in Times of Peace, Standing Armies, without the consent of our Legislatures.

He has affected to render the Military independent of and superior to the Civil Power.

He has combined with others to subject us to a Jurisdiction foreign to our Constitution, and unacknowledged by our Laws; giving his Assent to their Acts of pretended Legislation:

For quartering large Bodies of Armed Troops among us:

For protecting them, by a mock Trial, from Punishment for any Murders which they should commit on the Inhabitants of these States:

For cutting off our Trade with all Parts of the World:

For imposing Taxes on us without our Consent:

For depriving us, in many Cases, of the Benefits of Trial by Jury:

For transporting us beyond Seas to be tried for pretended Offences:

For abolishing the free System of English Laws in a neighbouring Province, establishing therein an arbitrary Government, and enlarging its Boundaries, so as to render it at once an Example and fit Instrument for introducing the same absolute Rule into these Colonies:

For taking away our Charters, abolishing our most valuable Laws, and altering fundamentally the Forms of our Governments:

For suspending our own Legislatures, and declaring themselves invested with Power to legislate for us in all Cases whatsoever.

He has abdicated Government here, by declaring us out of his Protection and waging War against us.

He has plundered our Seas, ravaged our Coasts, burnt our Towns, and destroyed the Lives of our People.

He is, at this Time, transporting large Armies of foreign Mercenaries to compleat the Works of Death, Desolation, and Tyranny, already begun with circumstances of Cruelty and Perfidy, scarcely paralleled in the most barbarous Ages, and totally unworthy the Head of a civilized Nation.

He has constrained our fellow Citizens taken Captive on the high Seas to bear Arms against their Country, to become the Executioners of their Friends and Brethren, or to fall themselves by their Hands.

He has excited domestic Insurrections amongst us, and has endeavoured to bring on the Inhabitants of our Frontiers, the merciless Indian Savages, whose known Rule of Warfare, is an undistinguished Destruction, of all Ages, Sexes and Conditions.

In every stage of these Oppressions we have Petitioned for Redress in the most humble Terms: Our repeated Petitions have been answered only by repeated Injury. A Prince, whose Character is thus marked by every act which may define a Tyrant, is unfit to be the Ruler of a free People.

Nor have we been wanting in Attentions to our British Brethren. We have warned them from Time to Time of Attempts by their Legislature to extend an unwarrantable Jurisdiction over us. We have reminded them of the Circumstances of our Emigration and Settlement here. We have appealed to their native Justice and Magnanimity, and we have conjured them by the Ties of our common Kindred to disavow these Usurpations, which, would inevitably interrupt our Connections and Correspondence. They too have been deaf to the Voice of Justice and of Consanguinity. We must, therefore, acquiesce in the Necessity, which denounces our Separation, and hold them, as we hold the rest of Mankind, Enemies in War, in Peace, Friends.

We, therefore, the Representatives of the UNITED STATES OF AMERICA, in General Congress, Assembled, appealing to the Supreme Judge of the World for the Rectitude of our Intentions, do, in the Name, and by Authority of the good People of these Colonies, solemnly Publish and Declare, That these United Colonies are, and of Right ought to be, Free and Independent States; that they are absolved from all Allegiance to the British Crown, and that all political Connection between them and the State of Great-Britain, is and ought to be totally dissolved; and that as Free and Independent States, they have full Power to levy War, conclude Peace, contract Alliances, establish Commerce, and to do all other Acts and Things which Independent States may of right do. And for the support of this Declaration, with a firm Reliance on the

Protection of divine Providence, we mutually pledge to each other our Lives, our Fortunes, and our sacred Honor.

Signed by Order and in Behalf of the Congress,

JOHN HANCOCK, President.

New-Hampshire.
{ Josiah Bartlett,
Wm. Whipple,
Matthew Thornton.

Massachusetts-Bay.
{ Saml. Adams,
John Adams,
Robt. Treat Paine,
Elbridge Gerry.

Rhode-Island and Providence, &c.
{ Step. Hopkins,
William Ellery.

Connecticut.
{ Roger Sherman,
Saml. Huntington,
Wm. Williams,
Oliver Wolcott.

New-York.
{ Wm. Floyd,
Phil. Livingston,
Frans. Lewis,
Lewis Morris.

New-Jersey.
{ Richd. Stockton,
Jno. Witherspoon,
Fras. Hopkinson,
John Hart,
Abra. Clark.

Pennsylvania.
{ Robt. Morris,
Benjamin Rush,
Benja. Franklin,
John Morton,
Geo. Clymer,
Jas. Smith,
Geo. Taylor,
James Wilson,
Geo. Ross.

Delaware.	{ Caesar Rodney, Geo. Read, (Tho M:Kean.)
Maryland.	{ Samuel Chase, Wm. Paca, Thos. Stone, Charles Carroll, of Carrollton.
Virginia.	{ George Wythe, Richard Henry Lee, Ths. Jefferson, Benja. Harrison, Thos. Nelson, jr. Francis Lightfoot Lee, Carter Braxton.
North-Carolina.	{ Wm. Hooper, Joseph Hewes, John Penn.
South-Carolina.	{ Edward Rutledge, Thos. Heyward, junr. Thomas Lynch, junr. Arthur Middleton.
Georgia.	{ Button Gwinnett, Lyman Hall, Geo. Walton.*

Attest: Charles Thomson, Secretary.

*Richard Henry Lee, of Virginia, introduced in the Continental Congress, on June 7, 1776, this resolution proposing a declaration of independence and thereafter articles of confederation:

Resolved, That these United Colonies are, and of right ought to be, free and independent States, that they are absolved from all allegiance to the British Crown, and that all political connection between them and the State of Great Britain is, and ought to be, totally dissolved.

That it is expedient forthwith to take the most effectual measures for forming foreign Alliances.

That a plan of confederation be prepared and transmitted to the respective Colonies for their consideration and approbation.

B. The Articles of Confederation and Perpetual Union (1776–1781)

ARTICLES OF CONFEDERATION

To all to whom these Presents shall come, we the under signed Delegates of the States affixed to our Names, send greeting.

Whereas the Delegates of the United States of America, in Congress assembled, did, on the 15th day of November, in the Year of Our Lord One thousand Seven Hundred and Seventy seven, and in the Second Year of the Independence of America, agree to certain articles of Confederation and perpetual Union between the States of Newhampshire, Massachusetts-bay, Rhodeisland and Providence Plantations, Connecticut, New York, New Jersey, Pennsylvania, Delaware, Maryland, Virginia, North-Carolina, South-Carolina, and Georgia in the words following, viz. "Articles of Confederation and perpetual Union between the states of Newhampshire, Massachusetts-bay, Rhodeisland and Providence Plantations, Connecticut, New-York, New-Jersey, Pennsylvania, Delaware, Maryland, Virginia, North-Carolina, South-Carolina and Georgia.

Article I. The Stile of this confederacy shall be "The United States of America."

Article II. Each state retains its sovereignty, freedom, and independence, and every Power, Jurisdiction and right, which is not by this confederation expressly delegated to the United States, in Congress assembled.

Article III. The said states hereby severally enter into a firm league of friendship with each other, for their common defence, the security of their Liberties, and their mutual and general wel-

245

fare, binding themselves to assist each other, against all force of-fered to, or attacks made upon them, or any of them, on account of religion, sovereignty, trade, or any other pretence whatever.

Article IV. The better to secure and perpetuate mutual friend-ship and intercourse among the people of the different states in this union, the free inhabitants of each of these states, paupers, vaga-bonds and fugitives from justice excepted, shall be entitled to all privileges and immunities of free citizens in the several states; and the people of each state shall have free ingress and regress to and from any other state, and shall enjoy therein all the privileges of trade and commerce, subject to the same duties, impositions and restrictions as the inhabitants thereof respectively, provided that such restriction shall not extend so far as to prevent the removal of property imported into any state, to any other state, of which the Owner is an inhabitant; provided also that no imposition, duties or restriction shall be laid by any state, on the property of the united states, or either of them.

If any Person guilty of, or charged with treason, felony, or other high misdemeanor in any state, shall flee from Justice, and be found in any of the united states, he shall, upon demand of the Governor or executive power, of the state from which he fled, be delivered up and removed to the state having jurisdiction of his offence.

Full faith and credit shall be given in each of these states to the records, acts and judicial proceedings of the courts and magistrates of every other state.

Article V. For the more convenient management of the general interests of the united states, delegates shall be annually appointed in such manner as the legislature of each state shall direct, to meet in Congress on the first Monday in November, in every year, with a power reserved to each state, to recal its delegates, or any of them, at any time within the year, and to send others in their stead, for the remainder of the Year.

No state shall be represented in Congress by less than two, nor by more than seven Members; and no person shall be capable of being a delegate for more than three years in any term of six years; nor shall any person, being a delegate, be capable of holding any office under the united states, for which he, or another for his ben-efit receives any salary, fees or emolument of any kind.

Each state shall maintain its own delegates in a meeting of the states, and while they act as members of the committee of the states.

In determining questions in the united states in Congress assembled, each state shall have one vote.

Freedom of speech and debate in Congress shall not be impeached or questioned in any Court, or place out of Congress, and the members of congress shall be protected in their persons from arrests and imprisonments, during the time of their going to and from, and attendance on congress, except for treason, felony, or breach of the peace.

Article VI. No state, without the Consent of the united states in congress assembled, shall send any embassy to, or receive any embassy from, or enter into any conference, agreement, alliance or treaty with any King prince or state; nor shall any person holding any office of profit or trust under the united states, or any of them, accept of any present, emolument, office or title of any kind whatever from any king, prince or foreign state; nor shall the united states in congress assembled, or any of them, grant any title of nobility.

No two or more states shall enter into any treaty, confederation or alliance whatever between them, without the consent of the united states in congress assembled, specifying accurately the purposes for which the same is to be entered into, and how long it shall continue.

No state shall lay any imposts or duties, which may interfere with any stipulations in treaties, entered into by the united states in congress assembled, with any king, prince or state, in pursuance of any treaties already proposed by congress, to the courts of France and Spain.

No vessels of war shall be kept up in time of peace by any state, except such number only, as shall be deemed necessary by the united states in congress assembled, for the defence of such state, or its trade; nor shall any body of forces be kept up by any state, in time of peace, except such number only, as in the judgment of the united states, in congress assembled, shall be deemed requisite to garrison the forts necessary for the defence of such state; but every state shall always keep up a well regulated and disciplined militia, sufficiently armed and accoutred, and shall provide and constantly have ready for use, in public stores, a due number of field pieces and tents, and a proper quantity of arms, ammunition and camp equipage.

No state shall engage in any war without the consent of the united states in congress assembled, unless such state be actually invaded by enemies, or shall have received certain advice of a resolution being formed by some nation of Indians to invade such state, and the danger is so imminent as not to admit of a delay till the united states in congress assembled can be consulted: nor shall any state grant commissions to any ships or vessels of war, nor letters of marque or reprisal, except it be after a declaration of war by the united states in congress assembled, and then only against the kingdom or state and the subjects thereof, against which war has been so declared, and under such regulations as shall be established by the united states in congress assembled, unless such state be infested by pirates, in which case vessels of war may be fitted out for that occasion, and kept so long as the danger shall continue, or until the united states in congress assembled, shall determine otherwise.

Article VII. When land-forces are raised by any state for the common defence, all officers of or under the rank of colonel, shall be appointed by the legislature of each state respectively, by whom such forces shall be raised, or in such manner as such state shall direct, and all vacancies shall be filled up by the State which first made the appointment.

Article VIII. All charges of war, and all other expences that shall be incurred for the common defence or general welfare, and allowed by the united states in congress assembled, shall be defrayed out of a common treasury, which shall be supplied by the several states in proportion to the value of all land within each state, granted to or surveyed for any Person, as such land and the buildings and improvements thereon shall be estimated according to such mode as the united states in congress assembled, shall from time to time direct and appoint.

The taxes for paying that proportion shall be laid and levied by the authority and direction of the legislatures of the several states within the time agreed upon by the united states in congress assembled.

Article IX. The united states in congress assembled, shall have the sole and exclusive right and power of determining on peace and war, except in the cases mentioned in the sixth article—of sending and receiving ambassadors—entering into treaties and alliances, provided that no treaty of commerce shall be made whereby the legislative power of the respective states shall be restrained from imposing such imposts and duties on foreigners as their own people are subjected to, or from prohibiting the exportation or importation of any species of goods or commodities, whatsoever—of establishing rules for deciding in all cases, what captures on land or water shall be legal, and in what manner prizes taken by land or naval forces in the service of the united states shall be divided or appropriated—of granting letters of marque and reprisal in times of peace—appointing courts for the trial of piracies and felonies committed on the high seas and establishing courts for receiving and determining finally appeals in all cases of captures, provided that no member of congress shall be appointed a judge of any of the said courts.

The united states in congress assembled shall also be the last resort on appeal in all disputes and differences now subsisting or that hereafter may arise between two or more states concerning boundary, jurisdiction or any other cause whatever; which authority shall always be exercised in the manner following. Whenever the legislative or executive authority or lawful agent of any state in controversy with another shall present a petition to congress stating the matter in question and praying for a hearing, notice thereof shall be given by order of congress to the legislative or executive authority of the other state in controversy, and a day assigned for the appearance of the parties by their lawful agents, who shall then be directed to appoint by joint consent, commissioners or judges to constitute a court for hearing and determining the matter in question: but if they cannot agree, congress shall name three persons out of each of the united states, and from the list of such persons each party shall alternately strike out one, the petitioners beginning, until the number shall be reduced to thirteen; and from that number not less than seven, nor more than nine names as congress shall direct, shall in the presence of congress be drawn out by lot, and the persons whose names shall be so drawn or any five of them, shall be commissioners or judges, to hear and finally determine the controversy, so always as a major part of the judges who shall hear the cause shall agree in the determination: and if either party shall neglect to attend at the day appointed, without showing reasons, which congress shall judge sufficient, or being present shall refuse to strike, the congress shall proceed to nominate three persons out of each state, and the secretary of congress shall strike in behalf of such party absent or refusing; and the judgment and sentence of the court to be appointed, in the manner before prescribed, shall be final and conclusive; and if any of the parties shall refuse to submit to the authority of such court, or to appear or defend their claim or cause, the court shall nevertheless proceed to pronounce sentence, or judgment, which shall in like manner be final and decisive, the judgment or sentence and other proceedings being in either case transmitted to congress, and lodged among the acts of congress for the security of the parties concerned: provided that every commissioner, before he sits in judgment, shall take an oath to be administered by one of the judges of the supreme or superior court of the state, where the cause shall be tried, "well and truly to hear and determine the matter in question, according to the best of his judgment, without favour, affection or hope of reward:" provided also, that no state shall be deprived of territory for the benefit of the united states.

All controversies concerning the private right of soil claimed under different grants of two or more states, whose jurisdictions as they may respect such lands, and the states which passed such grants are adjusted, the said grants or either of them being at the same time claimed to have originated antecedent to such settlement of jurisdiction, shall on the petition of either party to the congress of the united states, be finally determined as near as may be in the same manner as is before prescribed for deciding disputes respecting territorial jurisdiction between different states.

The united states in congress assembled shall also have the sole and exclusive right and power of regulating the alloy and value of coin struck by their own authority, or by that of the respective states—fixing the standard of weights and measures throughout the united states—regulating the trade and managing all affairs with the Indians, not members of any of the states, provided that the legislative right of any state within its own limits be not infringed or violated—establishing or regulating post-offices from one state to another, throughout all the united states, and exacting such postage on the papers passing thro' the same as may be requisite to defray the expences of the said office—appointing all officers of the land forces, in the service of the united states, excepting regimental officers—appointing all the officers of the naval forces, and commissioning all officers whatever in the service of the united states—making rules for the government and regulation of the said land and naval forces, and directing their operations.

The united states in congress assembled shall have authority to appoint a committee, to sit in the recess of congress, to be denominated "A Committee of the States," and to consist of one delegate from each state; and to appoint such other committees and civil officers as may be necessary for managing the general affairs of the united states under their direction—to appoint one of their number to preside, provided that no person be allowed to serve in the office of president more than one year in any term of three years; to ascertain the necessary sums of money to be raised for the service of the united states, and to appropriate and apply the same for defraying the public expences—to borrow money, or emit bills on the credit of the united states, transmitting every half year to the respective states an account of the sums of money so borrowed or emitted, —to build and equip a navy—to agree upon the number of land forces, and to make requisitions from each state for its quota, in proportion to the number of white inhabitants in such state; which requisition shall be binding, and thereupon the legislature of each state shall appoint the regimental officers, raise the men and cloath, arm and equip them in a soldier like manner, at the expence of the united states; and the officers and men so cloathed, armed and equipped shall march to the place appointed, and within the time agreed on by the united states in congress assembled: But if the united states in congress assembled shall, on consideration of circumstances judge proper that any state should not raise men, or should raise a smaller number than its quota, and that any other state should raise a greater number of men than the quota thereof, such extra number shall be raised, officered, cloathed, armed and equipped in the same manner as the quota of such state, unless the legislature of such state shall judge that such extra number cannot be safely spared out of the same, in which case they shall raise, officer, cloath, arm and equip as many of such extra number as they judge can be safely spared. And the officers and men so cloathed, armed and equipped, shall march to the place appointed, and within the time agreed on by the united states in congress assembled.

The united states in congress assembled shall never engage in a war, nor grant letters of marque and reprisal in time of peace, nor enter into any treaties or alliances, nor coin money, nor regulate the value thereof, nor ascertain the sums and expences necessary for the defence and welfare of the united states, or any of them, nor emit bills, nor borrow money on the credit of the united states, nor appropriate money, nor agree upon the number of vessels of war, to be built or purchased, or the number of land or sea forces to be raised, nor appoint a commander in chief of the army or navy, unless nine states assent to the same: nor shall a question on any other point, except for adjourning from day to day be determined, unless by the votes of a majority of the united states in congress assembled.

The congress of the united states shall have power to adjourn to any time within the year, and to any place within the united states, so that no period of adjournment be for a longer duration than the space of six Months, and shall publish the Journal of their proceedings monthly, except such parts thereof relating to treaties, alliances or military operations, as in their judgment require secrecy; and the yeas and nays of the delegates of each state on any question shall be entered on the Journal, when it is desired by any delegate; and the delegates of a state, or any of them, at his or their request shall be furnished with a transcript of the said Journal, except such parts as are above excepted, to lay before the legislatures of the several states.

Article X. The committee of the states, or any nine of them, shall be authorized to execute, in the recess of congress, such of the powers of congress as the united states in congress assembled, by the consent of nine states, shall from time to time think expedient to vest them with; provided that no power be delegated to the said committee, for the exercise of which, by the articles of confederation, the voice of nine states in the congress of the united states assembled is requisite.

Article XI. Canada acceding to this confederation, and joining in the measures of the united states, shall be admitted into, and entitled to all the advantages of this union: but no other colony shall be admitted into the same, unless such admission be agreed to by nine states.

Article XII. All bills of credit emitted, monies borrowed and debts contracted by, or under the authority of congress, before the assembling of the united states, in pursuance of the present confederation, shall be deemed and considered as a charge against the united states, for payment and satisfaction whereof the said united states, and the public faith are hereby solemnly pledged.

Article XIII. Every state shall abide by the determinations of the united states in congress assembled, on all questions which by this confederation are submitted to them. And the Articles of this confederation shall be inviolably observed by every state, and the union shall be perpetual; nor shall any alteration at any time hereafter be made in any of them; unless such alteration be agreed to in a congress of the united states, and be afterwards confirmed by the legislatures of every state.

And Whereas it hath pleased the Great Governor of the World to incline the hearts of the legislatures we respectively represent in congress, to approve of, and to authorize us to ratify the said articles of confederation and perpetual union, Know Ye that we the undersigned delegates, by virtue of the power and authority to us given for that purpose, do by these presents, in the name and in behalf of our respective constituents, fully and entirely ratify and confirm each and every of the said articles of confederation and perpetual union, and all and singular the matters and things therein contained: And we do further solemnly plight and engage the faith of our respective constituents, that they shall abide by the determinations of the united states in congress assembled, on all questions, which by the said confederation are submitted to them. And that the articles thereof shall be inviolably observed by the states we respectively represent, and that the union shall be perpetual. In Witness whereof we have hereunto set our hands in Congress. Done at Philadelphia in the state of Pennsylvania the ninth day of July, in the Year of our Lord one Thousand seven Hundred and Seventy-eight, and in the third year of the independence of America.

Josiah Bartlett,
John Wentworth, junr
   August 8th, 1778, } On the part & behalf of the
State of New Hampshire.

John Hancock,
Samuel Adams,
Elbridge Gerry,
Francis Dana,
James Lovell,
Samuel Holten, } On the part and behalf of the
State of Massachusetts
Bay.

William Ellery,
Henry Marchant,
John Collins, } On the part and behalf of the
State of Rhode-Island and
Providence Plantations.

Roger Sherman,
Samuel Huntington,
Oliver Wolcott,
Titus Hosmer,
Andrew Adams, } On the part and behalf of the
State of Connecticut.

Jas Duane,
Fra: Lewis,
Wm Duer,
Gouvr Morris, } On the part and behalf of the
State of New York.

Jno Witherspoon,
Nathl Scudder, } On the Part and in Behalf of
the State of New Jersey,
November 26th, 1778.

Robert Morris,
Daniel Roberdeau,
Jon. Bayard Smith,
William Clingar,
Joseph Reed,
   22d July, 1778, } On the part and behalf of the
State of Pennsylvania.

Thos McKean,
   Febr 22d, 1779,
John Dickinson,
   May 5th, 1779,
Nicholas Van Dyke, } On the part & behalf of the
State of Delaware.

John Hanson,
    March 1, 1781,   } On the part and behalf of the
Daniel Carroll, do   )   State of Maryland.

Richard Henry Lee,
John Banister,
Thomas Adams,   } On the Part and Behalf of the
Jno Harvie,   State of Virginia.
Francis Lightfoot Lee,

John Penn,
    July 21st, 1778,   } On the part and behalf of the
Corns Harnett,   State of North Carolina.
Jno Williams,

Henry Laurens,
William Henry Drayton,
Jno Mathews,   } On the part and behalf of the
Richd Hutson,   State of South Carolina.
Thos Heyward, junr,

Jno Walton,
    24th July, 1778,   } On the part and behalf of the
Edwd Telfair,   State of Georgia.
Edwd Langworthy,

C. Congressional Resolution Calling the Federal Convention (1787)

The United States
In CONGRESS Assembled,
February 21, 1787

Whereas there is provision in the Articles of Confederation & perpetual Union for making alterations therein by the assent of a Congress of the United States and of the legislatures of the several States; And whereas experience hath evinced that there are defects in the present Confederation, as a means to remedy which several of the States and particularly the State of New York by express instruction to their delegates in Congress have suggested a convention for the purposes expressed in the following resolution and such Convention appearing to be the most probable means of establishing in these states a firm national government

Resolved that in the opinion of Congress it is expedient that on the second Monday in May next a Convention of delegates who shall have been appointed by the several states be held at Philadelphia for the sole and express purpose of revising the Articles of Confederation and reporting to Congress and the several legislatures such alterations and provisions therein as shall when agreed to in Congress and confirmed by the states render the federal constitution adequate to the exigencies of Government & the preservation of the Union.*

---

*This resolution was in response to a report to their States by Commissioners from the States of New York, New Jersey, Pennsylvania, Delaware, and Virginia,

who had met in Annapolis, Maryland. That report, of September 14, 1786, included these observations:

> That there are important defects in the system of the Federal Government is acknowledged by the Acts of all those States, which have concurred in the present Meeting; That the defects, upon a closer examination, may be found greater and more numerous, than even these acts imply, is at least so far probable, from the embarrassments which characterise the present State of our national affairs, foreign and domestic, as may reasonably be supposed to merit a deliberate and candid discussion, in some mode, which will unite the Sentiments and Councils of all the States. In the choice of the mode, your Commissioners are of opinion, that a Convention of Deputies from the different States, for the special and sole purpose of entering into this investigation, and digesting a plan for supplying such defects as may be discovered to exist, will be entitled to a preference from considerations, which will occur, without being particularised.

> . . . Your Commissioners, with the most respectful deference, beg leave to suggest their unanimous conviction, that it may essentially tend to advance the interests of the union, if the States, by whom they have been respectively delegated, would themselves concur, and use their endeavours to procure the concurrence of the other States, in the appointment of Commissioners, to meet at Philadelphia on the second Monday in May next, to take into consideration the situation of the United States, to devise such further provisions as shall appear to them necessary to render the constitution of the Federal Government adequate to the exigencies of the Union; and to report such an Act for that purpose to the United States in Congress assembled, as when agreed to, by them, and afterwards confirmed by the Legislatures of every State, will effectually provide for the same.

The Annapolis Commissioners were Egbert Benson and Alexander Hamilton (New York), Abraham Clark, William Churchill Houston, and James Schureman (New Jersey), Tench Coxe (Pennsylvania), George Read, John Dickinson, and Richard Bassett (Delaware), and Edmund Randolph, James Madison, Jr., and St. George Tucker (Virginia).

D. The Northwest Ordinance (1787)

An Ordinance for the Government
of the Territory of the United States,
North-West of the River Ohio

[Section 1.] BE IT ORDAINED by the United States in Congress assembled, That the said territory, for the purposes of temporary government, be one district; subject, however, to be divided into two districts, as future circumstances may, in the opinion of Congress, make it expedient.

[Section 2.] Be it ordained by the authority aforesaid, That the estates both of resident and non-resident proprietors in the said territory, dying intestate, shall descend to, and be distributed among their children, and the descendants of a deceased child in equal parts; the descendants of a deceased child or grand-child, to take the share of their deceased parent in equal parts among them: And where there shall be no children or descendants, then in equal parts to the next of kin, in equal degree; and among collaterals, the children of a deceased brother or sister of the intestate, shall have in equal parts among them their deceased parents share; and there shall in no case be a distinction between kindred of the whole and half blood; saving in all cases to the widow of the intestate, her third part of the real estate for life, and one third part of the personal estate; and this law relative to descents and dower, shall remain in full force until altered by the legislature of the district—— And until the governor and judges shall adopt laws as herein after mentioned, estates in the said territory may be devised or bequeathed by wills in writing, signed and sealed by him or her, in whom the estate may be, (being of full age) and attested by three witnesses;—and real estates may be conveyed by lease and release, or bargain and sale, signed, sealed, and delivered by the person being of full age, in whom the estate may be, and attested by two witnesses, provided such wills be duly proved, and such conveyances be acknowledged, or the execution thereof duly proved, and be recorded within one year after proper magistrates, courts, and registers shall be appointed for that purpose; and personal property may be transferred by delivery, saving, however, to the French and Canadian inhabitants, and other settlers of the Kaskaskies, Saint Vincent's, and the neighbouring villages, who have heretofore professed themselves citizens of Virginia, their laws and customs now in force among them, relative to the descent and conveyance of property.

[Section 3.] Be it ordained by the authority aforesaid, That there shall be appointed from time to time, by Congress, a governor, whose commission shall continue in force for the term of three years, unless sooner revoked by Congress; he shall reside in the district, and have a freehold estate therein, in one thousand acres of land, while in the exercise of his office.

[Section 4.] There shall be appointed from time to time, by Congress, a secretary, whose commission shall continue in force for four years, unless sooner revoked, he shall reside in the district, and have a freehold estate therein, in five hundred acres of land, while in the exercise of his office; it shall be his duty to keep and preserve the acts and laws passed by the legislature, and the public records of the district, and the proceedings of the governor in his executive department; and transmit authentic copies of such acts and proceedings, every six months, to the secretary of Congress: There shall also be appointed a court to consist of three judges, any two of whom to form a court, who shall have a common law jurisdiction, and reside in the district, and have each therein a freehold estate in five hundred acres of land, while in the exercise of their offices; and their commissions shall continue in force during good behaviour.

[Section 5.] The governor and judges, or a majority of them, shall adopt and publish in the district, such laws of the original states, criminal and civil, as may be necessary, and best suited to the circumstances of the district, and report them to Congress, from time to time, which laws shall be in force in the district until the organization of the general assembly therein, unless disapproved of by Congress; but afterwards the legislature shall have authority to alter them as they shall think fit.

[Section 6.] The governor for the time being, shall be commander in chief of the militia, appoint and commission all officers in the same, below the rank of general officers; all general officers shall be appointed and commissioned by Congress.

[Section 7.] Previous to the organization of the general assembly, the governor shall appoint such magistrates and other civil officers, in each county or township, as he shall find necessary for the preservation of the peace and good order in the same: After the general assembly shall be organized, the powers and duties of magistrates and other civil officers shall be regulated and defined by the said assembly; but all magistrates and other civil officers, not herein otherwise directed, shall, during the continuance of this temporary government, be appointed by the governor.

[Section 8.] For the prevention of crimes and injuries, the laws to be adopted or made shall have force in all parts of the district, and for the execution of process, criminal and civil, the governor shall make proper divisions thereof—and he shall proceed from time to time, as circumstances may require, to lay out the parts of the district in which the Indian titles shall have been extinguished, into counties and townships, subject, however, to such alterations as may thereafter be made by the legislature.

[Section 9.] So soon as there shall be five thousand free male inhabitants, of full age, in the district, upon giving proof thereof to the governor, they shall receive authority, with time and place, to elect representatives from their counties or townships, to represent them in the general assembly; provided that for every five hundred free male inhabitants there shall be one representative, and so on progressively with the number of free male inhabitants, shall the right of representation increase, until the number of representatives shall amount to twenty-five, after which the number and proportion of representatives shall be regulated by the legislature; provided that no person be eligible or qualified to act as a representative, unless he shall have been a citizen of one of the United States three years and be a resident in the district, or unless he shall have resided in the district three years, and in either case shall likewise hold in his own right, in fee simple, two hundred acres of land within the same:—Provided also, that a freehold in fifty acres of land in the district, having been a citizen of one of the states, and being resident in the district; or the like freehold and two years residence in the district shall be necessary to qualify a man as an elector of a representative.

[Section 10.] The representatives thus elected, shall serve for the term of two years, and in case of the death of a representative, or removal from office, the governor shall issue a writ to the county or township for which he was a member, to elect another in his stead, to serve for the residue of the term.

[Section 11.] The general assembly, or legislature, shall consist of the governor, legislative council, and a house of representatives. The legislative council shall consist of five members, to continue in office five years, unless sooner removed by Congress, any three of whom to be a quorum, and the members of the council shall be nominated and appointed in the following manner, to wit: As soon as representatives shall be elected, the governor shall appoint a time and place for them to meet together, and, when met, they shall nominate ten persons, resident in the district, and each possessed of a freehold in five hundred acres of land, and return their names to Congress; five of whom Congress shall appoint and commission to serve as aforesaid; and whenever a vacancy shall happen in the council, by death or removal from office, the house of representatives shall nominate two persons, qualified as aforesaid, for each vacancy, and return their names to Congress; one of whom Congress shall appoint and commission for the residue of the term; and every five years, four months at least before the expiration of the time of service of the members of council, the said house shall nominate ten persons, qualified as aforesaid, and return their names to Congress, five of whom Congress shall appoint and commission to serve as members of the council five years, unless sooner removed. And the governor, legislative council, and house of representatives, shall have authority to make laws in all cases for the good government of the district, not repugnant to the principles and articles in this ordinance established and declared. And all bills having passed by a majority in the house, and by a majority in the council, shall be referred to the governor for his assent; but no bill or legislative act whatever, shall be of any force without his assent. The governor shall have power to convene, prorogue and dissolve the general assembly, when in his opinion it shall be expedient.

[Section 12.] The governor, judges, legislative council, secretary, and such other officers as Congress shall appoint in the district, shall take an oath or affirmation of fidelity, and of office, the governor before the president of Congress, and all other officers before the governor. As soon as a legislature shall be formed in the district, the council and house, assembled in one room, shall have authority by joint ballot to elect a delegate to Congress, who shall have a seat in Congress, with a right of debating, but not of voting, during this temporary government.

[Section 13.] And for extending the fundamental principles of civil and religious liberty, which form the basis whereon these republics, their laws and constitutions are erected; to fix and establish those principles as the basis of all laws, constitutions and governments, which for ever hereafter shall be formed in the said territory;—-to provide also for the establishment of states, and permanent government therein, and for their admission to a share in the federal councils on an equal footing with the original states, at as early periods as may be consistent with the general interest:

[Section 14.] It is hereby ordained and declared by the authority aforesaid, That the following articles shall be considered as articles of compact between the original states and the people and states in the said territory, and forever remain unalterable, unless by common consent, to wit:

Article the First. No person, demeaning himself in a peaceable and orderly manner, shall ever be molested on account of his mode of worship or religious sentiments in the said territory.

Article the Second. The inhabitants of the said territory shall always be entitled to the benefits of the writ of habeas corpus, and of the trial by jury; of a proportionate representation of the people in the legislature, and of judicial proceedings according to the course of the common law; all persons shall be bailable unless for capital offenses, where the proof shall be evident, or the presumption great; all fines shall be moderate, and no cruel or unusual punishments shall be inflicted; no man shall be deprived of his liberty or property but by the judgment of his peers, or the law of the land; and should the public exigencies make it necessary for the common preservation to take any person's property, or to demand his particular services, full compensation shall be made for the same;—-and in the just preservation of rights and property it is understood and declared, that no law ought ever to be made, or have force in the said territory, that shall in any manner whatever interfere with, or affect private contracts or engagements, bona fide and without fraud previously formed.

Article the Third. Religion, morality and knowledge, being necessary to good government and the happiness of mankind, schools and the means of education shall forever be encouraged. The utmost good faith shall always be observed towards the Indians; their lands and property shall never be taken from them without their consent; and in their property, rights and liberty, they never shall be invaded or disturbed, unless in just and lawful wars authorized by Congress; but laws founded in justice and humanity shall from time to time be made, for preventing wrongs being done to them; and for preserving peace and friendship with them.

Article the Fourth. The said territory, and the states which may be formed therein, shall forever remain a part of this confederacy of the United States of America, subject to the articles of confederation, and to such alterations therein as shall be constitutionally made; and to all the acts and ordinances of the United States in Congress assembled, conformable thereto. The inhabitants and settlers in the said territory, shall be subject to pay a part of the federal debts contracted or to be contracted, and a proportional part of the expences of government, to be apportioned on them by Congress, according to the same common rule and measure by which apportionments thereof shall be made on the other states; and the taxes for paying their proportion, shall be laid and levied by the authority and direction of the legislatures of the district or districts or new states, as in the original states, within the time agreed upon by the United States in Congress assembled. The legislatures of those districts, or new states, shall never interfere with the primary disposal of the soil by the United States in Congress assembled, nor with any regulations Congress may find necessary for securing the title in such soil to the bona fide purchasers. No tax shall be imposed on lands the property of the United States; and in no case shall non-resident proprietors be taxed higher than residents. The navigable waters leading into the Mississippi and St. Lawrence, and the carrying places between the same shall be common highways, and forever free, as well to the inhabitants of the said territory, as to the citizens of the United States, and those of any other states that may be admitted into the confederacy, without any tax, impost or duty therefor.

Article the Fifth. There shall be formed in the said territory, not less than three nor more than five states; and the boundaries of the states, as soon as Virginia shall alter her act of cession and consent to the same, shall become fixed and established as follows, to wit: The western state in the said territory, shall be bounded by the Mississippi, the Ohio and Wabash rivers; a direct line drawn from the Wabash and Post Vincent's due north to the territorial line between the United States and Canada, and by the said territorial line to the lake of the Woods and Mississippi. The middle state shall be bounded by the said direct line, the Wabash from Post Vincent's to the Ohio; by the Ohio, by a direct line drawn due north from the mouth of the Great Miami to the said territorial line, and by the said territorial line. The eastern state shall be bounded by the last mentioned direct line, the Ohio, Pennsylvania, and the said territorial line; Provided however, and it is further understood and declared, that the boundaries of these three states, shall be subject so far to be altered, that if Congress shall hereafter find it expedient, they shall have authority to form one or two states in that part of the said territory which lies north of an east and west line drawn through the southerly bend or extreme of lake Michigan: and whenever any of the said states shall have sixty thousand free inhabitants therein, such state shall be admitted by its delegates into the Congress of the United States, on an equal footing with the original states in all respects whatever; and shall be at liberty to form a permanent constitution and state government: Provided the constitution and government so to be formed, shall be republican, and in conformity to the principles contained in these articles, and so far as it can be consistent with the general interest of the confederacy, such admission shall be allowed at an earlier period, and when there may be a less number of free inhabitants in the state than sixty thousand.

Article the Sixth. There shall be neither slavery nor involuntary servitude in the said territory, otherwise than in punishment of crimes whereof the party shall have been duly convicted: Provided always, that any person escaping into the same, from whom labor or service is lawfully claimed in any one of the original states, such fugitive may be lawfully reclaimed and conveyed to the person claiming his or her labor or service as aforesaid.

Be it ordained by the authority aforesaid, That the resolutions of the 23d of April, 1784, relative to the subject of this ordinance, be, and the same are hereby repealed and declared null and void.

DONE by the UNITED STATES in CONGRESS assembled, the 13th day of July, in the year of our Lord 1787, and of their sovereignty and independence the 12th.*

*The following Act of the First Congress, approved August 7, 1789, reenacted the Northwest Ordinance as modified to conform to the United States Constitution of 1787:

An Act to provide for the government of the Territory
northwest of the river Ohio.

Whereas, in order that the ordinance of the United States in Congress assembled, for the government of the Territory northwest of the river Ohio may continue to have full effect, it is requisite that certain provisions should be made so as to adapt the same to the present Constitution of the United States:

Be it enacted, &c., That in all cases in which, by the said ordinance, any information is to be given, or communication made by the Governor of the said Territory to the United States in Congress assembled, or to any of their officers, it shall be the duty of the said Governor to give such information, and to make such communication to the President of the United States; and the President shall nominate, and by and with the advice and consent of the Senate shall appoint all officers which by the said ordinance were to have been appointed by the United States in Congress assembled, and all officers so appointed shall be commissioned by him; and in all cases where the United States in Congress assembled might, by the said ordinance, revoke any commission, or remove from any office, the President is hereby declared to have the same powers of revocation and removal.

Sec. 2. And be it further enacted, That in case of the death, removal, resignation, or necessary absence of the Governor of the said Territory, the Secretary thereof shall be, and he is hereby authorized and required to execute all the powers and perform all the duties of the Governor, during the vacancy occasioned by the removal, resignation, or necessary absence of the said Governor.

E. The United States Constitution (1787)

THE CONSTITUTION OF THE UNITED STATES

We the People of the United States, in Order to form a more perfect Union, establish Justice, insure domestic Tranquility, provide for the common defence, promote the general Welfare, and secure the Blessings of Liberty to ourselves and our Posterity, do ordain and establish this Constitution for the United States of America.

Article. I.

Section. 1. All legislative Powers herein granted shall be vested in a Congress of the United States, which shall consist of a Senate and a House of Representatives.

Section. 2. The House of Representatives shall be composed of Members chosen every second Year by the People of the several States, and the Electors in each State shall have the Qualifications requisite for Electors of the most numerous Branch of the State Legislature.

No person shall be a Representative who shall not have attained to the Age of twenty five Years, and been seven Years a Citizen of the United States, and who shall not, when elected, be an Inhabitant of that State in which he shall be chosen.

Representatives and direct Taxes shall be apportioned among the several States which may be included within this Union, according to their respective Numbers, which shall be determined by adding to the whole Number of free Persons, including those bound to Service for a Term of Years, and excluding Indians not taxed, three fifths of all other Persons. The actual Enumeration shall be made within three Years after the first Meeting of the Congress of the United States, and within every subsequent Term of ten Years, in such Manner as they shall by Law direct. The Number of Representatives shall not exceed one for every thirty Thousand, but each State shall have at Least one Representative; and until such enumeration shall be made, the State of New Hampshire shall be entitled to chuse three, Massachusetts eight, Rhode-Island and Providence Plantations one, Connecticut five, New-York six, New Jersey four, Pennsylvania eight, Delaware one, Maryland six, Virginia ten, North Carolina five, South Carolina five, and Georgia three.

When vacancies happen in the Representation from any State, the Executive Authority thereof shall issue Writs of Election to fill such Vacancies.

The House of Representatives shall chuse their Speaker and other Officers; and shall have the sole Power of Impeachment.

Section. 3. The Senate of the United States shall be composed of two Senators from each State, chosen by the Legislature thereof, for six Years; and each Senator shall have one Vote.

Immediately after they shall be assembled in Consequence of the first Election, they shall be divided as equally as may be into three Classes. The Seats of the Senators of the first Class shall be vacated at the Expiration of the second Year, of the second Class at the Expiration of the fourth Year, and of the third Class at the Expiration of the sixth Year, so that one third may be chosen every second Year; and if Vacancies happen by Resignation, or otherwise, during the Recess of the Legislature of any State, the Executive thereof may make temporary Appointments until the next Meeting of the Legislature, which shall then fill such Vacancies.

No Person shall be a Senator who shall not have attained to the Age of thirty Years, and been nine Years a Citizen of the United States, and who shall not, when elected, be an Inhabitant of that State for which he shall be chosen.

The Vice President of the United States shall be President of the Senate, but shall have no Vote, unless they be equally divided.

The Senate shall chuse their other Officers, and also a President pro tempore, in the Absence of the Vice President, or when he shall exercise the Office of President of the United States.

The Senate shall have the sole Power to try all Impeachments. When sitting for that Purpose, they shall be on Oath or Affirmation. When the President of the United States is tried, the Chief Justice shall preside: And no Person shall be convicted without the Concurrence of two thirds of the Members present.

Judgment in Cases of Impeachment shall not extend further than to removal from Office, and disqualification to hold and enjoy any Office of honor, Trust or Profit under the United States: but the Party convicted shall nevertheless be liable and subject to Indictment, Trial, Judgment and Punishment, according to Law.

Section. 4. The Times, Places and Manner of holding Elections for Senators and Representatives, shall be prescribed in each State by the Legislature thereof; but the Congress may at any time by Law make or alter such Regulations, except as to the Places of chusing Senators.

The Congress shall assemble at least once in every Year, and such Meeting shall be on the first Monday in December, unless they shall by Law appoint a different Day.

Section. 5. Each House shall be the Judge of the Elections, Returns and Qualifications of its own Members, and a Majority of each shall constitute a Quorum to do Business; but a smaller Number may adjourn from day to day, and may be authorized to compel the Attendance of absent Members, in such Manner, and under such Penalties as each House may provide.

Each House may determine the Rules of its Proceedings, punish its Members for disorderly Behaviour, and, with the Concurrence of two thirds, expel a Member.

Each House shall keep a Journal of its Proceedings, and from time to time publish the same, excepting such Parts as may in their Judgment require Secrecy; and the Yeas and Nays of the Members of either House on any question shall, at the Desire of one fifth of those Present, be entered on the Journal.

Neither House, during the Session of Congress, shall, without the Consent of the other, adjourn for more than three days, nor to any other Place than that in which the two Houses shall be sitting.

Section. 6. The Senators and Representatives shall receive a Compensation for their Services, to be ascertained by Law, and paid out of the Treasury of the United States. They shall in all Cases, except Treason, Felony and Breach of the Peace, be privileged from Arrest during their Attendance at the Session of their respective Houses, and in going to and returning from the same; and for any Speech or Debate in either House, they shall not be questioned in any other Place.

No Senator or Representative shall, during the Time for which he was elected, be appointed to any civil Office under the Authority of the United States, which shall have been created, or the Emoluments whereof shall have been encreased during such time; and no Person holding any Office under the United States, shall be a Member of either House during his Continuance in Office.

Section. 7. All Bills for raising Revenue shall originate in the House of Representatives; but the Senate may propose or concur with Amendments as on other Bills.

Every Bill which shall have passed the House of Representatives and the Senate, shall, before it become a Law, be presented to the President of the United States; If he approve he shall sign it, but if not he shall return it, with his Objections to that House in which it shall have originated, who shall enter the Objections at large on their Journal, and proceed to reconsider it. If after such Reconsideration two thirds of that House shall agree to pass the Bill, it shall be sent, together with the Objections, to the other House, by which it shall likewise be reconsidered, and if approved by two thirds of that House, it shall become a Law. But in all such Cases the Votes of both Houses shall be determined by yeas and Nays, and the Names of the Persons voting for and against the Bill shall be entered on the Journal of each House respectively. If any Bill shall not be returned by the President within ten Days (Sundays excepted) after it shall have been presented to him, the Same shall be a Law, in like Manner as if he had signed it, unless the Congress by their Adjournment prevent its Return in which Case it shall not be a Law.

Every Order, Resolution, or Vote to which the Concurrence of the Senate and House of Representatives may be necessary (except on a question of Adjournment) shall be presented to the President of the United States; and before the Same shall take Effect, shall be approved by him, or being disapproved by him, shall be repassed by two thirds of the Senate and House of Representatives, according to the Rules and Limitations prescribed in the Case of a Bill.

Section. 8. The Congress shall have Power To lay and collect

Taxes, Duties, Imposts and Excises, to pay the Debts and provide for the common Defence and general Welfare of the United States; but all Duties, Imposts and Excises shall be uniform throughout the United States;

To borrow Money on the credit of the United States;

To regulate Commerce with foreign Nations, and among the several States, and with the Indian Tribes;

To establish an uniform Rule of Naturalization, and uniform Laws on the subject of Bankruptcies throughout the United States;

To coin Money, regulate the Value thereof, and of foreign Coin, and fix the Standard of Weights and Measures;

To provide for the Punishment of counterfeiting the Securities and current Coin of the United States;

To establish Post Offices and post Roads;

To promote the Progress of Science and useful Arts, by securing for limited Times to Authors and Inventors the exclusive Right to their respective Writings and Discoveries;

To constitute Tribunals inferior to the supreme Court;

To define and punish Piracies and Felonies committed on the high Seas, and Offences against the Law of Nations;

To declare War, grant Letters of Marque and Reprisal, and make Rules concerning Captures on Land and Water;

To raise and support Armies, but no Appropriation of Money to that Use shall be for a longer Term than two Years;

To provide and maintain a Navy;

To make Rules for the Government and Regulation of the land and naval Forces;

To provide for calling forth the Militia to execute the Laws of the Union, suppress Insurrections and repel Invasions;

To provide for organizing, arming, and disciplining, the Militia, and for governing such Part of them as may be employed in the Service of the United States, reserving to the States respectively, the Appointment of the Officers, and the Authority of training the Militia according to the discipline prescribed by Congress;

To exercise exclusive Legislation in all Cases whatsoever, over such District (not exceeding ten Miles square) as may, by Cession of particular States, and the Acceptance of Congress, become the Seat of the Government of the United States, and to exercise like

Authority over all Places purchased by the Consent of the Legislature of the State in which the Same shall be, for the Erection of Forts, Magazines, Arsenals, dock-Yards, and other needful Buildings;—And

To make all Laws which shall be necessary and proper for carrying into Execution the foregoing Powers, and all other Powers vested by this Constitution in the Government of the United States, or in any Department or Officer thereof.

Section. 9. The Migration or Importation of such Persons as any of the States now existing shall think proper to admit, shall not be prohibited by the Congress prior to the Year one thousand eight hundred and eight, but a Tax or duty may be imposed on such Importation, not exceeding ten dollars for each Person.

The Privilege of the Writ of Habeas Corpus shall not be suspended, unless when in Cases of Rebellion or Invasion the public Safety may require it.

No Bill of Attainder or ex post facto Law shall be passed.

No Capitation, or other direct, Tax shall be laid, unless in Proportion to the Census or Enumeration herein before directed to be taken.

No Tax or Duty shall be laid on Articles exported from any State.

No Preference shall be given by any Regulation of Commerce or Revenue to the Ports of one State over those of another: nor shall Vessels bound to, or from, one State, be obliged to enter, clear, or pay Duties in another.

No Money shall be drawn from the Treasury, but in Consequence of Appropriations made by Law; and a regular Statement and Account of the Receipts and Expenditures of all public Money shall be published from time to time.

No Title of Nobility shall be granted by the United States: And no Person holding any Office of Profit or Trust under them, shall, without the Consent of the Congress, accept of any present, Emolument, Office, or Title, of any kind whatever, from any King, Prince, or foreign State.

Section. 10. No State shall enter into any Treaty, Alliance, or Confederation; grant Letters of Marque and Reprisal; coin Money; emit Bills of Credit; make any Thing but gold and silver Coin a

Tender in Payment of Debts; pass any Bill of Attainder, ex post facto Law, or Law impairing the Obligation of Contracts, or grant any Title of Nobility.

No State shall, without the Consent of the Congress, lay any Imposts or Duties on Imports or Exports, except what may be absolutely necessary for executing it's inspection Laws: and the net Produce of all Duties and Imposts, laid by any State on Imports or Exports, shall be for the Use of the Treasury of the United States; and all such Laws shall be subject to the Revision and Controul of the Congress.

No State shall, without the Consent of Congress, lay any Duty of Tonnage, keep Troops, or Ships of War in time of Peace, enter into any Agreement or Compact with another State, or with a foreign Power, or engage in War, unless actually invaded, or in such imminent Danger as will not admit of delay.

Article. II.

Section. 1. The executive Power shall be vested in a President of the United States of America. He shall hold his Office during the Term of four Years, and, together with the Vice President, chosen for the same Term, be elected, as follows

Each State shall appoint, in such Manner as the Legislature thereof may direct, a Number of Electors, equal to the whole Number of Senators and Representatives to which the State may be entitled in the Congress: but no Senator or Representative, or Person holding an Office of Trust or Profit under the United States, shall be appointed an Elector.

The Electors shall meet in their respective States, and vote by Ballot for two Persons, of whom one at least shall not be an Inhabitant of the same State with themselves. And they shall make a List of all the Persons voted for, and of the Number of Votes for each; which List they shall sign and certify, and transmit sealed to the Seat of the Government of the United States, directed to the President of the Senate. The President of the Senate shall, in the Presence of the Senate and House of Representatives, open all the Certificates, and the Votes shall then be counted. The Person having the greatest Number of Votes shall be the President, if such Number be a Majority of the whole Number of Electors appointed; and if there be more than one who have such Majority, and have an equal Number of Votes, then the House of Representatives shall immediately chuse by Ballot one of them for President; and if no Person have a Majority, then from the five highest on the List the said House shall in like Manner chuse the President. But in chusing the President, the Votes shall be taken by States, the Representation from each State having one Vote; A quorum for this Purpose shall consist of a Member or Members from two thirds of the States, and a Majority of all the States shall be necessary to a Choice. In every Case, after the Choice of the President, the Person having the greatest Number of Votes of the Electors shall be the Vice President. But if there should remain two or more who have equal Votes, the Senate shall chuse from them by Ballot the Vice President.

The Congress may determine the Time of chusing the Electors, and the Day on which they shall give their Votes; which Day shall be the same throughout the United States.

No Person except a natural born Citizen, or a Citizen of the United States, at the time of the Adoption of this Constitution, shall be eligible to the Office of President; neither shall any person be eligible to that Office who shall not have attained to the Age of thirty five Years, and been fourteen Years a Resident within the United States.

In Case of the Removal of the President from Office, or of his Death, Resignation, or Inability to discharge the Powers and Duties of the said Office, the Same shall devolve on the Vice President, and the Congress may by Law provide for the Case of Removal, Death, Resignation or Inability, both of the President and Vice President, declaring what Officer shall then act as President, and such Officer shall act accordingly, until the Disability be removed, or a President shall be elected.

The President shall, at stated Times, receive for his Services, a Compensation, which shall neither be encreased nor diminished during the Period for which he shall have been elected, and he shall not receive within that Period any other Emolument from the United States, or any of them.

Before he enter on the Execution of his Office, he shall take the following Oath or Affirmation: — "I do solemnly swear (or affirm) that I will faithfully execute the Office of President of the United

States, and will to the best of my Ability, preserve, protect and defend the Constitution of the United States."

Section. 2. The President shall be Commander in Chief of the Army and Navy of the United States, and of the Militia of the several States, when called into the actual Service of the United States; he may require the Opinion, in writing, of the principal Officer in each of the executive Departments, upon any Subject relating to the Duties of their respective Offices, and he shall have Power to grant Reprieves and Pardons for Offences against the United States, except in Cases of Impeachment.

He shall have Power, by and with the Advice and Consent of the Senate, to make Treaties, provided two thirds of the Senators present concur; and he shall nominate, and by and with the Advice and Consent of the Senate, shall appoint Ambassadors, other public Ministers and Consuls, Judges of the supreme Court, and all other Officers of the United States, whose Appointments are not herein otherwise provided for, and which shall be established by Law: but the Congress may by Law vest the Appointment of such inferior Officers, as they think proper, in the President alone, in the Courts of Law, or in the Heads of Departments.

The President shall have Power to fill up all Vacancies that may happen during the Recess of the Senate, by granting Commissions which shall expire at the End of their next Session.

Section. 3. He shall from time to time give to the Congress Information of the State of the Union, and recommend to their Consideration such Measures as he shall judge necessary and expedient; he may, on extraordinary Occasions, convene both Houses, or either of them, and in Case of Disagreement between them, with Respect to the Time of Adjournment, he may adjourn them to such Time as he shall think proper; he shall receive Ambassadors and other public Ministers; he shall take Care that the Laws be faithfully executed, and shall Commission all the Officers of the United States.

Section. 4. The President, Vice President and all civil Officers of the United States, shall be removed from Office on Impeachment for, and Conviction of, Treason, Bribery, or other high Crimes and Misdemeanors.

Article. III.

Section. 1. The judicial Power of the United States, shall be vested in one supreme Court, and in such inferior Courts as the Congress may from time to time ordain and establish. The Judges, both of the supreme and inferior Courts, shall hold their Offices during good Behaviour, and shall, at stated Times, receive for their Services, a Compensation, which shall not be diminished during their Continuance in Office.

Section. 2. The judicial Power shall extend to all Cases, in Law and Equity, arising under this Constitution, the Laws of the United States, and Treaties made, or which shall be made, under their Authority;—to all Cases affecting Ambassadors, other public Ministers and Consuls;—to all Cases of admiralty and maritime Jurisdiction;—to Controversies to which the United States shall be a Party;—to Controversies between two or more States;—between a State and Citizens of another State;—between Citizens of different States,—between Citizens of the same State claiming Lands under Grants of different States, and between a State, or the Citizens thereof, and foreign States, Citizens or Subjects.

In all Cases affecting Ambassadors, other public Ministers and Consuls, and those in which a State shall be a Party, the supreme Court shall have original Jurisdiction. In all the other Cases before mentioned, the supreme Court shall have appellate Jurisdiction, both as to Law and Fact, with such Exceptions, and under such Regulations as the Congress shall make.

The Trial of all Crimes, except in Cases of Impeachment, shall be by Jury; and such Trial shall be held in the State where the said Crimes shall have been committed; but when not committed within any State, the Trial shall be at such Place or Places as the Congress may by Law have directed.

Section. 3. Treason against the United States, shall consist only in levying War against them, or in adhering to their Enemies, giving them Aid and Comfort. No Person shall be convicted of Treason unless on the Testimony of two Witnesses to the same overt Act, or on Confession in open Court.

The Congress shall have Power to declare the Punishment of Treason, but no Attainder of Treason shall work Corruption of Blood, or Forfeiture except during the Life of the Person attainted.

Article. IV.

Section. 1. Full Faith and Credit shall be given in each State to the public Acts, Records, and judicial Proceedings of every other State. And the Congress may by general Laws prescribe the Manner in which such Acts, Records and Proceedings shall be proved, and the Effect thereof.

Section. 2. The Citizens of each State shall be entitled to all Privileges and Immunities of Citizens in the several States.

A Person charged in any State with Treason, Felony, or other Crime, who shall flee from Justice, and be found in another State, shall on Demand of the executive Authority of the State from which he fled, be delivered up, to be removed to the State having Jurisdiction of the Crime.

No Person held to Service or Labour in one State, under the Laws thereof, escaping into another, shall, in Consequence of any Law or Regulation therein, be discharged from such Service or Labour, but shall be delivered up on Claim of the Party to whom such Service or Labour may be due.

Section. 3. New States may be admitted by the Congress into this Union; but no new State shall be formed or erected within the Jurisdiction of any other State; nor any State be formed by the Junction of two or more States, or Parts of States, without the Consent of the Legislatures of the States concerned as well as of the Congress.

The Congress shall have Power to dispose of and make all needful Rules and Regulations respecting the Territory or other Property belonging to the United States; and nothing in this Constitution shall be so construed as to Prejudice any Claims of the United States, or of any particular State.

Section. 4. The United States shall guarantee to every State in this Union a Republican Form of Government, and shall protect each of them against Invasion; and on Application of the Legislature, or of the Executive (when the Legislature cannot be convened) against domestic Violence.

Article. V.

The Congress, whenever two thirds of both Houses shall deem it necessary, shall propose Amendments to this Constitution, or, on the Application of the Legislatures of two thirds of the several States, shall call a Convention for proposing Amendments, which, in either Case, shall be valid to all Intents and Purposes, as Part of this Constitution, when ratified by the Legislatures of three fourths of the several States, or by Conventions in three fourths thereof, as the one or the other Mode of Ratification may be proposed by the Congress; Provided that no Amendment which may be made prior to the Year One thousand eight hundred and eight shall in any Manner affect the first and fourth Clauses in the Ninth Section of the first Article; and that no State, without its Consent, shall be deprived of it's equal Suffrage in the Senate.

Article. VI.

All Debts contracted and Engagements entered into, before the Adoption of this Constitution, shall be as valid against the United States under this Constitution, as under the Confederation.

This Constitution, and the Laws of the United States which shall be made in Pursuance thereof; and all Treaties made, or which shall be made, under the Authority of the United States, shall be the supreme Law of the Land; and the Judges in every State shall be bound thereby, any Thing in the Constitution or Laws of any State to the Contrary notwithstanding.

The Senators and Representatives before mentioned, and the Members of the several State Legislatures, and all executive and judicial Officers, both of the United States and of the several States, shall be bound by Oath or Affirmation, to support this Constitution; but no religious Test shall ever be required as a Qualification to any Office or public Trust under the United States.

Article. VII.

The Ratification of the Conventions of nine States, shall be sufficient for the Establishment of this Constitution between the

States so ratifying the Same.

done in Convention by the Unanimous Consent of the States present the Seventeenth Day of September in the Year of our Lord one thousand seven hundred and Eighty seven and of the Independence of the United States of America the Twelfth In witness whereof We have hereunto subscribed our Names,

G. Washington—Presidt
and deputy from Virginia

New Hampshire
{ John Langdon
  Nicholas Gilman

Massachusetts
{ Nathaniel Gorham
  Rufus King

Connecticut
{ Wm Saml Johnson
  Roger Sherman

New York
Alexander Hamilton

New Jersey
{ Wil: Livingston
  David Brearley
  Wm Paterson
  Jona: Dayton

Pennsylvania
{ B. Franklin
  Thomas Mifflin
  Robt Morris
  Geo. Clymer
  Thos FitzSimons
  Jared Ingersoll
  James Wilson
  Gouv Morris

Delaware
{ Geo: Read
  Gunning Bedford jun
  John Dickinson
  Richard Bassett
  Jaco: Broom

Maryland
{ James McHenry
  Dan of St Thos Jenifer
  Danl Carroll

Virginia	{ John Blair— James Madison Jr.
North Carolina	{ Wm Blount Richd Dobbs Spaight Hu Williamson
South Carolina	{ J. Rutledge Charles Cotesworth Pinckney Charles Pinckney Pierce Butler
Georgia	{ William Few Abr Baldwin

Attest: William Jackson, Secretary

[The Amendments to the United States Constitution are collected in Appendix K.]

F. Chart for Article I, Section 8
(Lecture No. 5)

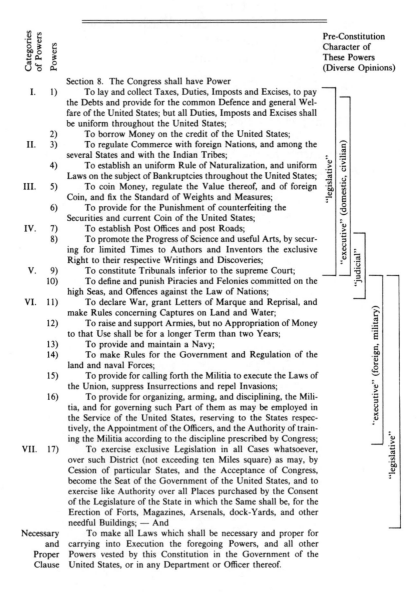

Categories of Powers	Powers		Pre-Constitution Character of These Powers (Diverse Opinions)
		Section 8. The Congress shall have Power	
I.	1)	To lay and collect Taxes, Duties, Imposts and Excises, to pay the Debts and provide for the common Defence and general Welfare of the United States; but all Duties, Imposts and Excises shall be uniform throughout the United States;	
	2)	To borrow Money on the credit of the United States;	
II.	3)	To regulate Commerce with foreign Nations, and among the several States and with the Indian Tribes;	"legislative"
	4)	To establish an uniform Rule of Naturalization, and uniform Laws on the subject of Bankruptcies throughout the United States;	
III.	5)	To coin Money, regulate the Value thereof, and of foreign Coin, and fix the Standard of Weights and Measures;	"executive" (domestic, civilian)
	6)	To provide for the Punishment of counterfeiting the Securities and current Coin of the United States;	
IV.	7)	To establish Post Offices and post Roads;	
	8)	To promote the Progress of Science and useful Arts, by securing for limited Times to Authors and Inventors the exclusive Right to their respective Writings and Discoveries;	"judicial"
V.	9)	To constitute Tribunals inferior to the supreme Court;	
	10)	To define and punish Piracies and Felonies committed on the high Seas, and Offences against the Law of Nations;	
VI.	11)	To declare War, grant Letters of Marque and Reprisal, and make Rules concerning Captures on Land and Water;	"executive" (foreign, military)
	12)	To raise and support Armies, but no Appropriation of Money to that Use shall be for a longer Term than two Years;	
	13)	To provide and maintain a Navy;	
	14)	To make Rules for the Government and Regulation of the land and naval Forces;	
	15)	To provide for calling forth the Militia to execute the Laws of the Union, suppress Insurrections and repel Invasions;	
	16)	To provide for organizing, arming, and disciplining, the Militia, and for governing such Part of them as may be employed in the Service of the United States, reserving to the States respectively, the Appointment of the Officers, and the Authority of training the Militia according to the discipline prescribed by Congress;	
VII.	17)	To exercise exclusive Legislation in all Cases whatsoever, over such District (not exceeding ten Miles square) as may, by Cession of particular States, and the Acceptance of Congress, become the Seat of the Government of the United States, and to exercise like Authority over all Places purchased by the Consent of the Legislature of the State in which the Same shall be, for the Erection of Forts, Magazines, Arsenals, dock-Yards, and other needful Buildings; — And	"legislative"
	Necessary and Proper Clause	To make all Laws which shall be necessary and proper for carrying into Execution the foregoing Powers, and all other Powers vested by this Constitution in the Government of the United States, or in any Department or Officer thereof.	

280

G. Resolutions of the Federal Convention Providing for Transmittal of the Proposed Constitution to the Confederation Congress (1787)

In CONVENTION, Monday September 17th, 1787.
Present
The States of New-Hampshire, Massachusetts, Connecticut,
Mr. *Hamilton* from New-York, New-Jersey,
Pennsylvania, Delaware, Maryland, Virginia,
North-Carolina, South-Carolina and Georgia:

RESOLVED,

That the preceding Constitution be laid before the United States in Congress assembled, and that it is the opinion of this Convention, that it should afterwards be submitted to a Convention of Delegates, chosen in each State by the People thereof, under the recommendation of its Legislature, for their assent and ratification; and that each Convention assenting to, and ratifying the same, should give Notice thereof to the United States in Congress assembled.

Resolved, That it is the opinion of this Convention, that as soon as the Conventions of nine States shall have ratified this Constitution, the United States in Congress assembled should fix a day on which Electors should be appointed by the States which shall have ratified the same, and a day on which the Electors should assemble to vote for the President, and the time and place for commencing proceedings under this Constitution. That after such publication the Electors should be appointed, and the Senators and Representatives elected: That the Electors should meet on the day fixed for the Election of the President, and should transmit their votes certifed, signed, sealed and directed, as the Constitution requires, to the Secretary of the United States in Congress assembled, that the Senators and Representatives should convene at the time and place assigned; that the Senators should appoint a President of the Senate, for the sole purpose of receiving, opening and counting the votes for President; and, that after he shall be chosen, the Congress, together with the President, should, without delay, proceed to execute this Constitution.

By the unanimous Order of the Convention,

George Washington, President

William Jackson, Secretary

H. Letter Transmitting the Proposed Constitution from the Federal Convention to the Confederation Congress (1787)

In CONVENTION, September 17, 1787.

[HIS EXCELLENCY,
The President of Congress]

SIR,

We have now the honor to submit to the consideration of the United States in Congress assembled, that Constitution which has appeared to us the most adviseable.

The friends of our country have long seen and desired, that the power of making war, peace and treaties, that of levying money and regulating commerce, and the correspondent executive and judicial authorities should be fully and effectually vested in the general government of the Union: but the impropriety of delegating such extensive trust to one body of men is evident—Hence results the necessity of a different organization.

It is obviously impracticable in the federal government of these States, to secure all rights of independent sovereignty to each, and yet provide for the interest and safety of all—Individuals entering into society, must give up a share of liberty to preserve the rest. The magnitude of the sacrifice must depend as well on situation and circumstance, as on the object to be obtained. It is at all times difficult to draw with precision the line between those rights which must be surrendered, and those which may be reserved; and on the present occasion this difficulty was encreased by a difference among the several States as to their situation, extent, habits, and particular interests.

In all our deliberations on this subject we kept steadily in our view, that which appears to us the greatest interest of every true American, the consolidation of our Union, in which is involved our prosperity, felicity, safety, perhaps our national existence. This important consideration, seriously and deeply impressed on our minds, led each State in the Convention to be less rigid on points of inferior magnitude, than might have been otherwise expected; and thus the Constitution, which we now present, is the result of a spirit of amity, and of that mutual deference and concession which the peculiarity of our political situation rendered indispensible.

That it will meet the full and entire approbation of every State is not perhaps to be expected; but each will doubtless consider, that had her interests been alone consulted, the consequences might have been particularly disagreeable or injurious to others; that it is liable to as few exceptions as could reasonably have been expected, we hope and believe; that it may promote the lasting welfare of that country so dear to us all, and secure her freedom and happiness, is our most ardent wish.

With great respect,

We have the honor to be,

SIR,

Your EXCELLENCY'S most

Obedient and humble Servants,

GEORGE WASHINGTON, President.

By unanimous Order of the CONVENTION.

I. Congressional Resolution Transmitting the Proposed Constitution to the States (1787)

The United States
In CONGRESS Assembled,
September 28, 1787

Congress assembled present Newhamphire Massachusetts Connecticut New York New Jersey Pennsylvania Delaware Virginia North Carolina South Carolina and Georgia and from Maryland Mr. Ross.

Congress having received the report of the [Federal] Convention lately assembled in Philadelphia

Resolved Unanimously that the said Report with the resolutions and letter accompanying the same be transmitted to the several legislatures in Order to be submitted to a convention of Delegates chosen in each state by the people thereof in conformity to the resolves of the Convention made and provided in that case.*

---

*The following circular letter, of September 28, 1787, was sent by the Secretary of the Confederation Congress to each of the Governors of the States:

In obedience to an unanimous resolution of the United States in Congress Assembled, a copy of which is annexed, I have the honor to transmit to Your Excellency, the Report of the Convention lately Assembled in Philadelphia, together with the resolutions and letter accompanying the same; And have to request that Your Excellency will be pleased to lay the same before the Legislature, in order that it may be submitted to a Convention of Delegates chosen in Your State by the people of the State in conformity to the resolves of the Convention, made & provided in that case.

J. Congressional Act for Putting the Constitution into Operation (1788)

The United States
In CONGRESS Assembled,
September 13, 1788

Whereas the convention assembled in Philadelphia, pursuant to the resolution of Congress of the 21st of February, 1787, did, on the 17th of September in the same year, report to the United States in Congress assembled, a constitution for the people of the United States; whereupon Congress, on the 28th of the same September, did resolve unanimously, "That the said report, with the resolutions and letter accompanying the same, be transmitted to the several legislatures, in order to be submitted to a convention of delegates chosen in each state by the people thereof, in conformity to the resolves of the convention made and provided in that case:" And whereas the constitution so reported by the convention, and by Congress transmitted to the several legislatures, has been ratified in the manner therein declared to be sufficient for the establishment of the same, and such ratifications* duly authenticated

---

*The Constitution was ratified by the several States in the following order:

Delaware, December 7, 1787, yeas, 30 (unanimous).
Pennsylvania, December 12, 1787, yeas, 43; nays, 23.
New Jersey, December 18, 1787, yeas, 38 (unanimous).
Georgia, January 2, 1788, yeas, 26 (unanimous).
Connecticut, January 9, 1788, yeas, 128; nays, 40.
Massachusetts, February 6, 1788, yeas, 187; nays, 168.
Maryland, April 28, 1788, yeas, 63; nays, 11.

have been received by Congress, and are filed in the office of the Secretary; therefore,

Resolved, That the first Wednesday in January next, be the day for appointing electors in the several states, which before the said day shall have ratified the said constitution; that the first Wednesday in February next, be the day for the electors to assemble in their respective states, and vote for a president; and that the first Wednesday in March next, be the time, and the present seat of Congress [New York City] the place for commencing proceedings under the said constitution.

South Carolina, May 23, 1788, yeas, 149; nays, 73.
New Hampshire, June 21, 1788, yeas, 57; nays, 46.
Virginia, June 26, 1788, yeas, 89; nays, 79.
New York, July 26, 1788, yeas, 30; nays, 27.
North Carolina, November 21, 1789, yeas, 194; nays, 77.
Rhode Island and Providence Plantations, May 29, 1790, yeas, 34; nays, 32.
Vermont, January 10, 1791, yeas, 105; nays, 4; admitted "as a new and entire member of the United States" by act of Congress approved February 18, 1791.

New Hampshire, on June 21, 1788, completed the nine States designated by Article VII as sufficient for the establishment of the Constitution between the States ratifying the same.

K. Amendments to the Constitution of the United States (1791–1971)

ARTICLES IN ADDITION TO, AND AMENDMENT OF,
THE CONSTITUTION OF THE UNITED STATES,
PROPOSED BY CONGRESS AND RATIFIED
BY THE SEVERAL STATES, PURSUANT TO THE FIFTH
ARTICLE OF THE ORIGINAL CONSTITUTION

Amendment I [1791]

Congress shall make no law respecting an establishment of religion, or prohibiting the free exercise thereof; or abridging the freedom of speech, or of the press; or the right of the people peaceably to assemble, and to petition the Government for a redress of grievances.

Amendment II [1791]

A well regulated Militia, being necessary to the security of a free State, the right of the people to keep and bear Arms, shall not be infringed.

Amendment III [1791]

No Soldier shall, in time of peace be quartered in any house, without the consent of the Owner, nor in time of war, but in a manner to be prescribed by law.

Amendment IV [1791]

The right of the people to be secure in their persons, houses, papers, and effects, against unreasonable searches and seizures, shall not be violated, and no warrants shall issue, but upon probable cause, supported by Oath or affirmation, and particularly describing the place to be searched, and the persons or things to be seized.

Amendment V [1791]

No person shall be held to answer for a capital, or otherwise infamous crime, unless on a presentment or indictment of a Grand Jury, except in cases arising in the land or naval forces, or in the Militia, when in actual service in time of War or public danger; nor shall any person be subject for the same offence to be twice put in jeopardy of life or limb; nor shall be compelled in any criminal case to be a witness against himself, nor be deprived of life, liberty, or property, without due process of law; nor shall private property be taken for public use, without just compensation.

Amendment VI [1791]

In all criminal prosecutions, the accused shall enjoy the right to a speedy and public trial, by an impartial jury of the State and district wherein the crime shall have been committed, which district shall have been previously ascertained by law, and to be informed of the nature and cause of the accusation; to be confronted with the witnesses against him; to have compulsory process for obtaining witnesses in his favor, and to have the Assistance of Counsel for his defence.

Amendment VII [1791]

In Suits at common law, where the value in controversy shall exceed twenty dollars, the right of trial by jury shall be preserved, and no fact tried by a jury, shall be otherwise re-examined in any Court of the United States, than according to the rules of the common law.

Amendment VIII [1791]

Excessive bail shall not be required, nor excessive fines imposed, nor cruel and unusual punishments inflicted.

Amendment IX [1791]

The enumeration in the Constitution, of certain rights, shall not be construed to deny or disparage others retained by the people.

Amendment X [1791]

The powers not delegated to the United States by the Constitution, nor prohibited by it to the States, are reserved to the States respectively, or to the people.

Amendment XI [1798]

The Judicial power of the United States shall not be construed to extend to any suit in law or equity, commenced or prosecuted against one of the United States by Citizens of another State, or by Citizens or Subjects of any Foreign State.

Amendment XII [1804]

The Electors shall meet in their respective states, and vote by ballot for President and Vice-President, one of whom, at least, shall not be an inhabitant of the same state with themselves; they shall name in their ballots the person voted for as President, and in distinct ballots the person voted for as Vice-President, and they shall make distinct lists of all persons voted for as President, and of all persons voted for as Vice-President, and of the number of votes for each, which lists they shall sign and certify, and transmit sealed to the seat of the government of the United States, directed to the President of the Senate;—The President of the Senate shall, in the presence of the Senate and House of Representatives, open all the certificates and the votes shall then be counted;—The person having the greatest number of votes for President, shall be the President, if such number be a majority of the whole number of Electors appointed; and if no person have such majority, then from the persons having the highest numbers not exceeding three on the list of those voted for as President, the House of Representatives shall choose immediately, by ballot, the President. But in choosing the President, the votes shall be taken by states, the representation from each state having one vote; a quorum for this purpose shall consist of a member or members from two-thirds of the states, and a majority of all the states shall be necessary to a choice. And if the

House of Representatives shall not choose a President whenever the right of choice shall devolve upon them, before the fourth day of March next following, then the Vice-President shall act as President, as in the case of the death or other constitutional disability of the President.—The person having the greatest number of votes as Vice-President, shall be the Vice-President, if such number be a majority of the whole number of Electors appointed, and if no person have a majority, then from the two highest numbers on the list, the Senate shall choose the Vice-President; a quorum for the purpose shall consist of two-thirds of the whole number of Senators, and a majority of the whole number shall be necessary to a choice. But no person constitutionally ineligible to the office of President shall be eligible to that of Vice-President of the United States.

Amendment XIII [1865]

Section 1. Neither slavery nor involuntary servitude, except as a punishment for crime whereof the party shall have been duly convicted, shall exist within the United States, or any place subject to their jurisdiction.

Section 2. Congress shall have power to enforce this article by appropriate legislation.

Amendment XIV [1868]

Section 1. All persons born or naturalized in the United States, and subject to the jurisdiction thereof, are citizens of the United States and of the State wherein they reside. No State shall make or enforce any law which shall abridge the privileges or immunities of citizens of the United States; nor shall any State deprive any person of life, liberty, or property, without due process of law; nor deny to any person within its jurisdiction the equal protection of the laws.

Section 2. Representatives shall be apportioned among the several States according to their respective numbers, counting the whole number of persons in each State, excluding Indians not taxed. But when the right to vote at any election for the choice of electors for President and Vice President of the United States, Representatives in Congress, the Executive and Judicial officers of a State, or the members of the Legislature thereof, is denied to any of the male inhabitants of such State, being twenty-one years of age, and citizens of the United States, or in any way abridged, except for participation in rebellion, or other crime, the basis of representation therein shall be reduced in the proportion which the number of such male citizens shall bear to the whole number of male citizens twenty-one years of age in such State.

Section 3. No person shall be a Senator or Representative in Congress, or elector of President and Vice President, or hold any office, civil or military, under the United States, or under any State, who, having previously taken an oath, as a member of Congress, or as an officer of the United States, or as a member of any State legislature, or as an executive or judicial officer of any State, to support the Constitution of the United States, shall have engaged in insurrection or rebellion against the same, or given aid or comfort to the enemies thereof. But Congress may by a vote of two-thirds of each House, remove such disability.

Section 4. The validity of the public debt of the United States, authorized by law, including debts incurred for payment of pensions and bounties for services in suppressing insurrection or rebellion, shall not be questioned. But neither the United States nor any State shall assume or pay any debt or obligation incurred in aid of insurrection or rebellion against the United States, or any claim for the loss or emancipation of any slave; but all such debts, obligations and claims shall be held illegal and void.

Section 5. The Congress shall have power to enforce, by appropriate legislation, the provisions of this article.

Amendment XV [1870]

Section 1. The right of citizens of the United States to vote shall not be denied or abridged by the United States or by any State on account of race, color, or previous condition of servitude.

Section 2. The Congress shall have power to enforce this article by appropriate legislation.

Amendment XVI [1913]

The Congress shall have power to lay and collect taxes on incomes, from whatever source derived, without apportionment among the several States, and without regard to any census or enumeration.

Amendment XVII [1913]

The Senate of the United States shall be composed of two Senators from each State, elected by the people thereof, for six years; and each Senator shall have one vote. The electors in each State shall have the qualifications requisite for electors of the most numerous branch of the State legislatures.

When vacancies happen in the representation of any State in the Senate, the executive authority of such State shall issue writs of election to fill such vacancies: *Provided*, That the legislature of any State may empower the executive thereof to make temporary appointments until the people fill the vacancies by election as the legislature may direct.

This amendment shall not be so construed as to affect the election or term of any Senator chosen before it becomes valid as part of the Constitution.

Amendment XVIII [1919]

Section 1. After one year from the ratification of this article the manufacture, sale, or transportation of intoxicating liquors within, the importation thereof into, or the exportation thereof from the United States and all territory subject to the jurisdiction thereof for beverage purposes is hereby prohibited.

Sec. 2. The Congress and the several States shall have concurrent power to enforce this article by appropriate legislation.

Sec. 3. This article shall be inoperative unless it shall have been ratified as an amendment to the Constitution by the legislatures of the several States, as provided in the Constitution, within seven years from the date of the submission hereof to the States by the Congress.

Amendment XIX [1920]

The right of citizens of the United States to vote shall not be denied or abridged by the United States or by any State on account of sex.

Congress shall have power to enforce this article by appropriate legislation.

Amendment XX [1933]

Section 1. The terms of the President and Vice President shall end at noon on the 20th day of January, and the terms of Senators and Representatives at noon on the 3d day of January, of the years in which such terms would have ended if this article had not been ratified; and the terms of their successors shall then begin.

Sec. 2. The Congress shall assemble at least once in every year, and such meeting shall begin at noon on the 3d day of January, unless they shall by law appoint a different day.

Sec. 3. If, at the time fixed for the beginning of the term of the President, the President elect shall have died, the Vice President elect shall become President. If a President shall not have been chosen before the time fixed for the beginning of his term, or if the President elect shall have failed to qualify, then the Vice President elect shall act as President until a President shall have qualified; and the Congress may by law provide for the case wherein neither a President elect nor a Vice President elect shall have qualified, declaring who shall then act as President, or the manner in which one who is to act shall be selected, and such person shall act accordingly until a President or Vice President shall have qualified.

Sec. 4. The Congress may by law provide for the case of the death of any of the persons from whom the House of Representatives may choose a President whenever the right of choice shall have devolved upon them, and for the case of the death of any of the persons from whom the Senate may choose a Vice President whenever the right of choice shall have devolved upon them.

Sec. 5. Sections 1 and 2 shall take effect on the 15th day of October following the ratification of this article.

Sec. 6. This article shall be inoperative unless it shall have been ratified as an amendment to the Constitution by the legislatures of three-fourths of the several States within seven years from the date of its submission.

Amendment XXI [1933]

Section 1. The eighteenth article of amendment to the Constitution of the United States is hereby repealed.

Sec. 2. The transportation or importation into any State, Territory, or possession of the United States for delivery or use therein of intoxicating liquors, in violation of the laws thereof, is hereby prohibited.

Sec. 3. This article shall be inoperative unless it shall have been ratified as an amendment to the Constitution by conventions in the several States, as provided in the Constitution, within seven years from the date of the submission hereof to the States by the Congress.

Amendment XXII [1951]

Section 1. No person shall be elected to the office of the President more than twice, and no person who has held the office of President, or acted as President, for more than two years of a term to which some other person was elected President shall be elected to the office of the President more than once. But this Article shall not apply to any person holding the office of President when this Article was proposed by the Congress, and shall not prevent any person who may be holding the office of President, or acting as President, during the term within which this Article becomes operative from holding the office of President or acting as President during the remainder of such term.

Sec. 2. This article shall be inoperative unless it shall have been ratified as an amendment to the Constitution by the legislatures of three-fourths of the several States within seven years from the date of its submission to the States by the Congress.

Amendment XXIII [1961]

Section 1. The District constituting the seat of Government of the United States shall appoint in such manner as the Congress may direct:

A number of electors of President and Vice President equal to the whole number of Senators and Representatives in Congress to which the District would be entitled if it were a State, but in no event more than the least populous State; they shall be in addition to those appointed by the States, but they shall be considered, for the purposes of the election of President and Vice President, to be electors appointed by a State; and they shall meet in the District and perform such duties as provided by the twelfth article of amendment.

Section 2. The Congress shall have power to enforce this article by appropriate legislation.

Amendment XXIV [1964]

Section 1. The right of citizens of the United States to vote in any primary or other election for President or Vice President, for electors for President or Vice President, or for Senator or Representative in Congress, shall not be denied or abridged by the United States or any State by reason of failure to pay any poll tax or other tax.

Section 2. The Congress shall have power to enforce this article by appropriate legislation.

Amendment XXV [1967]

Section 1. In case of the removal of the President from office or of his death or resignation, the Vice President shall become President.

Sec. 2. Whenever there is a vacancy in the office of the Vice President, the President shall nominate a Vice President who shall take office upon confirmation by a majority vote of both Houses of Congress.

Sec. 3. Whenever the President transmits to the President pro tempore of the Senate and the Speaker of the House of Representatives his written declaration that he is unable to discharge the powers and duties of his office, and until he transmits to them a written declaration to the contrary, such powers and duties shall be discharged by the Vice President as Acting President.

Sec. 4. Whenever the Vice President and a majority of either the principal officers of the executive departments or of such other body as Congress may by law provide, transmit to the President pro tempore of the Senate and the Speaker of the House of Representatives their written declaration that the President is unable to discharge the powers and duties of his office, the Vice President shall immediately assume the powers and duties of the office as Acting President.

Thereafter, when the President transmits to the President pro tempore of the Senate and the Speaker of the House of Representatives his written declaration that no inability exists, he shall resume the powers and duties of his office unless the Vice President and a majority of either the principal officers of the executive department or of such other body as Congress may by law provide, transmit within four days to the President pro tempore of the Senate and the Speaker of the House of Representatives their written declaration that the President is unable to discharge the powers and duties of his office. Thereupon Congress shall decide the issue, assembling within forty-eight hours for that purpose if not in session. If the Congress, within twenty-one days after receipt of the latter written declaration, or, if Congress is not in session, within twenty-one days after Congress is required to assemble, determines by two-thirds vote of both Houses that the President is unable to discharge the powers and duties of his office, the Vice President shall continue to discharge the same as Acting President; otherwise, the President shall resume the powers and duties of his office.

Amendment XXVI [1971]

Sec. 1. The right of citizens of the United States, who are eighteen years of age or older, to vote shall not be denied or abridged by the United States or by any State on account of age.

Sec. 2. The Congress shall have power to enforce this article by appropriate legislation.

L. Proposed Amendments to the Constitution Not Ratified by the States (1789–1978)

ARTICLES IN ADDITION TO, AND AMENDMENT OF, THE CONSTITUTION OF THE UNITED STATES, PROPOSED BY CONGRESS BUT NOT RATIFIED BY THE STATES

Proposal of 1789

Article I. After the first enumeration required by the first article of the Constitution, there shall be one Representative for every thirty thousand, until the number shall amount to one hundred, after which the proportion shall be so regulated by Congress, that there shall be not less than one hundred Representatives, nor less than one Representative for every forty thousand persons, until the number of Representatives shall amount to two hundred; after which the proportion shall be so regulated by Congress, that there shall not be less than two hundred Representatives, nor more than one Representative for every fifty thousand persons.

Proposal of 1789

Article II. No law varying the compensation for the services of the Senators and Representatives shall take effect, until an election of Representatives shall have intervened.

Proposal of 1810

If any citizen of the United States shall accept, claim, receive or retain any title of nobility or honour, or shall, without the consent of Congress, accept and retain any present, pension, office or emolument of any kind whatever, from any emperor, king, prince or foreign power, such person shall cease to be a citizen of the United States, and shall be incapable of holding any office of trust or profit under them, or either of them.

Proposal of 1861

No amendment shall be made to the Constitution which will authorize or give to Congress the power to abolish or interfere, within any State, with the domestic institutions thereof, including that of persons held to labor or service by the laws of said State.

Proposal of 1924

Section 1. The Congress shall have power to limit, regulate, and prohibit the labor of persons under 18 years of age.

Section 2. The power of the several States is unimpaired by this article except that the operation of State laws shall be suspended to the extent necessary to give effect to legislation enacted by the Congress.

Proposal of 1972

Section 1. Equality of rights under the law shall not be denied or abridged by the United States or by any State on account of sex.

Section 2. The Congress shall have the power to enforce, by appropriate legislation, the provisions of this article.

Section 3. This amendment shall take effect two years after the date of ratification.

Proposal of 1978

Section 1. For purposes of representation in the Congress, election of the President and Vice President, and article V of this Constitution, the District constituting the seat of government of the United States shall be treated as though it were a State.

Section 2. The exercise of the rights and powers conferred under this article shall be by the people of the District constituting the seat of government, and as shall be provided by the Congress.

Section 3. The twenty-third article of amendment to the Constitution of the United States is hereby repealed.

Section 4. This article shall be inoperative, unless it shall have been ratified as an amendment to the Constitution by the legislatures of three-fourths of the several States within seven years from the date of its submission.

M. The Gettysburg Address (1863)

FINAL TEXT OF THE ADDRESS DELIVERED AT THE DEDICATION OF THE CEMETERY AT GETTYSBURG

Four score and seven years ago our fathers brought forth on this continent, a new nation, conceived in Liberty, and dedicated to the proposition that all men are created equal.

Now we are engaged in a great civil war, testing whether that nation, or any nation so conceived and so dedicated, can long endure. We are met on a great battle-field of that war. We have come to dedicate a portion of that field, as a final resting place for those who here gave their lives that that nation might live. It is altogether fitting and proper that we should do this.

But, in a larger sense, we can not dedicate—we can not consecrate—we can not hallow—this ground. The brave men, living and dead, who struggled here, have consecrated it, far above our poor power to add or detract. The world will little note, nor long remember what we say here, but it can never forget what they did here. It is for us the living, rather, to be dedicated here to the unfinished work which they who fought here have thus far so nobly advanced. It is rather for us to be here dedicated to the great task remaining before us—that from these honored dead we take increased devotion to that cause for which they gave the last full measure of devotion—that we here highly resolve that these dead shall not have died in vain—that this nation, under God, shall have a new birth of freedom—and that government of the people, by the people, for the people, shall not perish from the earth.

Abraham Lincoln

November 19, 1863*

300

*It is instructive to read the Gettysburg Address with President Lincoln's Second Inaugural Address of March 4, 1865:

Fellow Countrymen:

At this second appearing to take the oath of the presidential office, there is less occasion for an extended address than there was at the first. Then a statement, somewhat in detail, of a course to be pursued, seemed fitting and proper. Now, at the expiration of four years, during which public declarations have been constantly called forth on every point and phase of the great contest which still absorbs the attention, and engrosses the energies of the nation, little that is new could be presented. The progress of our arms, upon which all else chiefly depends, is as well known to the public as to myself; and it is, I trust, reasonably satisfactory and encouraging to all. With high hope for the future, no prediction in regard to it is ventured.

On the occasion corresponding to this four years ago, all thoughts were anxiously directed to an impending civil-war. All dreaded it—all sought to avoid it. While the inaugural address was being delivered from this place, devoted altogether to *saving* the Union without war, insurgent agents were in the city seeking to *destroy* it without war—seeking to dissolve the Union, and divide effects, by negotiation. Both parties deprecated war; but one of them would *make* war rather than let the nation survive; and the other would *accept* war rather than let it perish. And the war came.

One eighth of the whole population were colored slaves, not distributed generally over the Union, but localized in the Southern part of it. These slaves constituted a peculiar and powerful interest. All knew that this interest was, somehow, the cause of the war. To strengthen, perpetuate, and extend this interest was the object for which the insurgents would rend the Union, even by war; while the government claimed no right to do more than to restrict the territorial enlargement of it. Neither party expected for the war, the magnitude, or the duration, which it has already attained. Neither anticipated that the *cause* of the conflict might cease with, or even before, the conflict itself should cease. Each looked for an easier triumph, and a result less fundamental and astounding. Both read the same Bible, and pray to the same God; and each invokes His aid against the other. It may seem strange that any men should dare to ask a just God's assistance in wringing their bread from the sweat of other men's faces; but let us judge not that we be not judged. The prayers of both could not be answered; that of neither has been answered fully. The Almighty has His own purposes. "Woe unto the world because of offences! for it must needs be that offences come; but woe to that man by whom the offence cometh!" If we shall suppose that American Slavery is one of those offences which, in the providence of God, must needs come, but which, having continued through His appointed time, He now wills to remove, and that He gives to both North and South, this terrible war, as the woe due to those by whom the offence came, shall we discern therein any departure from those divine attributes which the believers in a Living God always ascribe to Him? Fondly do we hope—fervently do we pray— that this mighty scourge of war may speedily pass away. Yet, if God wills that it continue, until all the wealth piled by the bond-man's two hundred and fifty years of unrequited toil shall be sunk, and until every drop of blood drawn with the lash, shall be paid by another drawn with the sword, as was said three thousand years ago, so still it must be said "the judgments of the Lord, are true and righteous altogether."

With malice toward none; with charity for all; with firmness in the right, as God gives us to see the right, let us strive on to finish the work we are in; to bind up the nation's wounds; to care for him who shall have borne the battle, and hor his widow, and his orphan—to do all which may achieve and cherish a just, and a lasting peace, among ourselves, and with all nations.

Notes

1. The *Loyola University of Chicago Law Journal* version of this Commentary provides an appendix of my publications on constitutional and related subjects, including accounts by me of the work and influence of two of my teachers, William Winslow Crosskey and Leo Strauss. (Vol. 18, pp. 225–33, Fall 1986; some corrections of those publications are indicated in that appendix.) Only a half dozen citations have been provided to my published work in the notes to this Commentary. These may be found in notes 6, 49, 85, 98, and 150. (Notes 6, 49, and 98 include citations to corrections for my three books.) The perspective from which I speak in this Commentary is further suggested by the following list of publications selected from my bibliography:

1. "The Declaration of Independence," *St. Louis University Law Journal* 9 (Spring 1965): 390–415.
2. "Self-Government and the Mass Media: A Practical Man's Guide," in *The Mass Media and Modern Democracy*, 161–232, ed. by Harry M. Clor (Chicago: Rand McNally, 1974). This article includes an analysis of the Pentagon Papers controversy and an extended argument for the abolition of broadcast television in the United States.
3. "The Occasions of Freedom of Speech," *Political Science Reviewer* 5 (Fall 1975): 383–402.
4. "Human Nature and the First Amendment," *University of Pittsburgh Law Review* 40 (Summer 1979): 661–778.
5. "Abraham Lincoln's Emancipation Proclamation," in *Constitutional Government in America*, 421–46, ed. by Ronald K. L. Collins (Durham, N.C.: Carolina Academic Press, 1980).
6. "Notes toward an 'Apologia pro vita sua,' " *Interpretation* 10 (May & September 1982): 319–52.
7. "Legal Realism, the New Journalism, and *The Brethren*," *Duke Law Journal* 1983 (November 1983): 1045–74.
8. "Mr. Crosskey, the American Constitution, and the Natures of Things," *Loyola University of Chicago Law Journal* 15 (Winter 1984): 181–260.

9. "How to Read the Constitution of the United States," *Loyola University of Chicago Law Journal* 17 (Fall 1985): 1–66.
10. *Encyclopedia Britannica*, 15th ed., 1985. S.v. "Censorship."
11. "Freedom of Speech and the Silence of the Law," *Texas Law Review* 64 (October 1985): 443–67.
12. "The Northwest Ordinance of 1787: Illinois' First Constitution," *Illinois Bar Journal* 75 (November 1986): 123–29.
13. "What Is Still Wrong with George Anastaplo? A Sequel to 366 U.S. 82 (1961)," *De Paul Law Review* 35 (Spring 1986): 551–647.
14. "Seven Questions for Professor Jaffa," *University of Puget Sound Law Review* 10 (Spring 1987): 507–69.
15. "On the Judging of Judges: The Case for Robert H. Bork," *University of Chicago Maroon* (October 6, 1987): 21; "Justice Brennan, Due Process, and the Freedom of Speech: A Celebration of *Speiser v. Randall*," *John Marshall Law Review* 20 (Fall 1986): 7–27; "William H. Rehnquist and the First Amendment," *Intercollegiate Review* (Spring 1987): 31–40; "Justice Brennan, Natural Right, and Constitutional Interpretation," *Cardozo Law Review* 10 (October 1988): 201–20; "Mr. Justice Black, His Generous Common Sense, and the Bar Admission Cases," *Southwestern University Law Review* 9 (1977): 977–1048.
16. "Church and State: Explorations," *Loyola University of Chicago Law Journal* 19 (Fall 1987): 61–193.
17. "We the People: The Rulers and the Ruled," in *The Great Ideas Today*, 1987: 52–72.

My forthcoming publications of relevance here include:

1. "*In re* Allan Bloom: A Respectful Dissent," in *The Great Ideas Today*, 1988;
2. "Slavery and the Constitution: Explorations," *Texas Tech Law Review*, 1989;
3. *The American Moralist: Essays on Law, Ethics, and Government* (Athens, Ohio: Swallow Press/Ohio University Press, 1990).

I did not include in my *Loyola Law Journal* bibliography the series of long introductions to ancient non-Western texts I have been preparing for the annual volumes of *The Great Ideas Today* (an *Encyclopedia Britannica* publication). These introductions are to the *Analects* of Confucius (1984), to the *Bhagavad Gita* (1985), to the *Gilgamesh* (1986), to the *Koran* (1989), and to Buddhist thought (1990). When one learns what has been done and said over millennia in ordering the characters and lives of other great peoples, one may better see and hence more deeply appreciate what was said and done in this Country between 1776 and 1789.

The sources of the seven epigraphs of this Commentary are the following:

1. Socrates: Plato, *Crito* 54D.
2. James Wilson: Pennsylvania Ratification Convention, November 24 (or 26), 1787; Jonathan Elliot, ed., *The Debates in the Several State Conventions on the Adoption of the Federal Constitution*, 2d ed. (Philadelphia: J. B. Lippincott, 1836), 3: 433.

3. Thomas Jefferson: letter to John Adams, October 28, 1813; quoted in Leo Strauss, *What Is Political Philosophy?* (Glencoe, Ill.: Free Press, 1959), 86.
4. William Winslow Crosskey: *Politics and the Constitution in the History of the United States* (Chicago: University of Chicago Press, 1953), 1: 674, 2: 1172.
5. Oliver Wendell Holmes, Jr.: this sentence serves as the epigraph for Crosskey, *Politics and the Constitution.* See also ibid., 2: 910, 1365, n. 90.
6. Gouverneur Morris: letter from Paris, France to President George Washington, January 24, 1790; quoted in George Anastaplo, "American Constitutionalism and the Virtue of Prudence: Philadelphia, Paris, Washington, Gettysburg," in Leo Paul S. de Alvarez, ed., *Abraham Lincoln, the Gettysburg Address, and American Constitutionalism* (Irving, Tex.: University of Dallas Press, 1976), 96.
7. Leo Strauss: *Spinoza's Critique of Religion* (New York: Schocken Books, 1965), 2.

LECTURES

1. The constitutions of the Americans, as reviewed in this opening lecture, are the following:

I. The Language of the English-Speaking Peoples
II. The British Constitution
III. The Declaration of Independence
IV. The Common Law
V. The Law of Public Bodies
VI. The State Constitution(s)
VII. The Best Regime (Temporal)
VIII. The Best Regime(s) (Spiritual)
IX. The Character of the People
X. The Law of Nations
XI. The Articles of Confederation
XII. The Constitution of 1787
XIII. The System of the World

See note 113, below.

Deliberate use is made in this Commentary of the old-fashioned mode of capitalizing words such as *State, Country,* and *Constitutional* (when they refer to the 1787 Constitution and its amendments). Also old-fashioned is the use of *General Government* and *National Courts* instead of *Federal Government* and *Federal Courts.* Those subdivisions of the Constitution conventionally referred to as Clauses are sometimes referred to in this Commentary, for the convenience of readers, as Sentences, Paragraphs, Provisions, or Sets of Powers.

The reader is urged to begin by reading the text of this book without reference to its notes. Cross-references within this book are to Lectures and Sections, to Appendixes, to notes, or to passages in the text keyed to notes.

2. On the other hand, some would argue that it is difficult to put serious philosophical discourse into English. See note 12, below. See also Lecture No. 3, Section VI (end). John Milton repeatedly indicates in his *Areopagitica* that the language of the liberty-loving English is ill-fitted for repressive measures. See also the text at note 51.

3. See Leonard W. Levy, Kenneth L. Karst, & Dennis J. Mahoney, eds., *Encyclopedia of the American Constitution* (New York: Macmillan Co., 1986), s.vv. "British Constitution", "Constitution", and "Unwritten Constitution". (Cited hereafter as *Ency. Am. Const.*) On "the succession of English constitutions," see Eugene F. Miller, "Hume on the Development of English Liberty," *Political Science Reviewer* 16 (1986): 127.

4. "The common law is a system of principles and rules grounded in universal custom or natural law and developed, articulated, and applied by courts in a process designed for the resolution of individual controversies. In this general sense, the common law is the historic basis of all Anglo-American legal systems. It is also an important element in the origin and plan of the United States Constitution." Ibid., 332. See also Lecture No. 2, Section V; Lecture No. 10; Lecture No. 11; and Lecture No. 15, Sections III and IV.

5. See Lecture No. 12, Sections VII and VIII.

6. See, on nature and on natural right, Lecture No. 2, Sections I, V, and VII; Lecture No. 4, Sections III and IV; Lecture No. 5, Sections IV and VII; Lecture No. 7, Sections II(ix), II(xi), II(xiv), and II(xv); Lecture No. 8, Sections VII and VIII; Lecture No. 10, Sections VI, VII, and IX; Lecture No. 11, Section II; Lecture No. 12, Sections II, IX, and XI; Lecture No. 14, Sections V, VIII, and IX; Lecture No. 15, Section IX; and Lecture No. 17, Sections IV, VIII, and IX. See also *Ency. Am. Const.*, s.v. "Natural Rights and the Constitution"; Leo Strauss, *Natural Right and History* (Chicago: University of Chicago Press, 1953); George Anastaplo, *Human Being and Citizen: Essays on Virtue, Freedom and the Common Good* (Chicago: Swallow Press/Ohio University Press, 1975), 45f, 74f. (For corrections of *Human Being and Citizen*, see page 371 of *The Artist as Thinker*, cited in note 49, below.)

7. See, for example, Lecture No. 15, Section IX.

8. See also Lecture No. 2, Section VII; and Lecture No. 16, Section VI.

9. See, on slavery, Lecture No. 1, Section XII; Lecture No. 2, Sections IV, V, VII, and VIII; Lecture No. 3, Sections III and V; Lecture No. 5, Section VI; Lecture No. 6, Sections II, III, VI, and VII; Lecture No. 7, Sections II(x) and II(xi); Lecture No. 10, Section VI; Lecture No. 11, Sections V and IX; Lecture No. 12, Section X; Lecture No. 13, Sections III and V-IX; Lecture No. 14, Sections VIII and IX; and Lecture No. 17, Sections IV-IX. See also *Ency. Am. Const.*, s.vv. "Lincoln, Abraham", "Slavery and the Constitution", and "Slavery in the Territories"; Harry V. Jaffa, *Crisis of the House Divided: An Interpretation of the Lincoln-Douglas Debates*, 2d ed. (Chicago: University of Chicago Press, 1982). See as well notes 14, 15, 42, and 145, below; and Appendix M.

10. See on the Tenth Amendment, Lecture No. 2, Section IX; Lecture No. 5, Sections II and VII; Lecture No. 6, Section IV; and Lecture No. 17, Sections

IV and V. A proper reading of the Tenth Amendment should recognize that *delegated, reserved,* and *States* may not mean quite what they are now commonly taken to mean. Does the Tenth Amendment subordinate the States to the United States Constitution in a way that had not been done before? See note 23, below. See, for the texts of all of the amendments, Appendix K.

11. The Eleventh Amendment protects a State from being sued by citizens of other States if it does not choose to be. This amendment was developed in response to *Chisholm* v. *Georgia,* 2 U.S. (2 Dall.) 419 (1793), which had permitted a State to be sued without its consent by a citizen of another State. See *Ency. Am. Const.,* s.vv. "*Chisholm* v. *Georgia*", "Eleventh Amendment", and "Judicial Power of the United States".

See, on the Twelfth Amendment, Lecture No. 8. See also *Ency. Am. Const.,* s.v. "Twelfth Amendment".

12. Martin Heidegger, whom I have had occasion to characterize as "the Macbeth of philosophy," argued that Greek, German, and perhaps Sanskrit are best for *thinking*. See the text at note 2.

13. William W. Crosskey, *Politics and the Constitution in the History of the United States* (Chicago: University of Chicago Press, 1953), 1: 199 (quoting Elbridge Gerry). (Cited hereafter as Crosskey.) Gerry was one of the three delegates present during the final meeting of the Federal Convention who refused to sign the Constitution. See the text at note 143.

14. See, on liberty, Lecture No. 1, Section VII; Lecture No. 2, Sections II, III, and V; Lecture No. 3, Sections V and XII; Lecture No. 4, Sections I and V; Lecture No. 5, Sections VI and VII; Lecture No. 6, Sections IV and VII; Lecture No. 7, Sections II(iii) and II(vii); Lecture No. 9, Section IV; Lecture No. 12, Section XI; Lecture No. 13, Sections V, VII, and VIII; Lecture No. 14, Section V; Lecture No. 15, Sections II and IX; Lecture No. 17, Sections III, VII, and IX. See also note 111, below.

I speak of the six ends set forth in the Preamble. A seventh end is evident in the Preamble as a whole: the ordaining and establishing of the Constitution itself. See note 109, below.

15. See, on equality, Lecture No. 1, Section XII; Lecture No. 3, Sections V, VI, VII, VIII, and IX; Lecture No. 4, Section V; Lecture No. 6, Sections VI and VII; Lecture No. 8, Section VI; Lecture No. 11, Section IX; Lecture No. 13, Sections VII and VIII; Lecture No. 14, Section VIII; Lecture No. 15, Section II; and Lecture No. 17, Section IX. See also note 9, above, and note 111, below.

16. See, on a republican form of government, Lecture No. 1, Section VII; Lecture No. 3, Section IV; Lecture No. 6, Section IV; and Lecture No. 13, Sections V and VII. See also *Ency. Am. Const.,* s.v. "Republican Form of Government".

See, on the *people* required for a republican form of government, Lecture No. 1, Sections VII and IX; Lecture No. 2, Sections II, IV, VII, and IX; Lecture No. 3; Lecture No. 4, Sections I-III; Lecture No. 5, Sections III and VII; Lecture No. 6, Sections II, IV, VI, and VII; Lecture No. 7, Section II(xi); Lecture No. 8, Section VII; Lecture No. 9, Section VIII; Lecture No. 11, Section IX;

Lecture No. 12, Sections X, XI, and XII; Lecture No. 13, Section VIII; Lecture No. 14, Sections V and IX; Lecture No. 15, Sections II and VII; Lecture No. 16, Section II; and Lecture No. 17, Sections VI, VII, and IX.

I published in 1965 an article in which I discuss the separation-of-powers implications of the references to divinity in the Declaration of Independence. (I first offered these suggestions in print in my 1964 University of Chicago doctoral dissertation at 508–511.) I have recently discovered that I may have been somewhat anticipated here by *Isaiah* 33: 22. Compare *Isaiah* 40: 18, 25. Compare also *Isaiah* 44: 6–20.

17. See Appendix H; Lecture No. 17, Section I.

18. The most instructive research into the possible significance of the Preamble and of the enumeration of powers in Section 8 of Article I remains the pioneering work of William Winslow Crosskey, *Politics and the Constitution* (note 13, above). See Malcolm P. Sharp, "Crosskey, Anastaplo and Meiklejohn on the United States Constitution," *University of Chicago Law School Record*, 1973: 3; C. Herman Pritchett, Book Review, *California Law Review*, 60: 1476 (1972).

See, on the Preamble, Lecture No. 1, Section VII; Lecture No. 2, Sections I–VI and IX; Lecture No. 3, Sections X and XIII; Lecture No. 4, Section VI; Lecture No. 5, Sections II and VI; Lecture No. 6, Section III; Lecture No. 9, Section V; Lecture No. 11, Section IX; Lecture No. 12, Sections III, VII, and X; Lecture No. 13, Section IX; Lecture No. 14, Section V; Lecture No. 17, Sections VI and VIII. Compare *Ency. Am. Const.*, s.v. "Preamble". See also note 30, below.

See, on the enumeration of powers, Lecture No. 5, Section IV; and Appendix F.

19. Jonathan Elliot, ed., *The Debates in the Several State Conventions on the Adoption of the Federal Constitution*, 2d ed., (Philadelphia: J. B. Lippincott Co., 1836), 2: 330. (Cited hereafter as Elliot.) These materials may also be found, with the original capitalization, spelling, punctuation, etc., in Herbert J. Storing & Murray Dry, eds., *The Complete Anti-Federalist* (Chicago: University of Chicago Press, 1981). I continue to cite the Elliot collection and the Farrand collection (note 31, below) because so much of my published work is already keyed to them.

20. See note 10, above.

21. See, on freedom of speech and of the press, Lecture No. 1, Section III; Lecture No. 2, Section VII; Lecture No. 3, Sections X and XII; Lecture No. 4, Sections I and IV; Lecture No. 5, Section VII; Lecture No. 6, Section IV; Lecture No. 7, Section II(iv); Lecture No. 8, Sections II, VIII, and IX; Lecture No. 9, Sections IV, VI, and IX; Lecture No. 12, Section XI; Lecture No. 13, Section V; Lecture No. 14, Section V; Lecture No. 17, Section III. See also note 98, below.

James Madison is recorded as having said in the Virginia Ratification Convention on June 24, 1788, "Mr. Chairman, nothing has excited more admiration in the world than the manner in which free governments have been established in America; for it was the first instance, from the creation of the world to the American revolution, that free inhabitants have been seen deliberating on a form of government, and selecting such of their citizens as possessed their confidence, to determine upon and give effect to it." Elliot, 3: 616. See also the opening paragraph of the *Federalist Papers*.

22. Mortimer J. Adler, *We Hold These Truths: Understanding the Ideas and the Ideals of the Constitution* (New York: Macmillan Co., 1987), 129. Compare ibid., 3–8, for a Calhounian rather than a Lincolnian interpretation of the relation between the Declaration of 1776 and the Constitution of 1787. See Lecture No. 17, Sections VI–IX.

The Chief of the Manuscript Division, Library of Congress, has examined "the most important documentary records surrounding the creation of the Constitution and has found them to be defective in varying degrees":

> [I]n all cases the resulting documents are not full, reliable records of the debates of the Constitutional and ratifying conventions. If we conclude that this array of defects has corrupted the historical documentation of the Constitution, it would appear to be impossible to rely upon the documentary record to discover the intentions of the Framers. A jurisprudence of original intention is not precluded by these findings, but it would be obliged to seek the intention of the Framers in the words of the Constitution, as the Framers themselves intended.

James H. Hutson, "The Creation of the Constitution: The Integrity of the Documentary Record," *Texas Law Review*, 65: 1, at 38–39 (1986). See note 71, below.

23. Cannot it be said that the Union permitted the emergence of the States, even though it does not generally empower them? See the text at note 163. See also note 10, above.

24. Elliot, 3: 22. See also ibid., 3: 23. Compare the text at note 163. See as well Elliot, 2: 99; 3: 28–29, 42–44, 98, 143; 4: 15–16, 23–25. Was "We the People" acceptable to some delegates in the Federal Convention only because it was not known which States would agree to the new constitutional arrangement?

25. The State constitutions referred to and quoted from in this Commentary may be found in, among other places, Benjamin P. Poore, ed., *The Federal and State Constitutions, Colonial Charters, and Other Organic Laws of the United States*, 2d ed. (Washington: Government Printing Office, 1878). (Cited hereinafter as *The Federal and State Constitutions*.) More precise citations are not needed in this Commentary either to State constitutions or to such documents as the Declaration of Independence, the Articles of Confederation, the Northwest Ordinance, and the United States Constitution. These four organic documents are set forth in their entirety in Appendixes A, B, D, and E.

26. In the House of Representatives, for which the Constitution originally provided 65 members, 44 votes were needed to override a Presidential veto instead of 33; in the Senate, with 26 Senators anticipated from 13 States, 18 votes were needed instead of 14. (I assume in each case that every eligible

State supplied all of its members. I disregard here the tie-breaking vote in the Senate available to the Vice-President.) See also Lecture No. 9, Section III; and Lecture No. 14, Section I.

Consider, with respect to the limits of the veto power, Senator Sam Nunn's comment in response to a Presidential threat to veto a defense authorization bill: "The President can veto, but he can't fund the Army, the Navy, the Air Force and the Marine Corps." *Chicago Tribune*, October 8, 1987, sec. 1, p. 27. See note 107, below.

27. See, on judicial review, Lecture No. 6, Section IV; Lecture No. 10, Sections I and IX; Lecture No. 11, Sections IV-VII; Lecture No. 12, Section XI; Lecture No. 14, Section VII; Lecture No. 15, Sections V, VI, and VII; and Lecture No. 17, Section VII. See also notes 111 and 139, below.

28. See note 18, above. It should be noticed, however, that the student of the Constitution today is apt to have available to work with (because of the many volumes of records and other sources recently collected and annotated by zealous scholars) far more seventeenth and eighteenth century materials bearing upon Constitutional issues than any public man in this Country would have had available to him in the 1776–1789 period. There may be something deeply misleading, as well as much that is useful, about such abundance. It should also be remembered that the records of debates in the Federal Convention and in the State Ratification Conventions are in various ways unreliable. See note 22, above, note 71, below. See also Lecture No. 3, Section XIII; Lecture No. 4, Section II (end); Lecture No. 4, Section IX; Lecture No. 6, Section I; and Lecture No. 17, Section I.

29. Interpreters of the Constitution have long assumed that much more can be done for the common defense by the General Government than can be done by it for the general welfare, even though the Constitutional authority for the latter seems much the same in scope as the Constitutional authority for the former. See notes 44 and 168, below.

30. *Expressly* had been used in comparable circumstances in the Articles of Confederation, with its considerably weaker powers for the Legislature. See note 10, above, and Lecture No. 17, Section IV.

See, on the purposes of the Preamble, Crosskey, 1: 374, 376. See, on rules of interpretation, ibid., 1: 24, See also William W. Crosskey and William Jeffrey, Jr., *Politics and the Constitution in the History of the United States* (Chicago: University of Chicago Press, 1980), 3: 16–23. See as well note 18, above.

31. Max Farrand, ed., *The Records of the Federal Convention of 1787* (New Haven: Yale University Press, 1937), 1: 469. (Cited hereafter as Farrand.) A paperback edition of James Madison's *Notes of Debates in the Federal Convention of 1787*, which is found in the first two Farrand volumes, is available from Ohio University Press. That instructive text is also available in volume 5 of the Elliot collection and, along with many other materials, throughout Philip B. Kurland & Ralph Lerner, eds., *The Founders' Constitution*, (Chicago: University of Chicago Press, 1987). The comprehensive Kurland & Lerner collection is anticipated by two useful guides to Constitu-

tional sources: (1) David Hutchison, *The Foundations of the Constitution* (Secaucus, N.J.: University Books, 1975) (originally published in 1928); (2) Arthur Taylor Prescott, ed., *Drafting the Constitution* (University, La.: Louisiana State University Press, 1941). See note 19, above.

32. The chart is appended to these lectures as Appendix F. See also note 18, above.

33. Of our seventeen sets of powers, the central one is that of constituting tribunals inferior to the Supreme Court. See also the text at note 41. My numbering of sets of powers in Section 8 corresponds to the numbering of clauses conventionally used here by courts and scholars.

34. The five groupings are suggested in the right-hand margin of the Appendix F chart. The considerable overlapping among them reflects the disputed character of these powers. Perhaps even more overlapping is called for. I again emphasize the tentative character of these speculations, which are designed to elicit comparable, and perhaps much better informed, speculations by others.

35. I restate what I have just been saying by observing that the symmetry is such that the first and last groups of powers here were formerly regarded by some as "legislative"; the second and the next-to-last groups of powers were formerly regarded by some as "executive"; and the central group was formerly regarded by some as "judicial". Under the Articles of Confederation, Congress exercised almost all of the powers exercised by the General Government, but this was early recognized as not a happy state of affairs.

Still another reason for listing some of the powers in Section 8 of Article I is suggested in Section VIII of this lecture (Lecture No. 5). The narrowing of the crime of treason in Section 3 of Article III also called for enumeration of certain powers in Section 8 of Article I, such as with respect to counterfeiting. Comparable precautions contributed to the enumeration of other powers.

36. See, for example, *Wickard* v. *Filburn*, 317 U.S. 111 (1942).

37. See *Gibbons* v. *Ogden*, 22 U.S. (9 Wheat.) 1 (1824). It is said at the end of the Declaration of Independence that the United States claimed they had "full Power to levy War, conclude Peace, contract Alliances, establish Commerce, and to do all other Acts and Things which Independent States may of right do." The first three powers listed here are related to the foreign affairs of the Country, while the commerce power referred to is related primarily to the economy of the Country. Thus, the commerce power of the United States is the great domestic power, along with the revenue power, drawn upon in the Declaration. All this is in a context that finds the representatives of the United States speaking "in the Name, and by Authority of the good People of these Colonies." (In the opening lines of the Declaration they had spoken of "one People" and elsewhere of "their Country.") We are again reminded of why Abraham Lincoln and others could insist that the Union was older than the States. See notes 22 and 23, above, note 162, below.

38. See William Blackstone, *Commentaries on the Laws of England* (1765–1769), 4: 420–21, 424, on the considerable extent of "branches of commerce," "commerce in general," and "a great commercial people." (Cited hereafter as

Blackstone. I use here the four volumes republished recently by the University of Chicago Press.)

See, on the continuing multiplicity of corporation codes in the United States, Alfred F. Conard, *Corporations in Perspective* (Mineola, N.Y.: Foundation Press, 1976), 4–6. "Most similar to the United States' situation is that of Canada, where each of ten provinces has its own companies act. . . . [But] the federal government has adopted a Canada Corporations Act, under which most large, nationwide companies have chosen to be incorporated." Ibid., 6.

39. Elliot, 3: 171. "Southerners feared congressional regulation of interstate traffic in slaves, and consequently sought to interpret the commerce clause narrowly." *Ency. Am. Const.*, 2: 529. See Elliot, 3: 598. See, on consolidation, Appendix H. See also the text at note 24.

40. See, on the Bill of Rights, Lecture No. 1, Section XII; Lecture No. 6, Section IV; and Lecture No. 17, Section III. See also note 113, below. The first two of the twelve amendments proposed for the "Bill of Rights" by the First Congress in 1789 were not ratified by the States. They are set forth in Appendix L. See Lecture No. 3, Section III; and Lecture No. 17, Section III.

41. Jack W. Peltason, *Corwin and Peltason's Understanding the Constitution*, 10th ed. (New York: Holt, Rinehart, and Winston, 1985), 84. (Cited hereafter as Peltason.)

It is salutary to keep in mind throughout this Commentary the reservations expressed by one of my readers, reservations that take as their point of departure the Congressional control of appropriations:

> I think you are wrong in your praise of the American Congress. It is a spending machine that won't stop. It is pacifistic and obstructionist in foreign policy. It has been unable either to reform itself or its policies, or to give leadership in any direction. While it may provide some constituent service and a forum for popular expression, it has maintained no reasonable oversight of the executive bureaucracy. I am not optimistic about its leadership in the future. Therefore, I think prudence would suggest that the Executive should be strengthened further, especially in foreign policy and in its control over spending.

Would strengthening further the Executive lead to more or less "reasonable oversight of the executive bureaucracy"? Consider in this connection the material on the Iranian-arms and Contra-aid controversy cited in note 41 of the *Loyola University of Chicago Law Journal* version of this Commentary (18: 15–249). See also note 85, below and the text at note 131. It is salutary to notice in this connection that a "conservative" administration has been obliged to acknowledge that patriots can properly invoke the Fifth Amendment self-incrimination plea. See "Pleading the Fifth Is No Crime," *New York Times*, Dec. 5, 1986, sec. 1, p. 30.

It is instructive as well to be reminded by all this that when a grand accounting is required within the General Government, it is to the Congress that such an accounting is made. See note 109, below.

42. Peltason, 80. See note 39, above. See also Elliot, 4: 19, 100–102, 272–77, 285–86, 296–97; *Ency. Am. Const.*, 3: 483. The use in the first paragraph of Section 10 of Article I of "the States now existing" suggests to Harry V. Jaffa and others that the Framers expected that slavery would be limited to the original thirteen States. See, to the same effect, the reference to "the original States" in the fugitive slave provision in Article VI of the Northwest Ordinance (Appendix D).

43. Peltason, 59.

44. Farrand, 2: 445. See also 2: 276–77. See as well Appendix H. Are not the common defense, the general welfare, etc., the ends to which the considerable powers with respect to war, commerce and revenue should be devoted? See note 29, above, and the text at note 152.

45. Peltason, 80.

46. See Lecture No. 10, Section I. See also Crosskey, 625; *Ency. Am. Const.*, s.v. "Habeas Corpus".

47. See *Ency. Am. Const.*, s.v. "Contract Clause". Compare Crosskey, 1: 352–60. In support of the challenging Crosskey interpretation of the Contracts Clause is the fact that whatever the States are forbidden to do is not something so inherently questionable that the General Government should also be forbidden to do it. See, on sleeping giants, note 121, below.

48. Alexis de Tocqueville, *Democracy in America*, George Lawrence, trans. (Garden City, N.Y.: Doubleday & Company, 1969). See also ibid., 732. Compare ibid., 493.

49. George Anastaplo, *The Artist as Thinker: From Shakespeare to Joyce* (Athens, Ohio: Swallow Press/Ohio University Press, 1983), 373–74 (quoting P. A. Rollins).

50. Farrand, 3: 405.

51. David Bevington, ed., *The Complete Works of Shakespeare*, 3d ed. (Glenview Ill.: Scott, Foresman, 1980), 10–11. See note 2, above.

52. Ibid., 2, 4.

53. Ibid., 2. The population of the United States at the time of the Declaration of Independence in 1776 and at the time of the Federal Convention in 1787 was between three and four million people. Great Britian had, by then, a population of about ten million people, with perhaps eight million in England alone. See, on American State-by-State population figures in 1787, Elliot, 4: 282.

54. William Shakespeare, *Henry VIII*, V, v, 47 (emphasis added).

55. Farrand, 2: 541.

56. On the political and religious conflicts at the time of the English History Plays, see Bevington, ed., *The Complete Works of Shakespeare*, 9–15.

57. The lessons I have culled from Shakespeare's English History Plays that bear on modern constitutionalism are with respect to the following matters:

I. On constitutional government being taken for granted

II. The primacy of the political

III. Liberty and the republican tradition
IV. The rights of Englishmen
V. Legislative supremacy
VI. Judicial prerogatives
VII. The allure and attributes of a monarch
VIII. The mode of selection of the chief executive
IX. The relation of legitimacy to merit
X. Heredity and honor
XI. The character of the people
XII. The importance of oaths
XIII. The evils of usurpation
XIV. The relation of the moral and spiritual virtues to political virtue
XV. The common good as a standard
XVI. The rule of law
XVII. On the human things served by political life.

58. In many ways, indeed, the President resembles the colorful tail tied to a high-flying kite: for the most part, the tail (which may be useful for balance) seems to be along only for the ride and for show (which, too, can be useful). Difficulties develop, however, when the tail decides it can and should go off on its own. See note 41, above, and note 85, below.

59. Farrand, 2: 501.

60. There is still another curious place left for chance in the system here. If there should ever be a tie within a State in the popular vote for Presidential electors, that highly unlikely tie can be broken, as in Illinois, by lot, with all of that State's electoral votes going to the candidate thus singled out by Providence. See Ill. Rev. Stat. ch. 46, para. 23–27 (1985).

See, on chance, Lecture No. 1, Section IX; Lecture No. 2, Section V; Lecture No. 5, Section I; Lecture No. 8, Sections I, II, VII, and IX; Lecture No. 9, Sections VII and VIII; Lecture No. 10, Section VII; Lecture No. 11, Section I; Lecture No. 13, Section VII; and Lecture No. 14, Section IX.

61. *Congressional Record*, 123: 319–20 (Jan. 6, 1977). Capital letters are used in the *Congressional Record* for the names of current members of Congress. The Vice-President on this occasion was Nelson Rockefeller.

62. Ibid.

63. Ibid., 123: 320. See, for State-by-State totals, ibid., 123: 319.

64. Elliot, 3: 58.

65. *Congressional Record*, 123: 8814 (March 23, 1977).

66. "Electoral College: Retire the Relic," *Chicago Sun-Times*, Nov. 6, 1976, p. 31. Compare Martin Diamond, *The Electoral College and the American Idea of Democracy* (Washington: American Enterprise Institute, 1977).

67. I have been told that the only State which has had this arrangement in recent decades is Maine. See Maine Rev. Stat. Ann. tit. 21-A, sec. 805(2) (Supp. 1986).

68. All this, too, could be done without a Constitutional amendment, since Congress could announce, before each election, the way the Presidential contest will be decided in the unlikely event the upcoming contest is left to the

House of Representatives for resolution. The States could thereafter so vote as States, in the House of Representatives, as both to satisfy the Constitutional requirement and to produce a choice in accordance with the results of the previously announced mode of voting by Members. See, on similar arrangements for popular elections of Senators before the Seventeenth Amendment, *Ency. Am. Const.*, 4: 1665.

A solemn declaration in advance by Congress would not satisfy everyone, however, even though much in our Constitutional system depends upon well-established understandings and traditions that have no formal Constitutional sanction. Some would insist, therefore, upon a Constitutional amendment incorporating the change I have tentatively proposed for study. (For one thing, it is difficult for one Congress to bind its successors.)

69. A creative use, with respect to primaries, of the power and duty of Congress to make sure that Presidential electors shall give their votes on the same day "throughout the United States" could well be experimented with here.
See note 150, below.

70. John Adams, letter to Abigail Adams, December 19, 1793. Adams also observed, "I am Vice President. In this I am nothing, but I may be everything." Donald Young, *American Roulette: The History and Dilemma of the Vice Presidency* (New York: Holt, Rinehart, and Winston, 1965), 10. See also *Ency. Am. Const.*, s.vv. "Adams, John" and "Vice-Presidency". The Twelfth Amendment has reduced significantly the political foundation upon which the Vice Presidency originally stood.

71. Thus, in one recent compilation of all records left by delegates to the Federal Convention, there are 923 pages devoted to Article I, 215 pages devoted to Article II, 56 pages to Article III, 60 pages to Article IV, 10 pages to Article V, 51 pages to Article VI, and 47 pages to Article VII (or twice as much to the Legislative Article as to all the other parts of the Constitution combined). See Wilbourn E. Benton, ed., *1787: Drafting the U. S. Constitution* (College Station, Texas: Texas A & M University Press, 1986).

The authors of the *Federalist Papers*, in attempting to explain what the new Constitution meant, needed to devote only a small part of their analyses to the Presidency. In the State Ratification Conventions, as well, the principal discussions were usually of the Legislative Article of the proposed Constitution. Systematic commentaries upon the entire document are not recorded in the materials available to us from the Ratification Campaign period. See notes 22 and 28, above.

72. P.L. No. 93–148, 87 Stat. 555 (1973) (War Powers Resolution).

73. John R. Silber, "Presidential Handcuffs: Can We Afford the War Powers Act?", *New Republic*, Feb. 18, 1985, pp. 14, 15.

74. Ibid., 15.

75. Ibid.

76. Ibid. Compare *Youngstown Sheet & Tube Co.* v. *Sawyer*, 343 U.S. 572, at 613 (1952) (Frankfurter, J., concurring): "It has not been our tradition to envy such governments." See, note 85 (end), below.

77. *Youngstown Sheet & Tube Co.* v. *Sawyer*, 343 U.S. 572 (1952). See also *Ency. Am. Const.*, 4: 1761. Is a proper executive prerogative comparable to the judicial prerogative (that is, the equity power of a judge)? This permits, in each instance, the appropriate public servant to deal with problems not foreseen by the legislature. Does not John Locke suggest, however, that it is quite a different matter when the legislature has already addressed, and dealt in its own way with, a problem? See, on the problems in applying Locke's executive-prerogative doctrine to the American constitutional system which alone legitimates the President himself, Larry Arnhart, " 'The God-Like Prince': John Locke's Executive Prerogative and the American Presidency," *Presidential Studies Quarterly*, 9: 121 (1979). It is observed in *Federalist* No. 51, "In republican government, the legislature necessarily predominates." In a true "mixed regime," would not the monarchic and aristocratic elements have independent, if not even hereditary, bases for their powers and prerogatives?

78. Silber, 16. Three recent graduates of the National War College sum up in this fashion their discussion of American experience with the War Powers Resolution:

> We recognize that the President's ability to deploy military forces for sustained periods depends on his ability to convince the country of the merits of his policies. It is a political fact that even when a President receives early support for his action his ability to sustain the use of military force depends on the long-term support of the American public. . . .
>
> In the final analysis, the War Powers Resolution will continue to act as a constraint on the President's ability to wage prolonged undeclared war. As a symbol of congressional interest in war, peace, and foreign affairs it will continue to remind both the Congress and the President that each has a legitimate role in these matters.

Robert D. Clark, Andrew M. Egeland, Jr., & David B. Sanford, *The War Powers Resolution* (Washington, D.C.: National Defense University Press, 1985), 42–43.

79. William R. Neikirk, "Cabinet Openings Unearth Dissension in GOP," *Chicago Tribune*, Jan. 10, 1986, sec. 1, p. 1.

80. Ibid.

81. Another "jarring" condition laid down by the prospective Secretary of Agriculture was that "he could fire most of the top officials of the Agriculture Department." Ibid., sec. 1, p. 1.

82. Ever since the First Congress in 1789, the question has been asked whether the President can remove unilaterally an officer whose nomination had been consented to by the Senate. A similar question has been asked with respect to the abrogation of treaties. See *Ency. Am. Const.*, s.vv. "Appointing and Removal Power, Presidential" and "Treaty Power". See also notes 85 and 137, below.

83. Would the use of "The executive Power of the United States" have suggested that there may be executive power that does not depend upon the Constitution? Does "The executive Power," standing thus alone in the Constitu-

tion, oblige us to consider what that executive power is keyed to? What else can it be keyed to but the scope of the General Government indicated in the Preamble and developed primarily in the Legislative Article? See Lecture No. 3, Section II; Lecture No. 5, Section II; and Lecture No. 9, Section I.

84. The Vice President is the presiding officer, in a different and much more limited way, over the Senate. I have found instructive a long paper prepared by Harvey Flaumenhaft of St. John's College for a Liberty Fund Symposium, "Presiding in the New Republic" (1986). It exhibits President Washington's commendable restraint in deferring to the extensive legislative prerogatives recognized in the Constitution. It is observed, at the midpoint of the Flaumenhaft paper, "Washington's first term as President was characterized by a *deference* that would make it possible for national *energy* to grow; his second term, by an *assertiveness* that would make it possible for national *security* to be provided for."

85. Even the President's conduct of foreign policy, which is often made much of, can always be decisively shaped by Congressional directives. Consider, for example, Congress's critical intervention in foreign affairs, despite a Presidential veto, by the imposition of sanctions upon South Africa in 1986. See also Lecture No. 3, Section IX, and the text at note 41. See as well Edmund S. Muskie, "The Chains of Liberty: Congress, President, and American Security," *Cornell Law Forum*, 14: 2 (1988); "Congress Can Control Arms, Too," *New York Times*, Aug. 14, 1986, sec. 1, p. 22. Consider also the materials drawn upon in note 85 of the *Loyola University of Chicago Law Journal* version of this Commentary (18: 15–249).

The President, in preparing and executing his Iran-arms and Contra-aid programs, was deprived of those sound political assessments without which important foreign policy initiatives by this Country are likely to fail, assessments that veteran politicians in Congress would have provided him if they had been properly consulted. One could be reminded by the 1987 Iran-Contra hearings that veteran politicians tend to be far more astute and far more knowledgeable, including about the Constitution, than they are often given credit for. The ultimate dependence of Congress upon the people was summed up by Senator Warren Rudman's observation of July 13, 1987: "The American people have the constitutional right to be wrong." A less provocative way of putting this is to notice that intrinsic to the principles of the Constitution is the recognition that a bad law may still be Constitutional. See also note 41, above.

Underlying this kind of controversy may be fundamental differences between Legislature and Executive under the Constitution. Consider, for a comment on these differences, the concluding paragraph of the conservative Willmoore Kendall's noteworthy 1960 essay, "The Two Majorities":

> If the foregoing analysis is correct, the tension between Executive and Legislative has a deeper meaning—one which, however, begins to emerge only when we challenge the notion that the "high principle" represented by the President and the bureaucracy is indeed high principle, and that the long run

task is to somehow "educate" the congressmen, and out beyond the congressmen the electorate, to acceptance of it. That meaning has to do with the dangerous gap that yawns between high principle as it is understood in the intellectual community (which makes its influence felt through the President and
the bureaucracy) and high principle as it is understood by the remainder of
the population (which makes its influence felt through the Congress). To put
it differently: the deeper meaning emerges when we abandon the fiction
(which I have employed above for purposes of exposition) that we have on
the one hand an Executive devoted to high principle, and a Legislature whose
majority simply refuse to live up to it, and confront the possibility that what
we have is in fact two *conceptions* of high principle about which reasonable
men may legitimately differ. Whilst we maintain the fiction, the task we must
perform is indeed that of "educating" the congressmen, and off beyond them,
the electorate, "up" to acceptance of high principle; once we abandon it, the
task *might* become that of helping the congressmen to "educate" the intellectual community "up" to acceptance of the principles that underlie congressional resistance to executive proposals. In the one case (whilst we maintain the
fiction), discussion is unnecessary; in the other case (where we recognize that
what we stand over against are two sharply differing conceptions of the des-
tiny and perfection of America and of mankind, each of which conceivably
has something to be said for it), discussion is indispensable; and in order to
decide, as individuals, whom to support when executive-legislative tension
arises, we must reopen (that is, cease to treat as closed), reopen in a context
of mutual good faith and respect, the deepest issues between American conservatism and American liberalism. Reopen them, and, I repeat, discuss
them; which we are much out of the habit of doing.

Nellie Kendall, ed., *Willmoore Kendall Contra Mundum* (New Rochelle,
N.Y.: Arlington House, 1971), 226–27. (Does not "the intellectual community" tend to side also with the Judiciary against the Legislature?) Mr. Kendall
observed that "the American system," as "its Framers intended it to be," is
"one in which the final decisions upon at least the important determinations
of policy are hammered out, in accordance with 'the republican principle,' in
a deliberative assembly made up of uninstructed representatives, chosen by
their neighbors because they are the 'virtuous' men . . ." Ibid., 206. Mr. Kendall tended to identify the conservative cause with the legislative mode under
the Constitution. Have not the Reagan Administration and its partisans
shown us that American conservatism, too, is apt, when "in power," to side
with the Executive against the Legislature, thereby disturbing the intended
Constitutional equilibrium?

Consider also the insistence by Abraham Lincoln, in his 1838 Lyceum
Speech, upon the necessity of law-abidingness if our political institutions are
to be perpetuated. See note 169, below. Another disturbing feature of the
1986 Iranian-arms and Contra-aid revelations is that they can help undermine
the moral standing, as well as the reputation and hence the capacity for statesmanship, of the United States around the world. Consider George Anastaplo,
"What Is Still Wrong with George Anastaplo?," *DePaul Law Review*, 35: 551,

at 559, n. 41 (1986). I quote there from the talk about Karl von Clausewitz's treatise on war I gave at a Defense Intelligence College seminar in Washington, D.C., August 28, 1986. The passage quoted from my Clausewitz talk begins, "We should be on guard against that cleverness which can be easily mistaken for prudence, thereby lulling us into a general thoughtlessness . . . Thoughtlessness may be seen in the temptation to try to imitate the Russians in the conduct of our own affairs at home as well as abroad." See Lecture No. 7, Section II(vii).

In any event, it is salutary *in our present circumstances* to challenge the fashionable characterization of the President as "the architect of American foreign policy." It has become easy to overlook the decisive powers of Congress to declare war, to appropriate funds for the army and navy, to establish (and to limit) foreign aid programs, and to make other laws that empower, guide, and circumscribe the President. Then there are the considerable powers of the Senate with respect to appointments and treaties. See *Ency. Am. Const.*, s.v. "Political Philosophy of the Constitution".

86. *Marbury* v. *Madison*, 5 U.S. (1 Cranch) 137 (1803).

87. William Pfaff, "Why Treat Presidents Like Gods?," *Chicago Tribune*, May 28, 1985, sec. 1, p. 15.

88. Ibid. I do not believe George Washington ever was seriously offered a crown to refuse.

89. Ibid.

90. Ibid.

91. Ibid. Mr. Pfaff concluded this column with these observations:

> What has changed in American life that we should pay such servile, even obscene, attention, then, to the Presidential incumbent, his wife, his entourage? Ronald Reagan, Jimmy Carter, Gerald Ford—these are ordinary and decent men whom we put at the top of the insecure pile of American politics for a few years. Why are they treated like gods? Who is being flattered or appeased? Ourselves? Is that what it's all about? Is it national ego, self-adoration, self-aggrandizement? I don't know, but I think it is time that it stops.

See also W. Dale Nelson, "The President's Cocoon," *Chicago Tribune*, April 5, 1988, sec. 5, p. 1. Compare Blackstone, 1: 289: the king is recognized as "the one visible magistrate in whom the majesty of the public resides." But see ibid., 1: 226: "The principal duty of the king is, to govern his people according to law." See, on the assassination of a remarkably unprotected Swedish Prime Minister (Olof Palme), William Pfaff, "Burying a Certain Idea of Sweden," *Chicago Tribune*, March 18, 1986, sec. 1, p. 11.

92. *Marbury* v. *Madison*, 5 U.S. (1 Cranch) 137 (1803).

93. These two terms seem to have been used interchangeably, since something that is referred to as a *Controversy* is shortly thereafter referred to as a *Case*: that is, references are made to those controversies, or cases, "in which a State shall be a Party."

94. See, for example, *Swift* v. *Tyson*, 41 U.S. (16 Pet.) 1 (1842). Common-law adjudications by the National Courts are taken for granted in, among

other places, Article III, Section 2, paragraph 2 of the Constitution and the Seventh Amendment. See, on the common law, note 4, above. Compare Michael Conant, "The Commerce Clause, the Supremacy Clause and the Law Merchant: *Swift* v. *Tyson* and the Unity of Commercial Law," *Journal of Maritime Law and Commerce*, 15: 153 (1984). See, for an instructive consideration of these matters by a State appellate judge, Richard Neely, *The Product Liability Mess: How Business Can Be Rescued from the Politics of State Courts* (New York: The Free Press, 1988).

95. *Erie Railroad Co.* v. *Tompkins*, 304 U.S. 64 (1938).

96. Ibid., 77–80. One can properly acknowledge that the two-headed system of determining the applicable common law in diversity cases had become intolerable well before 1938. See Crosskey, 2: 910–17. Much is to be said for a system of law which insures that "litigants with the same kind of case would have their rights measured by the same legal standards of liability." *Pope & Talbot, Inc.* v. *Hawn*, 346 U.S. 406, at 410 (Black, J.). See Henry J. Friendly, "In Praise of *Erie*—and of the New Federal Common Law," *New York University Law Review*, 39: 383 (1964). But what I am probing in this lecture, and in the opening sections of my next lecture, is the change in jurisprudential opinion about the nature of law that led both to the problem of the justly-decried "two-headed" common-law system and to the recourse to the dubious *Erie* solution for that problem.

97. See, for example, the dissenting opinion by Justice Oliver W. Holmes, Jr., in *Black & White Taxicab Co.* v. *Brown and Yellow Taxicab and Transfer Co.*, 276 U.S. 518, 532–36 (1928).

Justice Holmes conceded this much to the traditional understanding of the Anglo-American common law:

> Books written about any branch of the common law treat it as a unit, cite cases from this court, from the circuit courts of appeal, from the state courts, from England and the Colonies of England indiscriminately, and criticize them as right or wrong according to the writer's notions of a single theory. It is very hard to resist the impression that there is one august corpus, to understand which clearly is the only task of any court concerned. If there were such a transcendental body of law outside of any particular state but obligatory within it unless and until changed by statute, the courts of the United States might be right in using their independent judgment as to what it was.

Ibid., 533. Justice Holmes then adds, "But there is no such body of law." Ibid. I believe he is mistaken, along with many others of like mind today. The common law takes for granted enduring standards of right and wrong that judges discover and apply to the cases that happen to come before them. Such judges can be most flexible, and otherwise sensible, without being relativists. And so it could once be accepted that the opinions of judges are not the law but rather are evidence of the law. Is there not something deeply realistic about this? Underlying the contemporary controversy here is the one between the Aristotelian and the Hobbesian positions. See Anastaplo, *Human Being and Citi-*

zen, Essays No. 4 and No. 6. See also Berns, "Aristotle," cited in note 169, below.

98. See also George Anastaplo, *The Constitutionalist: Notes on the First Amendment* (Dallas: Southern Methodist University Press, 1971), pp. 169–201 (reprinted in Mary Pollinque, ed., *Readings in American Government*, 2d ed. (Dubuque, Iowa: Kendall/Hunt Publishing Co., 1976), 88–99).

The argument of *The Constitutionalist* has been summed up by me in this way:

> The First Amendment to the Constitution prohibits Congress, in its law-making capacity, from cutting down in any way or for any reason freedom of speech and of the press. The extent of this freedom is to be measured not merely by the common-law treatises and cases available on December 15, 1791—the date of the ratification of the First Amendment—but also by the general understanding and practice of the people of the United States who insisted upon, had written for them, and ratified (through their State legislatures) the First Amendment. An important indication of the extent of this freedom is to be seen in the teachings of the Declaration of Independence and in the events leading up to the Revolution.
>
> Although the prohibition in the First Amendment is absolute—we see here a restraint upon Congress that is unqualified, among restraints that *are* qualified—the absolute prohibition does not relate to all forms of expression but only to that which the terms, *freedom of speech, or of the press* were then taken to encompass, political speech, speech having to do with the duties and concerns of self-governing citizens. Thus, for example, this Constitutional provision is not primarily or directly concerned with what we now call artistic expression or with the problems of obscenity. Rather, the First Amendment acknowledges that the sovereign citizen has the right freely to discuss the public business, a privilege theretofore claimed only for members of legislative bodies.
>
> Absolute as the Constitutional prohibition may be with respect to Congress, it does not touch directly the great State power to affect freedom of speech and of the press. In fact, I shall argue, one condition for effective negation of Congressional power over this subject (which negation is important for the political freedom of the American people) is that the States should retain some power to regulate political expression. It seems to me, however, that the General Government has the duty to police or restrain the power of the States in this respect, a duty dictated by such commands in the Constitution of 1787 as that which provides that the "United States shall guarantee to every State in this Union a Republican Form of Government."

Ibid., 15–16. See also note 21, above.

99. 5 U.S. (1 Cranch) 137 (1803). See, on judicial review, note 27, above.

100. The considerable literature on this subject includes useful discussions in the *Encyclopedia of the American Constitution*, 3: 1053, 1054f, 1199, 1202, 1214–1215, 1349; 4: 1813–1814, 1816–1817, 1827–1828. The most challenging

study of the case remains that by Mr. Crosskey in his *Politics and the Constitution*.

101. It was the Judiciary Act of 1789 (1 Stat. 73 (1789)) that got the national judicial system going. See *Ency. Am. Const.*, s.v. "Judiciary Act of 1789".

102. Other provisional arrangements include the designation in the 1787 Constitution of the number of members in the House of Representatives from each State, pending the first census, and the designation of the date Congress is to meet, which date is identified by the Constitution as subject to Congressional revision. See Lecture No. 4, Section III.

103. *Dred Scott* v. *Sandford*, 60 U.S. (19 How.) 393 (1857). The Supreme Court did confirm the constitutionality of various acts of Congress, especially in response to challenges by States, during the half-century between *Marbury* and *Dred Scott*. Was this somewhat like the British Monarch's automatic signing of bills even as he claimed an absolute veto power? See note 107, below.

104. 1 Stat. 50 (1789). See the end of Appendix D.

105. See, for example, *Schechter Poultry Corp.* v. *United States*, 295 U.S. 495 (1935); *Carter* v. *Carter Coal Co.*, 298 U.S. 238 (1936).

106. Farrand, 1: 21, 97–104, 138–40; 2: 73–80, 298–301 (with means provided for the legislature to overcome judicial disapproval of a law). See also ibid., 2: 92–93, 376, 440; note 139, below; Lecture No. 6, Section IV (end). *Federalist* No. 78 makes a plausible argument for judicial review, as do others. But the question is not whether this or that polemicist could make an argument for judicial review during the Ratification Campaign and thereafter but rather whether the Federal Convention had been persuaded by such arguments in its framing of the judicial power. Consider also the remarkable silence about judicial review in *Federalist* No. 33, in circumstances which called for it to be at least referred to if it had been understood to have been available. Be that as it may, judicial review would not have mattered as much as it has during the past century if the Constitution had been generally recognized to provide Congress the extensive commerce and other powers that it does. On the other hand, the meaning of various Constitutional powers would not have been made as much of as they have been, or rather in the way they have been, if it had always been understood that the principal authoritative interpretation of the Constitution would be done by Congress and the President, not by the Courts.

107. See, for example, Blackstone, 1: 182 (on "the vast authority" of Parliament). See also ibid., 1: 49, 91, 138, 156–57, 178. Compare ibid., 1: 239 (actions by the Crown "contrary to reason" are considered void). See as well ibid., 1: 42–62.

The power in Congress to make laws over the objections of the President is indicative of where the ultimate power lies among the branches of the General Government of the United States. See note 26, above. When Blackstone said that "the power of making law constitutes the supreme authority," was he not thinking of a Parliament in which the Monarchy exercises, at least in principle, an absolute veto? See Blackstone, 1: 52; Lecture No. 4, Section VI. See also note 103, above. See as well note 77, above.

108. Ibid., 1: 155, 158–59.

109. Blackstone had recognized the members of Parliament as "the guardians of the English constitution." Ibid., 1: 9. Congress is bound by the Constitution in a way that Parliament is not. See Elliot, 4: 64. Although, as we have seen, judicial review is referred to here and there during the Ratification Campaign, by and large a vigilant people is relied upon to keep the Congress in check. See, for example, ibid., 4: 71–72. See, also, note 41 (end), above.

It is salutary to notice again that it is the Congress alone, among the branches of the General Government, which is said to have the power to "ordain and establish" (this is in Section 1 of Article III), a power that the people exercise in the Preamble. The people, that is, do the ultimate legislating, subject of course to the "Laws of Nature and of Nature's God." See note 14, above.

110. The Framers, many of whom had been condemned as traitors by the British, were sensitive about this crime, it seems. See on the various species of treason, Blackstone, 4: 74–92, 203–4. See also Elliot, 2: 469.

111. Edward Dumbauld, *The Bill of Rights* (Westport, Ct.: Greenwood Press, 1979), 9. A dedication to equality easily tends toward radical democracy. A sensible people that has been "conceived in Liberty" may be inclined, in order to correct the excessive egalitarianism sometimes indulged in since the eighteenth century, to defer to a somewhat aristocratic element in the regime, in the form of judicial review.

Does not liberty naturally aspire to excellence, just as equality naturally aspires to justice? See Lecture No. 17, Section IX.

112. The documents drawn upon in Sections II and III of this lecture (Lecture No. 12) may readily be found in Samuel E. Morison, ed., *Sources and Documents Illustrating the American Revolution 1764–1788 and the Formation of the Federal Constitution*, 2d. ed. (New York: Oxford University Press, 1929).

113. See, for the State constitutions drawn upon here, *The Federal and State Constitutions;* note 25, above.

The Ninth Amendment attempts to protect against the risks of a necessarily incomplete enumeration of rights in the Bill of Rights. That there are rights in addition to those enumerated may implicitly recognize one or more constitutions for Americans in addition to those that are written. See Lecture No. 1, Section XIII; and Lecture No. 17, Section III. Among the rights protected by the Ninth Amendment may be the right of revolution. See, for disavowals of "the notion of non-resistance," Blackstone, 1: 157, 237–38, 356. See also note 169, below.

114. Massachusetts had done the same, as a stopgap measure, for a few years after 1776. See Allan Nevins, *The American States During and After the Revolution 1775–1789* (New York: Augustus M. Kelley, 1924), 127–28.

115. Ibid., 126–27.

116. Ibid., 138–39. Some recent works on State constitutions are cited in

note 116 of the *Loyola University of Chicago Law Journal* version of this Commentary (18: 15–249).

117. Alexander Hamilton is reported to have said on June 21, 1788, in the New York State Ratification Convention, that "the true principle of a republic is, that the people should choose whom they please to govern them." Elliot, 2: 257. See note 16, above.

118. See, for example, *Baker* v. *Carr*, 369 U.S. 186 (1962); *Reynolds* v. *Sims*, 377 U.S. 533 (1964).

119. See Peltason, 124.

120. See, for example, *Luther* v. *Borden*, 48 U.S. (7 How.) 1 (1849); *Pacific States Telephone and Telegraph* v. *Oregon*, 223 U.S. 118 (1912). See also note 16, above.

121. Senator Charles Sumner called the Guarantee "a sleeping giant." Peltason, 124.

122. See ibid., 127–28. See also *Ency. Am. Const.*, s.v. "Amending Process". The twenty-six amendments to the Constitution are collected in Appendix K. The seven amendments proposed by Congress that have not been ratified by the States are collected in Appendix L.

123. *Ency. Am. Const.*, 3: 1511. See also *Coleman* v. *Miller*, 307 U.S. 433, 453 (1939).

124. Edward S. Corwin, *The Constitution and What It Means Today* (Princeton: Princeton University Press, 1973), 219 (citing Article I, Section 5, Paragraph 1 of the Constitution). (Cited hereafter as Corwin.) See, on the numbers required by the Constitution on various occasions, Lecture No. 3, Section XII; Lecture No. 4, Section VI; and Lecture No. 9, Section III.

125. See, for example, Walter Dellinger, "The Balanced Budget Amendment Hoax," *New Republic*, Apr. 7, 1986, p. 10.

126. Peltason, 125.

127. See, for example, John T. Noonan Jr., "Calling for a Constitutional Convention," *National Review*, July 26, 1985, p. 25. (Cited hereafter as Noonan.)

128. See, for example, *Roe* v. *Wade*, 410 U.S. 113 (1973); *Doe* v. *Bolton*, 410 U.S. 179 (1973).

129. See Peltason, 271. The prospect of two more Democratic Party members in the Senate has "naturally" stiffened Republican Party opposition to this change. Would the consent be required of any State that originally ceded territory solely for the District of Columbia? See Article I, Section 8, Clause 17 and Article IV, Section 3 of the Constitution.

130. James J. Kilpatrick, "Balanced Budget Amendment: Good Riddance (Let's Hope)," *Chicago Sun-Times*, Apr. 3, 1986, p. 52. (The Senate speech drawn upon by Mr. Kilpatrick was by Gary Hart of Colorado.) The column continues with these observations:

> This resolution invites a hundred questions having to do with outlays, receipts, fiscal years, estimates of revenue and the like. The Treasury would live in constant uncertainty that the government's checks might unconstitutionally bounce.

Under this resolution, three-fifths of each house could provide for a "specific excess of outlays over receipts." This is bizarre. As Hart observed, it takes only a simple majority of those voting to take the nation to war. What sense does it make to require a three-fifths majority to raise the ante for soil conservation?

Proponents respond that such super-majorities should be required to prevent endless exceptions that would defeat the purpose of the amendment. But the amendment, said Hart, "could easily be circumvented through at least six major loopholes, including phony economic forecasts."

Hart wondered how the amendment would be enforced. Suppose outlays did in fact exceed receipts? Would it be left to the federal courts to pass on the accuracy of budget estimates? Would the Supreme Court decree cuts in spending or increases in revenue? The resolution would virtually mandate judicial activism on federal taxing and spending.

131. Ibid. See also "Unbalancing the Constitution," *Chicago Tribune,* Mar. 31, 1986, sec. 1, p. 10; "Making the System Work," *Christian Science Monitor,* Mar. 27, 1986, p. 15. Compare Noonan, p. 25.

132. The one exception was in the ratification of the Twenty-first Amendment repealing the Eighteenth Amendment. See *Ency. Am. Const.,* s.v. "Twenty-first Amendment".

133. Peltason, 125. See also Corwin, 221–22; Lecture No. 8, Section VII.

134. Peltason, 129 (quoting Woodrow Wilson).

135. Corwin, 221.

136. *Coleman* v. *Miller,* 307 U.S. 433, 457–58 (1939) (Black, J., concurring) (emphasis added).

137. See *Ency. Am. Const.,* s.vv. "Alien and Sedition Acts", "Embargo Acts", and "Tariff Act of 1828". Particularly instructive is Louis Fisher, "Constitutional Interpretation by Members of Congress," *North Carolina Law Review,* 63: 707 (1985). Compare Abner J. Mikva, "How Well Does Congress Support and Defend the Constitution?," *North Carolina Law Review,* 61: 587 (1983). See also Louis Fisher, *Constitutional Dialogues: Interpretation as Political Process* (Princeton: Princeton University Press, 1988).

138. See, for a chronology of the origins and implementation of the Constitution of 1787, *Ency. Am. Const.,* 4: 2114–17. See also Appendix J.

139. Is this a form of judicial review to be exercised by State courts? The acts of a State legislature would not be assessed in the light of the State constitution, however, but in the light of a clearly superior national system of Constitution, laws, and treaties. Even so, the evident impropriety of any court's disregard of the dictates of *its own constitution* or of its own legislature may have been such as to require this explicit authorization in the United States Constitution for something so unusual. See notes 27 and 111, above.

140. I devote as much space as I do here to the "religious Test" problem, which is far more than the space I devote to the Supremacy Clause problem, because supremacy is not seriously questioned today, especially when it is noticed that the Supremacy Clause is directed only to State government pro-

ceedings. But the meaning of religious liberty, including what a government, State or National, may do in cooperation with religion, is very much a problem today.

What I say in this Commentary about the Framers' public opinions about religion and the law seems congruent with John Locke's argument in his *Letter Concerning Toleration* that a general belief in God is required for moral conduct and a responsible integrity. Consider also the argument of the Savoyard Vicar in Jean-Jacques Rousseau's *Emile*. Are not those passages Lockean in spirit which are quoted in Section IX of Lecture No. 15 from the Virginia Declaration of Rights and from the 1777 New York Constitution?

See, on the character of the American people, Lecture No. 2, Section IX; Lecture No. 8, Section IX; Lecture No. 9, Section IV; Lecture No. 12, Section XII; Lecture No. 15, Section VIII; and Lecture No. 17, Section III. See, on attacks upon States "on account of religion" as a "pretence," Articles of Confederation, Article III (Appendix B).

One can see in these early State constitutions that the legislation of morality was considered a proper concern, even a duty, of government. See notes 168 and 169, below.

141. This article in the 1776 Maryland Constitution provides,

That, as it is the duty of every man to worship God in such manner as he thinks most acceptable to him; all persons, professing the Christian religion, are equally entitled to protection in their religious liberty; wherefore no person ought by any law to be molested in his person or estate on account of his religious persuasion or profession, or for his religious practice; unless, under colour of religion, any man shall disturb the good order, peace or safety of the State, or shall infringe the laws of morality, or injure others, in their natural, civil, or religious rights; nor ought any person to be compelled to frequent or maintain, or contribute, unless on contract, to maintain any particular place of worship, or any particular ministry; yet the Legislature may, in their discretion, lay a general and equal tax, for the support of the Christian religion; leaving to each individual the power of appointing the payment over of the money, collected from him, to the support of any particular place of worship or minister, or for the benefit of the poor of his own denomination, or the poor in general of any particular county: but the churches, chapels, glebes, and all other property now belonging to the church of England, ought to remain to the church of England forever. And all acts of Assembly, lately passed, for collecting monies for building or repairing particular churches or chapels of ease, shall continue in force, and be executed, unless the Legislature shall, by act, supersede or repeal the same: but no county court shall assess any quantity of tobacco, or sum of money, hereafter, on the application of any vestry-men or church-wardens; and every encumbent of the church of England, who hath remained in his parish, and performed his duty, shall be entitled to receive the provision and support established by the act, entitled "An act for the support of the clergy of the church of England, in this Province," till the November court of this present year, to be held for the county in which his parish shall lie, or partly lie, or for such time as he hath remained in his parish, and performed his duty.

See also the Maryland oath set forth in Section VIII of this lecture.

142. Farrand, 2: 643.

143. Ibid., 2: 648–49.

144. Ibid., 1: 528.

145. Matthew 6:34. Compare Niccolò Machiavelli, *The Prince*, Leo Paul S. de Alvarez, trans. (Irving, Texas: University of Dallas Press, 1980), 16:

> But the Romans, seeing from afar the inconveniences, always remedied them; and they never let them follow in order to avoid a war, because they knew that war is not to be avoided, but is only deferred to the advantage of others . . . Nor did that which is ordinarily in the mouth of the wise of our times, "to enjoy the benefit of time," ever please them, but [they chose] rather [to take] such benefit [as came] from their virtue and prudence; for time drives forward everything, and can bring along with it the good as well as the bad, and the bad as well as the good.

Compare Lecture No. 6, Section VII; and Lecture No. 13, Section VI (on the merits of abolitionists' avoiding in 1787 an immediate confrontation with slavery).

146. Farrand, 1: 450–52.

147. Ibid., 2: 648.

148. See, for example, Morton J. Frisch & Richard G. Stevens, eds., *The Political Thought of American Statesmen* (Itasca, Ill.: F. E. Peacock, 1973), 130, 141–42, 156. (Cited hereafter as Frisch & Stevens.)

149. Ibid., 152.

150. George Anastaplo, "American Constitutionalism and the Virtue of Prudence: Philadelphia, Paris, Washington, Gettysburg," in Leo Paul S. de Alvarez, ed., *Abraham Lincoln, The Gettysburg Address, and American Constitutionalism* (Irving, Texas: University of Dallas Press, 1976), 92. See also Lecture No. 2, Section IV; Lecture No. 3, Section VIII; and Lecture No. 6, Section VI. See as well note 111, below.

It might seem prudent, in our present circumstances, to consider, as the Federal Convention did in 1787, whether selection of Presidents and Vice-Presidents, for fixed terms, from among a slate of five candidates somehow chosen by the people in the several States, might not be better entrusted to the Congress. Is the Congress more apt to be able to know better and to judge properly the candidates than an electorate that has become woefully dependent upon television? Thus, the final selection would be made in early January rather than in early November. On the other hand, since it is not likely that any changes made at this time in the selection of Presidents will be sensible, it might be best to leave the Constitution as it now is, especially since the people at large are obviously reluctant to give up the right they now believe they have to choose the President. See also Lecture No. 8, Section IX.

151. See Anastaplo, "American Constitutionalism and the Virtue of Prudence," 80.

152. Appendix H; Farrand, 2: 666. See note 44, above.

153. Nathaniel Gorham, a delegate to the Federal Convention from Massa-

chusetts, asked on July 23, 1787: "But will any one say, that all the States are to suffer themselves to be ruined, if Rho. Island should persist in her opposition to general measures?" Ibid., 90. Patrick Henry said in the Virginia Ratification Convention, on June 12, 1788: "As to North Carolina, it is *a poor, despised place*. Its dissent will not have influence to introduce any amendments." Elliot, 3: 314. See, for the dates of the States' ratifications, Appendix J.

154. Frisch & Stevens, 126.

155. See, for example, ibid., 121, 130. See also ibid., 140, 143. See as well *Dred Scott* v. *Sandford*, 60 U.S. (19 How.) 393, at 435 (1857).

156. See *Annals of Congress* (Washington: Gales and Seaton, 1834), 1: 761. See also Lecture No. 5, Section II; note 10, above.

157. Frisch & Stevens, 144.

158. Ibid., 145.

159. Ibid., 130.

160. Ibid., 135.

161. Ibid., 153. See also ibid., 150, 154.

162. See Lecture No. 12, Section VI; Lecture No. 15, Section II; notes 22 and 37, above. See also Roy P. Basler, ed., *The Collected Works of Abraham Lincoln* (New Brunswick, N.J.: Rutgers University Press, 1953), 4: 434. (Cited hereafter as *Collected Works of Lincoln*.) See as well Farrand, 1: 467–68; Elliot, 4: 301–2; *Dred Scott* v. *Sandford*, 60 U.S. (19 How.) 393, at 434, 441, 502.

163. See, for example, *Collected Works of Lincoln*, 4: 436–37. See also note 23, above. Compare the text at note 24.

164. Frisch & Stevens, 145. The quotation from the Virginia Resolutions is italicized by Calhoun. See also ibid., 134.

165. See, for example, ibid., 149, 150, 154.

166. Ibid., 137.

167. Ibid. See also ibid., 141.

168. See ibid., 121, 157. "The same view is believed to be applicable to the power of regulating commerce, as well as all the other powers." Ibid., 160. See also note 137, above. Compare note 29, above.

The United States Supreme Court has recognized that Congress, in using various of its powers, has repeatedly "legislat[ed] against moral wrongs." *Heart of Atlanta Motel* v. *United States*, 379 U.S. 241, at 257 (1964) (Clark, J.). See also Lecture No. 5, Section VII; note 140, above. This sort of thing goes back to the First Session of the First Congress (as in the discussion there of how the tax power may be used to discourage the consumption of rum).

169. Compare President Lincoln's discussion, upon his inauguration in 1861, of whether the South was *entitled* at that time to invoke the right of revolution:

> That there are persons who seek to destroy the Union at all events, and are glad of any pretext to do it, I will neither affirm or deny; but if there be such, I need address no word to them. To those, however, who really love the Union, may I not speak?

Before entering upon so grave a matter as the destruction of our national Union, would it not be wise to ascertain precisely why we do it? Will you hazard so desperate a step, while there is any possibility that any portion of the ills you fly from have no real existence? Will you while the certain ills you fly to, are greater than all the real ones you fly from? Will you risk the commission of so fearful a mistake?

All profess to be content in the Union, if all constitutional rights can be maintained. Is it true, then, that any right, plainly written in the Constitution, has been denied? I think not. Happily the human mind is so constructed, that no party can reach to the audacity of doing this. Think, if you can, of a single instance in which a plainly written provision of the Constitution has ever been denied. If, by the mere force of numbers, a majority should deprive a minority of any clearly written constitutional right, it might, in a moral point of view, justify revolution—certainly would, if such right were a vital one,—but such is not our case. All the vital rights of minorities, and of individuals, are so plainly assured to them, by affirmations and negations in the Constitution, that controversies never arise concerning them. But no organic law can ever be framed with a provision specifically applicable to every question which may occur in practical administration. No foresight can anticipate, nor any document of reasonable length contain express provisions for all possible questions.

Collected Works of Lincoln, 4: 255–56. See also ibid., 4: 432–37. See, on the right of revolution, Farrand, 1: 249, 282, 338; 2: 468–69, 476–77; 366 U.S. 82, 95–96, 99–103 (1961); Lecture No. 1, Sections II and III; Lecture No. 7, Sections II(iv) and II(ix); Lecture No. 12, Section XI; Lecture No. 13, Section IV; Lecture No. 14, Sections V and IX; Lecture No. 15, Section III; and Lecture No. 17, Section IX.

South Carolina, in its "Declaration of the Causes of Secession," December 1860, accused the Free States of (1) violations or half-hearted enforcement of the Fugitive Slave Acts, (2) toleration of abolitionist agitation, and (3) election of a Presidential candidate pledged to the eventual abolition of slavery. See *Ency. Am. Const.*, 4: 1712. These proslavery grievances were hardly of the dignity anticipated by the Declaration of Independence. See note 113, above. See as well Appendix M.

It should be evident from the guidance provided us by men such as Lincoln that, legislative supremacy notwithstanding, the Constitution depends upon, and provides ample scope for, gifted men, in and out of the Presidency. See Anastaplo, "American Constitutionalism and the Virtue of Prudence," 165–68, n. 64; Laurence Berns, "Aristotle and the Moderns on Freedom and Equality," in Kenneth L. Deutsch and Walter Soffer, eds., *The Crisis of Liberal Democracy: A Straussian Perspective* (Albany: State University of New York Press, 1987). See also the concluding paragraph of Lecture No. 9, Section VI.

Or as John Mercer, a delegate to the Federal Convention from Maryland, said on August 14, 1787: "It is a great mistake to suppose that the paper [the Constitution] we are to propose will govern the U. States. It is the men whom it will bring into the Governt. and interest in maintaining it that is to govern them. The paper will only mark out the mode & the form— Men are the substance and must do the business." Farrand, 2: 289. See, on the character of the American people, note 140, above.

See, on the intended equilibrium rather than the equality between the branches of the General Government, note 85, above.

Index

Rousseau, Jean-Jacques, 326 n.140
Rule of law, xviii, 18, 63, 66, 67, 80, 86,
118, 134, 169, 176, 191, 314 n.57, 318
n.85, 319 n.91. *See also* Constitutional proprieties
Rules of interpretation. *See* Interpretation, mode of

Safety, self-preservation, 16, 72, 73,
239
Sanford, David B., 316 n.78
Schechter Poultry Corp. v. *United
States* (1935), 143, 322 n.105
Secession, 177. *See also* Calhoun, John
C.; Rebellion against the United
States
Self-incrimination, privilege against,
289, 312 n.41
Separation of powers, 21, 41, 44, 66,
119, 163, 308 n.16
Seventeenth Amendment, 45, 315 n.68;
text, 293
Seventh Amendment, 146, 320 n.94;
text, 289
Shakespeare, William, 1, 11, 13, 74–88,
125, 150, 213, 313 nn.49, 51, 313–14
n.57, 315 n.73
Sharp, Malcolm P., 308 n.18
Silber, John R., 113, 115, 315 n.73
Slavery, xiv, 8, 11, 19, 22, 28–30, 58,
62–65, 71–72, 83, 130, 138, 142, 147,
162, 167, 169, 170, 176–78, 193, 194,
228–33, 264–65, 267, 271, 291–92,
299, 300–2, 304 n.1, 306 n.9, 312
n.39, 313 n.42, 327 n.145, 329 n.169;
collected references, 306 n.9. *See also*
Calhoun, John C.
Socrates, ix, 304 n.1. *See also*
Philosophy
Soffer, Walter, 329 n.169
Speiser v. *Randall* (1958), 304 n.1
States: constitutions, 5, 21, 74, 149–66,
213, 305 n.1, 323 nn.113, 116; original thirteen, 62, 71–72, 171–72, 276,
313 n.42; representation in the Senate, 31, 33, 35, 45, 192, 194, 195,
223; States' Rights, xiv, 10, 12, 23,
24, 28–29, 37–38, 66, 70–71, 131, 147,
167–79, 222, 233, 245, 307 n.11. *See
also* Federal Conventions called by

the States; Tenth Amendment; Union
older than the States
Stevens, Richard G., 327 n.148
Storing, Herbert J., 308 n.19
Strauss, Leo, x, xvii, 303 n.1, 305 n.1,
306 n.6, 329 n.169
Stuarts, 43
Succession, rules of, 35, 77, 79, 81, 82,
86
Suffrage, universal adult, 162. *See also*
Equality principle
Sumner, Charles, 324 n.121
Supremacy Clause, 196, 198–203, 277,
320 n.94, 325–26 n.140; *text*, 277
Supreme Court of the United States:
compensation 125; jurisdiction, 118,
124, 139–45, 319 n.93; size, 125, 139;
tenure, 125. *See also* Judicial review
Swift v. *Tyson* (1842), 128–29, 319–20
n.94. *See also* Common law

Tariffs, 202, 228, 232, 325 n.137
Tax powers, revenue bills, 29, 30, 43–
45, 50, 51, 54, 57, 60, 62, 63, 65, 68,
77, 78, 91, 114, 165, 249, 266, 269–
70, 271, 283, 292, 313 n.44
Television, 39, 106, 303 n.1, 327 n.150
Tenth Amendment, 11, 21, 24, 52, 228–
29, 310 n.30; *collected references*,
306–7 n.10, *text*, 290
Territories, 142, 167, 306 n.9
Thirteenth Amendment, 65, 11–12, 233;
text, 291
Titles of nobility, 62, 63, 64, 71, 72, 82,
123, 146, 147, 162, 271, 272, 298–99
Tocqueville, Alexis de, 75, 313 n.48
Treason, 66, 146, 147, 245, 268, 301,
311 n.35, 323 n.110
Treaty powers and obligations, 111,
112, 113, 198, 199, 201, 247, 249,
252, 274, 316 n.82, 319 n.85
Trial by jury: *See* Jury, trial by
Truman, Harry S., 144
Twelfth Amendment, 11, 88, 93, 99,
228, 306–7 n.10, 307 n.11, 315 n.70;
text, 290–91
Twentieth Amendment, 100; *text*, 294
Twenty-fifth Amendment, 100, 107,
116; *text*, 296–97

George Anastaplo is
Lecturer in the Liberal Arts
at the University of Chicago,
Professor Emeritus of Political Science and of Philosophy
at Rosary College,
and Professor of Law
at Loyola University of Chicago.